BASIC CONCEPTS
OF
LEGAL THOUGHT

BASIC CONCEPTS
OF
LEGAL THOUGHT

George P. Fletcher

New York   Oxford
OXFORD UNIVERSITY PRESS
1996

Oxford University Press

Oxford   New York
Athens   Auckland   Bangkok   Bombay
Calcutta   Cape Town   Dar es Salaam   Delhi
Florence   Hong Kong   Istanbul   Karachi
Kuala Lumpur   Madras   Madrid   Melbourne
Mexico City   Nairobi   Paris   Singapore
Taipei   Tokyo   Toronto

and associated companies in
Berlin   Ibadan

Copyright © 1996 by George P. Fletcher

Published by Oxford University Press, Inc.
198 Madison Avenue, New York, New York 10016

Oxford is a registered trademark of Oxford University Press, Inc.

Library of Congress Cataloging-in-Publication Data
Fletcher, George P.
Basic concepts of legal thought / George P. Fletcher.
p.   cm.   Includes bibliographical references.
ISBN-13 978–0–19–508336–1
ISBN 0–19–508335–0
ISBN 0–19–508336–9 (pbk.)
1. Law—Philosophy.   2. Jurisprudence.   3. Rule of law.
I. Title.
K237.F58   1996
340′.1—dc20   95–13332

8 9

Printed in the United States of America
on acid-free paper

*For Herbert Morris and all my teachers
who introduced me to the beauties
and mysteries of the law.*

Contents

BASIC CONCEPTS
OF
LEGAL THOUGHT

Introduction

Shakespeare did not think much of lawyers. He mocked their language, satirized their reasoning, and spoofed their procedures. Most of the joking is less ominous than the threat by the rebel Dick the Butcher in *Henry VI, Part Two*: "The first thing we do, let's kill all the lawyers." Insiders to legal reasoning laugh with the gravedigger in *Hamlet* when he misnames the doctrine of *se defendendo* as *se offendendo*. The malapropism in Latin is equivalent to coming into court and pleading "I killed him in self-offense, your Honor."

Shakespeare found the reasoning of lawyers as amusing as their language. Legal scholars have traditionally thought that it made an important difference whether someone slays another by thrusting his sword into a passive body or by standing motionless as the victim impales himself on the sword. The former is an action; the latter, merely an omission, carrying a lesser degree of responsibility. Here is how the gravedigger in *Hamlet* adapts this distinction to whether Ophelia "acted" in throwing herself into a river and drowning:

> Here lies the water; good: here stands the man; good; if the man go to this water, and drown himself it is, will he, nill he, he goes; mark you that; but if the water come to him and drown him, he drowns not himself: argal, he that is not guilty of his own death shortens not his own life.

If this kind of reasoning does not adequately mock legal argument, just think about Portia, the betrothed of Bassanio, in turn, the close

3

friend of Antonio, disguising herself as a traveling scholar and insinuating herself into the judgment of Antonio's dispute with Shylock. Friends are not generally regarded as unbiased judges, and Portia certainly was partial to Antonio. The procedure is as patently inane as Portia's strict construction of the contract that permits Shylock to claim his pound of flesh provided he not spill a drop of Antonio's blood. *The Merchant of Venice* is, of course, a comedy, and for Shakespeare, there was no better subject for comedy than the pretenses of lawyers.

We still laugh at lawyer jokes. "A lawyer and a physician fall overboard. The sharks eat the physician but leave the lawyer alone. Why is that? Professional courtesy, of course," We express disdain for lawyers, but we cannot live without them. The public becomes angry and disillusioned by the O. J. Simpson case, but they continue to watch the proceedings on television.

Law has become the American civil religion. The newspapers are filled with stories about trials, about pending legislation, about new decisions by the courts. Legally trained executives now run major motion picture studios, corporations, and universities. They speak to each other in the lingo of jurisprudence. Understanding the law has become, in fact, an essential part of literacy in a culture dominated by lawyers.

We demand more of the law than it can possibly deliver. For twentieth-century immigrant lawyers, the U.S. Constitution is the embodiment of everything true and beautiful. The recent effort to amend the Bill of Rights to protect the American flag struck many lawyers as sacrilegious: tampering with the basic charter of American civil liberties would be as dangerous as amending the Bible. Law embodies our aspirations, our sense of ultimate justice, our commitments as a nation of diverse ethnicities and religions.

Most lawyers learn to ply their craft, but they seldom learn to reflect philosophically about what they are doing. They know how to make arguments of justice and morality, but they are not in a position to speak thoughtfully about either. There in fact lies the deep philosophical issue behind Shakespeare's spoof about whether the water came to Ophelia or Ophelia came to the water. Should acts be treated differently from omissions and how do we decide whether drowning is one or the other? Alas, lawyers rarely have the pleasure, in their education or in their practice, of pondering these deeper issues.

As much as lawyers are often ignorant of the conceptual grammar of their thinking, most students of the humanities and social sciences pass through college without learning the curious ways of that richly textured culture called the law. Learning something about the basic concepts of legal thought should be part of every complete education in philosophy, government, history, sociology—not to mention business and economics. Shakespeare could not have written so wittily about lawyers unless he had first mastered the byways of their language, arguments, and concepts.

I wrote this book because I could not find a good slim volume that eases law students into the mysteries of legal philosophy as well as providing an introduction to nonlawyers who seek to understand the legal mind. But this introduction to legal thought is more than a review of the received wisdom. I have a distinctive jurisprudential point of view that derives from many years of working and writing in the field of comparative law.

When American lawyers speak of "the law," they have in mind their own legal system. At most, they might be referring to the Anglo-American common law system, a body of ideas and principles that crystallized in the course of English history and then took hold in the former English colonies, including the United States. There are, of course, other legal traditions. The most notable are the two that have developed in Continental Europe—one centered on the French and the other on the German legal system. American writers frequently lump these two traditions under the single term "civil law." Asian legal cultures provide yet another perspective on law as it bears on social relations. A comparative perspective enables one to appreciate the different shapes that the law can take.

Language matters more than most observers realize in shaping the contours of the law. The common law and the English language have a strong affinity for each other. The English common law has flourished in countries where English is the language of legal discourse. Some countries influenced by English law, notably Israel, have endeavored to translate English terms into the native lexicon, but there seems to be as much lost in the translation of law as in the translation of Shakespeare. There is no way to convey the connotations of "due process," "reasonable doubt," and "malice aforethought" in any language except English. The relationship also runs the other way. No anglophone culture has successfully adopted and nourished any other system of law. Some people claim that Louisiana has kept the French system alive in the English language, but the pressures of language seem to have overwhelmed Louisiana's original commitment to French culture.

By remaining committed to the French language, Quebec has succeeded in going its own way, both linguistically and legally. Napoleon's *Code Civil* and its surrounding modes of thought have flourished in cultures based on French or other Romance languages, such as Spanish, Portuguese, and Romanian. The German system of thought has prospered in many non-English cultures, including Russia, Greece, and Japan, largely because local lawyers have succeeded in adapting German terms into their own legal languages.

Language is hardly a neutral field for legal thought to play itself out. Early in my scholarly career, I addressed and rejected the Whorfian

thesis that language determines legal thought. A colleague had asserted
that the Soviet Communists had not adopted "presumption of innocence" because Russian had no concept like the Latin-based term "presumption." The view that language dictates the horizons of thought is
clearly wrong, but there is nonetheless some not-fully-understood connection between language and legal thought. I explore this connection
in this book by showing, where possible, the ways in which concepts
change their hues as the linguistic terrain takes on different shadows.
Some terms like "equality" and "consent" readily translate across Western languages, but others do not. When a concept is embedded in the
English language, we should be aware of this peculiar union of form and
substance. The attempt to generate this self-consciousness about our
language accounts for the many passages in this book in which I explore
the problem of translating terms like "law" and "discretion" into foreign
languages.

The book begins with a set of topics grouped around perennial
puzzles about what it means to live under law and the rule of law. The
more one ponders these elementary questions, the more intransigent
they seem. The first four chapters, then, are designed to give the reader a
basic orientation about seemingly obvious ideas such as the rule of law
and deciding cases under the law.

The middle four chapters turn to the ultimate values that political
and moral philosophers ponder in their efforts to fathom the criteria for
deciding whether a legal system as a whole meets criteria of legitimacy.
The notions of justice, desert, consent, and equality figure prominently
in judging our legal cultures as sound and legitimate.

Chapters nine to eleven ponder morality in the law. There is no
escaping the influence of moral principles in resolving legal disputes. The
problem lies in deciding which moral principles should take precedence.
A three-front battle defines the heartland of moral controversy in the
law. The utilitarians and the economists are allied against those who
believe in rights and Kantian principles of moral duty. And both of these
individualistic and liberal camps stand against the thrust of new communitarian thinking, as expressed in values like loyalty. In the final chapter,
I struggle with the problem of consistency in law. The question is
whether it is possible to bring together all these ideas, outlined in the
course of eleven chapters, in one coherent picture of the law's foundations. I hope to keep the reader in suspense about whether consistency
in the law is a possible ideal.

In the course of the 1994–95 academic year, I asked many first year
students at Columbia Law School to read this book in draft form. Many
improvements follow directly from their reactions and suggestions. One
recurrent comment was that it is difficult for a novice in legal philosophy
to follow the argument without a guide to the participants whose names
figure in the great philosophical debates of the past and present. The

beginning reader needs, as it were, a program to identify and follow the players. Thus I include an appendix of short biographies that provide a few tidbits of history about names that appear in the text. The contingency of the discussion determines, by and large, the names of those highlighted in the text. There are obviously many, if not most important writers today who, for one accidental reason or another, are left out of the *Dramatis Personae.* May my colleagues forgive any unintended slight.

The first draft of four of these chapters—on law, discretion, justice, and morality—provided the foundation for a series of talks I gave as the Second Cardozo Lectures in Law in Trento, Italy in April, 1992. I am grateful to Ugo Mattei, P. G. Monateri, and Elisabetta Grande for hosting me on that occasion. I managed to complete most of the first draft of the entire book during a productive and pleasant stay at the Collegium Budapest in the spring of 1993. My sojourn in Budapest was successful due, in no small part, to the efforts of the Rector of the Collegium Lajos Vékás.

There are many other people whose contribution to this project merits a special note of appreciation. Peter Widulski and Russell Christopher worked long and hard as critics of my drafts. The book would not have been possible without their assistance. Lewis Farberman checked the footnotes and made several helpful suggestions. Ron Shapira, Kent Greenawalt, Arthur Jacobson, and Meir Dan-Cohen provided me with sensible suggestions on aspects of the argument. One hopes that these gestures of assistance have made the text easier to follow. May the argument bring the novice to appreciate an undervalued phenomenon of beauty—the law.

I

THE LEGAL
SYSTEM

1

The Rule of Law

Of the all the dreams that drive men and women into the streets, from Buenos Aires to Budapest, the "rule of law" is the most puzzling. We have a pretty good idea what we mean by "free markets" and "democratic elections." But legality and the "rule of law" are ideals that present themselves as opaque even to legal philosophers. Many American jurists treat the rule of law as though it were no more than governance by rules. Thus we find Justice Scalia arguing explicitly that the rule of law is no more than the law of rules.[1] And philosophers, such as Friedrich Hayek and Joseph Raz, make the same assumption that the rule of law means that the government "is bound by rules fixed and announced beforehand."[2] Playing by the rules is, in some dubious contexts, a great achievement, but once societies have minimized graft and arbitrary rule, the "rule of law" seems to promise more than blindly playing the game. After all, the rules of the game might be horribly unjust.

There are in fact two versions of the rule of law, a modest version of adhering to the rules and a more lofty ideal that incorporates criteria of justice. We shuffle back and forth between them because we are unsure of the import of the term "law" in the expression "rule of law." To explicate a rarely perceived ambiguity in English, we turn to a distinction between two concepts of law that is widely recognized in other languages but ignored in English.

Continental European languages, for example, use one term for law

11

that expresses the idea of laws enacted—laid down, legislated—by an authoritative body. Thus Germans use the term *Gesetz*, French *loi*, Russians *zakon*, Spanish *ley*, and speakers of Hebrew *ḥok*. All these languages also contain a second word for law that expresses a higher notion of Law as binding because it is sound in principle.[3] This alternative conception of law is expressed in the Continental European languages as *Recht* in German, *droit* in French, *pravo* in Russian, *derecho* in Spanish, and *mishpat* in Hebrew.[4] The closest translation of these terms in English would be "Right," an archaic expression for Law sometimes used in the translation of philosophical works.[5] The connotation of Right (or Law with a capital L) is typically that of good or just law, which is binding on us because it is good or just. In many modern European languages (not Hebrew) the term for Law in this higher sense is used to refer to personal rights in the plural (*Rechte, droits, prava, derechos*). The appeal to human rights, therefore, is an indirect appeal to the same word "Right" that in European languages signifies Law in a higher sense.[6] When we speak today of protecting human rights, such as the rights to life, liberty, and dignity, we always have in mind rights that appeal to us because they are just as a matter of principle.[7]

Each of these two terms for law generates a distinct conception of the rule of law. If someone argues that the "rule of law" simply means that "the government is bound by rules fixed and announced beforehand,"[8] they would be content with having the rules laid down by an authoritative lawgiver or legislature. This is what the Germans would call a *Gesetzesstaat* or the Communists once labelled "socialist legality" (*sotsialisticheskaja zakonnost'*). The rules are binding whether they are good or bad.

Those who think that the rule of law is an ideal for good government stress the dimension of Right in the rule of law. The vision of a state based on ideal law is captured in the German notion of a *Rechtsstaat*. The European notion of the "rule of law" is based always on the term for Law in the higher sense. In the dying days of the Soviet Union, President Mikhail Gorbachev, a lawyer, expressed his commitment to reentering European culture by reformulating the ideal of Soviet law. For several generations, the governing aspiration of Soviet law was "socialist legality" or, in Justice Scalia's terms, conformity to the rules enacted by the state (except, of course, when the Party ordered a temporary deviation). As the state became more democratic in the Western sense, the ideal of law became the *Rechtsstaat*—the state based on higher law, expressed in Russian as *pravovoe gosudarstvo*. Gorbachev attempted to shift the foundational value of his legal system to the ideal version of the rule of law. The terminological shift that Gorbachev introduced is used today as Russia slouches toward a Western-style legal system.

In English, we are never quite sure what we mean by the "rule of law." Do we mean rule by the laws laid down—whether the legal rules are good or bad? Or do we mean "rule by Law," by the right rules, by the rules that meet the tests of morality and justice? Because we have only one word for law in place of the two commonly found in other legal systems, we suffer and perhaps cultivate this ambiguity.

Unlike typical European constitutions, the basic charter of the United States says nothing about a commitment to the rule of law. The closest constitutional analogue is the phrase prohibiting the deprivation of "life, liberty, or property without due process of law."[9] The notion of "due process" provides a conduit for our best understanding of justice and principles of Right. In the language of Justice Cardozo the due process clause expresses "the concept of ordered liberty."[10] The practice of bringing to bear higher law in constitutional interpretation constitutes part of the American commitment to "constitutionalism."[11] The same vision of a civilized legal order is embedded in the European conception of a *Rechtsstaat*. American legal thinkers seem, therefore, to split their faith in legality between two different notions of the rule of law. The quotidian work of the legal system conforms to Hayek's and Scalia's prescription: the rule of law means following the rules laid down. The invocation of higher law, of the principles that infuse justice in the legal order, is reserved for interpretation of the Constitution and, in particular, of the due process clause.

But what does it mean to live under rules governed by "the concept of ordered liberty" or "due process" or in a *Rechtsstaat*? It is not easy to specify the characteristics of this ideal. A minimum requirement might well be a commitment to some form of equality, at least to the avoidance of arbitrary discrimination between equally situated persons.[12] Another requirement would be the maintenance of fair procedures for resolving disputes. These are, of course, merely the bare bones. The effort to introduce substantive values into "the concept of ordered liberty" has produced great controversy. In 1905 the Supreme Court ruled that unrestrained freedom of contract was one of these higher values;[13] in 1973, the focus had shifted to the right to have an abortion.[14] Very few people support both decisions. Many on the political left condemn the former decision and support the latter; some on the political right condemn the latter and support the former. The rejection of both decisions has spawned a school of interpretation called "originalism," which insists that all basic rights be spelled out in the Constitution.[15]

In the end, it might be as difficult to specify the characteristics of this ideal of due process or of a *Rechtsstaat* as it is to define the physical ideal of good health. The best approximation of health might be this: an organism is healthy if it is not ill. The burden falls on perceiving illness, and if there is no illness, the organism is healthy. We recognize breakdowns more easily than we can define the positive ideal.[16] In the same way, lawyers have a strong sense for the perversions that prevent a legal system from realizing the rule of law. One of them is willy-nilly decision making by judges who either do not follow the rules or exercise too much discretion. Another is retroactive criminal justice, or punishing people for a crime committed before the law is announced. But even this approach of documenting perversions of the rule of law may run dry rather quickly. No one has yet given an adequate account, by this approach or any other, of the ideal conception of the rule of law.

In this chapter I take a novel approach to this nagging problem of definition by reflecting on three case studies taken from recent pages of post-Communist political life. After the changes of 1989, the Eastern European governments were in a state of great sensitivity to the ultimate value that should guide their new democratic orders. The events in Hungary from 1990 to 1993 provide a good window on one society's struggle to establish the rule of law in the wake of forty-five years of dictatorship and repression. The three case studies that will engage us will be the taxi strike in the fall of 1990; the decision to prosecute a man named Miklós Végvári who violated the old law in the name of new democratic values; and the legal activism of the newly created Hungarian Constitutional Court. Each of these tales has something to teach us about the rule of law as a democratic ideal.

The Taxi Strike

It is worth beginning with the taxi strike, for it is one of the most unusual phenomena of post-Communist political life. On Thursday night, October 25, 1990, the government made a sudden announcement that the price of gas would increase at the pumps. The new prices would be slightly higher than in Austria, the closest Western country. The price increase came as an obvious consequence of tensions in Iraq and other oil-producing countries, of price hikes in the world market for oil, and of increasing efforts by the Soviets to shut off the spigot of subsidized gas that had flowed freely when Hungary was a dutiful colony. For Hungarians, nurtured on Communist subsidies, this was the first direct experience with the capitalist idea that consumers must pay the full (unsubsidized) price of the goods they buy.

The taxi drivers were upset not only by the price increase, but by the government's apparent duplicity in planning the move. The government actually had promised repeatedly not to raise the price of gas. The sudden declaration of the increase was designed to catch people off guard and when they were still exuberant after having celebrated on October 23 their national epic, the abortive 1956 revolution. With several days off from work, most people were in a good mood. This was the first time since the transition to democracy that the Hungarians had openly and joyfully celebrated the passionate agony of 1956.

In 1990 it was not tanks but taxi cabs that clogged the streets and bridges of Budapest. Within a few hours after the government announced the price increase, the strikers managed to shut down the major traffic arteries in the city. They parked their taxies on all the major bridges, and threw up blockades around the city. Taxi drivers and private truck drivers cooperated spontaneously to generate blockades in provincial cities.

In the fall of 1990 I was in Budapest as a visiting professor at the local law school. I woke up that fateful Friday without advance warning of the strike. From my balcony overlooking the Danube, I noticed a large crowd milling around the *Szabadsághid*—the "Freedom Bridge" leading from the Old Market in Pest across the murky blue river to the palatial Gellért Hotel in Buda. I went out among the crowd. "Strike" was the word on the lips of the angry drivers hanging out by their cars blocking the bridge.

Events on Friday began to hint that this was more than a strike. The drivers had cordoned off the airport in Budapest; unless foreign businessmen were willing to walk the last few miles, they were better off sitting on their suitcases in the lobbies of luxury hotels. This ragtag collection of apolitical, tough-talking guys also managed to close the border to Austria. As in 1956, the only way to cross was to go through the fields and bypass the official checkpoints.

Business came to a standstill; shops closed early. Somehow people could get home, even if they lived and worked on opposite sides of the river. Though the subway was still running under the river, streetcars and private cars could not cross the Danube. The crowded subway stations became rumor mills. Reports began to circulate that food supplies were running low, that the hospitals could not receive deliveries of medicine. No one knew what was going to happen. The government was the fragile expression of a democratic order. Would it fail this first test?

The leaders of the leading half-dozen parties started speaking out, but in muted tones. The government, then run by the Hungarian Democratic Forum party, tried to rally support by staging a counterdemonstration. The opposition parties, the Free Democrats and the Young Democrats, did nothing to exploit the situation. Their attitude was to keep their distance, watch what was going on, and urge a peaceful resolution. On Saturday, October 27, the mood began to stabilize. Standstill became the norm. Though the streets were still blockaded, the crisp fall day invited strolling. Budapest came out onto the streets. Baby carriages and bicycles took over the lanes normally clogged with polluting vehicles. My sense on "Freedom Bridge" was that most people were beginning to enjoy "sticking it" to the government. Then came the news that the police chief of Budapest had announced that, if the government ordered intervention, he would resign.

This was a curious situation for a country accustomed to order first and to law second. A group of workers now blocks the major traffic

arteries of the city and everyone seems to applaud. At one level an act
of force meets with general approval or, at least, indifference. Worka-
day citizens are deprived of their right to use the bridges, and they do
not complain. They do not insist that labor be kept in its place. There
was no doubt in my mind that if the Teamsters tried to shut down the
bridges to Manhattan, the police would immediately don their battle
gear.

But this is Budapest, not New York or Los Angeles. The common
enemy of the last 45 years has not been organized labor but organized
government. The Hungarian Constitution, as reformed in October 1989,
prohibited the President from using the army to quell domestic rebellion.
The analogue in the United States would be the abolition of the National
Guard. Can you imagine how federal and state chief executives would
cope with urban violence if they could not call in the National Guard?
What would have happened without the National Guard in Los Angeles
in the post-verdict Rodney King riot of April 1992? The Hungarian
government had deliberately disarmed itself. The abuses of the past
made the people distrustful of armed intervention and the new constitutional limitation survived the temptation to crush the taxi strike by
bringing in military troops.

The taxi strike turned out to be an in-house affair. Its closest analogy
would be a 1960s-style college sit-in. The drivers protested the gas hike
in much the same way that American students protested the Vietnam
War by closing down universities. The government stood in their minds—
as university administrations functioned in the minds of students—as
the symbol of all authority. The drivers "parked in" on the bridge, they
ceased doing "business as usual," and their fellow denizens thought it
just fine to make life difficult for the parental surrogates called the government.

Some intellectuals began to speak of the "park-in" [my term] as an
act of civil disobedience. But acts of civil disobedience raise fundamental
issues of right and wrong. There was no moral issue at stake in the taxi
strike. This was a bread-and-butter question. When I buttonholed people and asked, "Why shouldn't taxis simply raise their rates to offset the
gas price increase?" the typical response was, "But then no one could
afford to use taxis." This is the logic of those who still do not accept the
vicissitudes of living under capitalism. As of 1990 Hungarians were still
looking to their government as their providers, as the guarantors of their
welfare.

On Sunday the strike leaders entered into negotiations with the
government. Remarkably, the negotiations were broadcast, nonstop, on
Hungarian television. Citizens sat glued to their sets with the rapt attention Americans reserve for trials of football heroes accused of murder. It
appeared as though the conflicting sides were reaching an agreement in
front of the television cameras. They suspended the meeting for about an

hour, came back and then Sunday night announced a compromise that would lower the price of gas temporarily as taxi strikers went back to work and life returned to normal.

My impression was that very few people in Budapest cared about the symbolic importance of maintaining the proper legal framework for a dispute between a small group of driver-citizens and the government as oil supplier. The minds of Hungarians were on taboos other than breaching the rule of law. No one wanted another violent confrontation on the streets of Budapest. Having just observed the anniversary of the 1956 uprising, everyone was horrified at the prospect of blood flowing once again on the banks of the Danube. Using force to open the bridges was simply out of the question.

There is much to be learned from this episode. First, it seems that the rule of law hardly makes sense in a situation in which the citizenry still sees itself as negotiating with the government as employees negotiate with management. Alas, this is the legacy of Communism and central planning. The Party did, indeed, function as the management of Hungary, Inc. The round-table discussions leading to democratic elections carried forward the mentality of employees negotiating benefits from their masters. In a centrally planned economy and controlled society, it is hard to think otherwise.

Yet the rule of law, it seems, requires a vision of government closer to the liberal theory of the state as a disinterested arbiter. The state's officials must be above the conflicts that lend themselves to regulation under law. So long as the government—as sole supplier of gas—is a party to a dispute, one cannot expect the matter to be resolved under the neutral standard called law.[17] Also, the rule of law requires governmental distance in another sense. The state cannot enforce the law consistently and evenhandedly if it thinks of itself as a surrogate parent for its citizens, as bearing ultimate responsibility for their welfare. The kind of indulgence shown by college administrations in the late 1960s—and by the Hungarian government in 1990—reflects an identity of interests with the citizenry rather than the kind of distance required for the neutral arbitration of disputes. The Hungarian government and the masses on the streets shared a common interest in avoiding a repetition of past traumas, and this common interest weighed more heavily than the commitment to secure the rights of citizens to free access to the streets and bridges.

Prosecutorial Discretion

The connection between the rule of law and full enforcement of the law (at least the criminal law) is revealed in ongoing disputes, both in the United States and in Europe, about the acceptability of prosecutorial discretion. We, in the United States, have learned to accept prosecutorial discretion as normal and, as some might say, inevitable in a legal system administered by people, not machines. Yet the dispute about full enforcement is still very much alive on the Continent. The camp in favor of full enforcement invokes the principle of legality on its side; they rely on the expression *Legalitätsprinzip* [legality principle] to designate full enforcement. Under this "legality principle," prosecutors may not make special deals with particular suspects in return for their cooperation. The discretionary approach—known as the *Opportunitätsprinzip* [opportunity principle]—permits prosecutors to pick and choose their cases and invest their resources to maximize their effectiveness.

The conflict between the principles of full and discretionary enforcement came to a head in Hungary's transition to democratic rule. The occasion was the prosecution of a onetime loyal officer of the Hungarian Secret Service, Miklós Végvári, who changed sides and invited dissident groups into the heart of the surveillance system that was eavesdropping on the round table negotiations between the dissidents and the Communist Party. On Christmas day 1989, Végvári invited a television crew from the "Black Box"—an alternative TV group—into the inner sancta of the Secret Service building in Budapest. The group filmed files and other secret corners of the operation and showed the film on television. The resulting scandal came to be known as "Dunagate": a label that suggested a certain pride in Hungary's generating a Western-style scandal.

Keep in mind that the first free elections took place in February 1990, three months after Végvári breached his official duties as an intelligence officer. There is little doubt that his acts constituted criminal violations under the criminal code then in force. And indeed, in principle, if we may abstract from the political conflict of the moment, his acts should constitute criminal offenses under any system of criminal law. Every legal system, whether democratic or Communist, maintains a secret service; and to invade its official quarters is not defensible however good the political motive. Under ordinary circumstances Végvári would have been prosecuted and convicted.

The Communist chief prosecutor decided, however, not to prosecute. This was a decision based not so much on expediency as on a recognition of Végvári's good faith and perhaps a sense that the changing political climate rendered him more of a hero than a villain. In June 1990, the newly constituted democratic government appointed a new chief prosecutor, Kálmán Györgyi, who was a distinguished professor of criminal procedure, well schooled in the German literature on the imperative of the "legality principle." Paradoxically, the new democratically minded chief prosecutor decided that he must prosecute Végvári. The principle of legality required that he bring to trial a man who had served the cause of the democratic transition.

When the case finally came to trial in the fall of 1990, the process revealed a curious mixture of Soviet and Western legal ideas. On the one hand, the decision to prosecute reflected a yearning to identify with the principles of legality that prevailed in the West, or at least in those few countries officially committed to the "legality principle." On the other hand, the central legal dispute reflected the ongoing influence of Soviet doctrines and terminology. Végvári's defense was that his conduct was justified because, as Soviet lawyers used to say, it was not "socially dangerous." He was aiding the democratic movement, and indeed the movement had won. In what sense could one say that his conduct constituted a danger to the legitimate interests of the emerging democratic order?

The answer to the question depends, of course, on how we define Végvári's conduct. If we look just at what he did, namely, reveal official secrets, his conduct was surely criminal regardless of his motives. If we focus on this conduct in context, however, it takes on the appearance of justified civil disobedience. The military court that heard the case (as an intelligence officer Végvári was under military jurisdiction) cannot be criticized for not being able to resolve this conundrum. The prosecution ended in November 1990 in a compromise verdict. The court issued an official sanction of Végvári's conduct, but this sanction was an informal reprimand, short of an official conviction.

The notion of a reprimand short of a conviction reveals the same kind of paternalistic thinking we noted in the resolution of the taxi strike. In the United States, we assume that the potential criminal liability of adults is an either/or matter. Either you are guilty and subject to sanction or you remain a free person. There is no gray zone in which you are subject to official reprimands from state officials. The indulgence that the government showed the taxi strikers represents the other side of the paternal coin. The same surrogate parent that shows caring regard also reprimands those who disappoint her. It will take years of reform to eliminate this way of thinking from a society that despised, but nonetheless became used to "big brother" in government.

An Activist Constitutional Court

One of the slogans that has captured the imagination of legal thinkers everywhere is the protection of "human rights." The ideal of the Right now shines most clearly in this expression that motivates reformers in English as well as other languages. The challenge for every emergent democracy is defining what these rights are and setting up institutions for interpreting and enforcing these definitions. The transition to democracy in Eastern Europe has meant, in most cases, subscribing to the rights spelled out in the European Convention of Human Rights, as applied by the European Court of Human Rights in Strasbourg, France. The ambition of every new democracy in the region is to join the Council of

Europe, namely the group of more than twenty-five nations that accept the jurisdiction of the human rights court in Strasbourg.

In addition, the new democracies have established constitutional courts for interpreting and enforcing their local constitutional safeguards of human rights. The Hungarian Constitutional Court, modeled after the German Constitutional Court, consists of nine sitting judges, virtually all of whom are professorial types who were appointed from research or teaching positions. The judges serve terms of fifteen years. They have had to confront and resolve more controversial cases than the U.S. Supreme Court assayed in its first hundred years, partly because their jurisdiction includes the "abstract review" of statutes on their face, without a specific case or controversy before the court. Any citizen can petition the court to hear a constitutional question. The jurisdiction of the U.S. Supreme Court is more circumspect: only actual cases and controversies, involving people who suffer the ill effects of a disputed statute, come before the Court.

The Eastern European democracies face the same set of problems bequeathed by their Communist past. First, what should they do about crimes committed under the Communists but never prosecuted? Second, what should they do about the widespread use of capital punishment in view of the Council of Europe's strongly disfavoring capital punishment? Further, what should they do about property rights that were sacrificed in the programs of nationalization of property carried out by the Communists? Of these recurrent problems in the region, I will focus on the resolution of two by the Hungarian Constitutional Court— punishment of crimes of the past and the future of capital punishment.

The hallmark of dictatorship is the government's participation in committing crimes against citizens. Because the government controls the prosecutorial establishment, these crimes are never prosecuted. (This explains some of the sensitivity connected to the Végvári case.) Some of the most egregious instances in the region occurred in 1956 and 1968 when Soviet tanks rolled into Budapest and Prague to squelch the movement toward democracy. Many executions followed both invasions. At the border between East and West Germany, other instances of violence were commonplace. The border guards of the former German Democratic Republic (GDR) shot and killed their own citizens who were trying to scale the wall and flee to the West.

Understandably, after the transition to democracy, the victims of this repression called for prosecution of those who were responsible. After unification of the two Germanies on October 3, 1990, the government began prosecuting the border guards who allegedly used excessive force at the border. The guards, in turn, claimed that statutes in force at the time, authorized them to use the force necessary to prevent unlawful exit from the country. The West Germans responded that these statutes violated the basic human right of freedom of movement, recognized in international law. As a result, the statutes were not really law in the sense of Right and therefore they provided no justification for attempting to kill the escaping East Germans. Not surprisingly, the West German view prevailed in the courts. This debate illustrates the conflict between two senses of the rule of law. The border guards relied on the law as the rules laid down by the legislature of the GDR. The Western courts relied on the higher notion incorporated in their idea of a *Rechtsstaat*—a state based not only on law but on respect for basic human rights.[18]

For the Hungarians, the major issue of justice in the transition to democracy was prosecuting those who collaborated in the repression of the 1956 uprising. For those crimes, the statute of limitations, typically twenty years, had already run. This meant that under ordinary circumstances, the prosecution was barred; the government's hands should have been tied. The parry to this argument was that under the Communist regime, political interests stood in the way of prosecution, and therefore the passing of time should not have had its normal effect.

The Hungarian Parliament responded in November 1991 to the popular demand for prosecution by enacting a law that tolled (i.e., suspended) the statute of limitations for the crimes of treason, murder, and related crimes of violence, when the reason for nonprosecution was political. Significantly, the period of limitations would begin running on May 1, 1990, the date on which the first freely elected post-Communist government took power. The assumption behind the statute was that the Communists were complicitous in these unprosecuted crimes of violence and therefore they naturally refused to prosecute them. The President of the Republic delayed signing and promulgating the law and in the interim asked the Constitutional Court for an opinion about the statute's constitutionality.

In March 1992 the Constitutional Court ruled that the statute was unconstitutional as a violation of the provision in the Constitution, as amended in October 1989, that recognized Hungary as an "independent, democratic *Rechtsstaat* [a state governed by the rule of law]."[19] The Court's opinion relies upon a variety of characteristics associated with the rule of law. One is that all citizens should be able to rely on rights vested by the express command of the legal system. If the statute of limitations has run, the citizen acquires a right not to be prosecuted for the crime. The attempt to suspend the statute's running during the Communist regime, therefore, represented an effort to deprive citizens of their rights. This argument is supported by common expectation that after the statute of limitations runs, the state will not try to counter the effect of the time limitation and prosecute the case. After the limitation period is satisfied, those who might have faced prosecution rely upon their immunity. They lead their lives with greater ease. They expose themselves to the risk of arrest. Under these circumstances, it makes sense to say that they also have a right to rely on their immunity from prosecution. The right derives from the common expectation that the law will not suddenly change to their detriment.[20]

The second argument advanced by the Court is that the rule of law requires certainty and predictability. The vague requirement for tolling the statute of limitations—that the previous failure to prosecute be based on political reasons—made it difficult, if not impossible, to predict when the law would apply and when it would not. This is a sound point.

Yet the third argument in the opinion is more dubious. The court argued that increasing the term of limitation after the commission of the crime violated the constitutional principle that all crimes must be legislatively defined prior to their commission.[21] The argument is that tolling the statute of limitations was something like increasing the penalty after the crime was committed. Suppose that on November 1, 1956, when the crime is punishable by ten years in prison, Béla commits an aggravated assault. Thereafter the legislature seeks to raise the penalty for aggravated assault to fifteen years; this would clearly be unconstitutional as an ex post facto law. The Constitutional Court reasoned that lengthening the statute of limitations was analogous to increasing the penalty. In both cases the offender faces a law at trial harsher than that in effect when he committed the offense. On the basis of this reasoning, the Constitutional Court declared the law unconstitutional even as to cases in which the statute had not yet run (i.e., to crimes committed in the 1980s).

The third argument is dubious because it overlooks a well-established legal principle. The general position of legal systems is that procedural changes are not part of the "crime" that must be defined prior to the time of commission. Suppose the state changes the rules of evidence or the number of judges or lay people who sit in judgment of the case. Do offenders have the right to rely upon the procedural institutions in force at the time of committing their offense? The answer is no. No legal system in the world recognizes that every suspect has the right to be tried under precisely the same set of legal institutions that were in force at the time of the crime. The principle is that the offender may rely on the substantive law in effect at the time of the alleged violation, but the state may design and redesign the rules that govern the effort to seek the truth about whether the suspect committed the crime.

Note that this distinction between the substantive rules defining the crime and the procedural rules governing the mode of trial is a fundamental tool of analysis in every legal system. Yet nowhere is the distinction definitely spelled out in the positive law of the jurisdiction. The existence and importance of this distinction between substance and procedure testifies to the inescapability of unwritten principles of law. It is hard to imagine a legal system that could function without this particular distinction.

In any event, the Constitutional Court reached the novel conclusion that the "rule of law" or the principles of a *Rechtsstaat* prohibited changing the statute of limitations even in a case in which the statute had not run. The German Constitutional Court had reached the opposite conclusion: amending the statute of limitations prior to its expiration was a procedural and not a substantive change.[22] But the Hungarians paid no attention to this or other holdings on the distinction between substance and procedure. The Court expressed acute sensitivity to the value of the rule of law and therefore ruled against any change of the law that accrued to the detriment of the defendant. This ruling may tell us more about the postcommunist historical situation of the Hungarian court than about the issues decided.

Another example of the same mode of reacting against the abuses of Communism occurred in the Court's decision on a challenge to the constitutionality of capital punishment. In October, 1990, just before the taxi strike, the newly constituted Constitutional Court in Budapest heard a complaint by a law professor from Miskolc, a provincial city to the northeast, challenging the constitutionality of the death penalty in Hungary. Of course, under the American consitution, it would be hard to imagine an ordinary citizen, even a political activist, challenging the constitutionality of the death penalty unless he or she was personally facing execution.

After a brief oral argument, the Court convened and with apparent ease declared capital punishment unconstitutional as an arbitrary violation of the right to life.[23] This was a much bigger event in constitutional history than the Court seemed to note. No other court, anywhere in the world, had categorically and irreversibly outlawed the oldest form of punishment—the taking of life. There was no widespread abuse of capital punishment in Hungary, as there was in the former Soviet Union. Under the reform Communists of the 1980s, Hungary was relatively progressive. The death penalty was threatened only for various forms of aggravated homicide, burglary resulting in death, genocide, other life-threatening, highly dangerous acts, such as terrorist acts and hijacking, and certain military offenses committed in wartime. All of these offenses, or almost all of them, would pass muster under American constitutional standards as the kind of offenses that render the death penalty permissible.[24] So far as one could tell, the vast majority of the Hungarian population strongly supported the death penalty.

If there were a clear provision on point in the reformed Hungarian Constitution, one might profile the judges as acting under a simple constitutional imperative. But there was no relevant clause that could generate a knockout syllogism against the death penalty. There was nothing more compelling than the vague language of the American Eighth Amendment prohibiting "cruel and unusual punishment." Article 54(1) of the amended Hungarian Constitution provides:

In the Hungarian Republic everyone has the inherent right to life and
human dignity to which no one may be subject to arbitrary deprivation.
And no one shall be subject to torture or to cruel and inhumane or
degrading treatment or punishment. And no one shall be subject without his free consent to medical or scientific experiment.

The key phrase in this provision proved to be "arbitrary deprivation." At one time, a plurality of Justices on the U.S. Supreme Court
thought that the way American courts decide to impose the death penalty was excessively discretionary and therefore arbitrary.[25] The Hungarian judges had a different sense of the word in mind. They focused
not on the arbitrariness inherent in the process of prosecution and sentencing but on the substantive arbitrariness of a legal system that did not
have compelling reasons for threatening and using the death penalty.
The claim was that the death penalty has no sound supporting reason
and if that was so, it must be viewed as arbitrary. Life so taken was taken
arbitrarily.

Now how would one conclude that the death penalty has no sound,
supporting reason? It is fairly easy to cast doubt on the statistics supporting deterrence as a rationale for the death penalty. But the death penalty
did not become established as a standard form of punishment because
people thought that executing some would deter potential murderers
more than lesser penalties could. If there was ever a point to the death
penalty, it is that retributive justice requires that the norm against killing
be vindicated by turning the crime back on the criminal, making him
suffer as he made his victim suffer. In Western philosophical thought,
notably in Kant and in Hegel, the principle of equivalence came to be a
stable component in our thinking about just punishment. Yet the majority of the Justices on the Hungarian Constitutional Court ignored the
retributive justification for capital punishment. Limiting their focus to
deterrence and its inadequacies, the judges concluded, without much
ado, that the death penalty was arbitrary and therefore unconstitutional.

Although Article 54 of the Hungarian Constitution is almost a ver-
batim adaptation of Articles 6(1) and 7 in the 1966 International Covenant on Civil and Political Rights,[26] there is little international authority
for the Hungarian Court's decision. However valuable the right to life
may be, there is nothing in these antecedent international documents
that outlaws capital punishment. On the contrary, they are all drafted to
recognize an exception for capital punishment. For example, the rest of
Article 6 in the International Covenant details the way in which the
death penalty is appropriately applied. And the parallel provision in the
European Convention on Human Rights explicitly recognizes that offenders may be sentenced to death and may be executed according to the
judgments of a court. As far as I know, no international document flatly
prohibits the death penalty. It is true that voluntary protocols to both the
International Covenant and the European Convention require subscrib-

ing states to forswear death as a sanction, but protocols, it is worth repeating, are not binding on member states. Great Britain, Belgium, and other respectable states have so far refused to sign.

Interpreting their amended constitution to prohibit the death penalty had great symbolic significance for the Hungarian Court. One could almost say that in this decision, as well as in the subsequent decision on suspending the statute of limitations, the Hungarian jurists were trying to posture themselves as exponents of Western values. They were becoming, in effect, more Western than the Westerners.

Some strict constructionists might argue that the Hungarian Court exceeded its mandate by construing the relevant provisions of the Hungarian Constitution so boldly. But that is not my view. Preliminarily, how do we know precisely what the mandate of the Hungarian Constitutional Court is? That mandate is being worked out as the Court takes a bold step, encounters criticism, and then either cuts back or goes forward with its innovations. It cannot be the case that at all times, in all places, the rule demands only that judges apply statutes or their constitution precisely as written. Indeed, the Communist conception of socialist legality required that judges surrender their personalities to the political view embodied in the statutory law. Independent judges must be able to think imaginatively and innovatively about the law they are called upon to interpret. The judges of the Hungarian Constitutional Court are not to be faulted on the ground that they might have thought a little too creatively about their problem.

Western observers may make the mistake of thinking of these constitutional courts in Eastern Europe as courts in the narrow sense. The better analogy for the Hungarian Constitutional Court might be that it functions like an upper house of Parliament—something like the House of Lords. There is only one chamber in the Hungarian Parliament. When the court rejects a statute as unconstitutional, the lawmakers set about the task of finding a version of the legislation that will pass muster. Their response to the decision on the statute of limitations was to enact another bill based on a distinct theory—namely that the statute of limitations does not run on war crimes committed in 1956. They used the same technique of responding with altered legislation in the field of privatization, which legislation bounded back and forth between the Court and Parliament several times. Also, it is important to keep in mind that the Hungarian Parliament can amend the Constitution by the simple procedure of mobilizing a two-thirds vote. Thus the rejections of legislation by the Constitutional Court have no more power than a veto by the American President:[27] in each case, the rejection can be overturned by a two-thirds vote of the legislature.

The quest for the rule of law in Eastern Europe has moved from the streets to the arenas of political discourse and to the step-by-step dismantling of the Communist infrastructure in legal and political thought.

The paternalist residue of Communist thinking profiles the government in the taxi strike as a surrogate parent, in the Végvári dispute as a chiding teacher, and in the behavior of the Constitutional Court as wise philosophers restraining the will of the masses. These images of the parent, the teacher, and the philosopher seem to be the residue of an authoritarian legal tradition. The transition to democracy may well require a lowering of expectation and a deflating of images. The rule of law seems to flourish when power is expressed in orderly bureaucratic behavior. On this view, the law takes the place of the authority expressed by parents, teachers, and philosophers.

Notes

1. Antonin Scalia, *The Rule of Law as a Law of Rules*, 56 UNIVERSITY OF CHICAGO LAW REVIEW 1175 (1989).

2. Joseph Raz, *The Rule of Law and Its Virtue*, in JOSEPH RAZ, THE AUTHORITY OF LAW 210 (1979) (This is Friedrich Hayek's definition, endorsed by Raz).

3. Ronald Dworkin has distinguished himself by arguing this view in a variety of contexts. *See infra* the exposition of his views at pp. 32, 35, 37.

4. On the the use of the Hebrew term in the Bible, see the discussion of the debate between God and Abraham in *Genesis* 18, 19 discussed in Chapter 9 below.

5. *See, e.g.*, G.W.F. HEGEL, PHILOSOPHY OF RIGHT (T.M. Knox trans. 1952).

6. This is not necessarily the case. A legal culture could well collapse the distinction between *Recht* and *Gesetz*, and treat the rules laid down as conclusive on the content of the Right. This approach is apparent in the positivism of Hans Kelsen. *See infra* the discussion of positivism at pp. 32–33.

7. *See, e.g.*, CARLOS NINO, THE ETHICS OF HUMAN RIGHTS (1991); RICHARD TUCK, NATURAL RIGHTS THEORIES: THEIR ORIGIN AND DEVELOPMENT (1979).

8. *See supra* notes 1 and 2.

9. U.S. CONST. amend. V, and amend. XIV, § 1.

10. Palko v. Connecticut, 302 United States Reports 319 (1937).

11. *See* Herman Belz, *Constitutionalism* in THE OXFORD COMPANION TO THE SUPREME COURT OF THE UNITED STATES 190–92 (Kermit L. Hall ed., 1992).

12. For further discussion of equality, see *infra* Chapter 10.

13. Lochner v. New York, 198 United States Reports 45 (1905).

14. Roe v. Wade, 410 United States Reports 113 (1973).

15. *See* ROBERT H. BORK, THE TEMPTING OF AMERICA: THE POLITICAL SEDUCTION OF LAW 143–85 (1990).

16. One is reminded of Justice Stewart's famous aphorism about pornography: "I know it when I see it." Jacobellis v. Ohio, 378 United States Reports 184, 197 (1964) (concurring opinion).

17. Some American leftists seem to doubt whether law can ever be a neutral standard. *See* THE POLITICS OF LAW: A PROGRESSIVE CRITIQUE (David Kairys ed., 1982); Joseph W. Singer, *The Player and the Cards: Nihilism and Legal Theory*, 94 YALE LAW JOURNAL 1 (1984).

18. For more on the theoretical aspects of this debate, see George P.

Fletcher, *The Nature of Justification*, in ACTION AND VALUE IN CRIMINAL LAW (Steven Shute et al. eds., 1993).

19. HUNGARIAN CONST. art. 2 § 1: The Hungarian term *jogállam* is a literal translation of the German *Rechtsstaat*.

20. This summary of the court's opinion is based on the English translation of the Resolution of the Constitutional Court of Hungary, No. 11/1992. (III.5)AB, on file with the author.

21. *Id.* art. 57, § 4. The language of this provision is in fact ambiguous. It does not require prior legislative definition of offenses but merely that at the time of commission the offense is unlawful according to principles of *Recht* (*magyar jog szerint*).

22. BVerfGE 25, 269 (Decision of the Constitutional Court 1969).

23. The Death Penalty Case, Alkotmánybiróság [Constitutional Court] 107 Magyar Közlöny, U.T., 1, 1 (1990).

24. For an analysis of conflicting trends in the earlier Supreme Court jurisprudence on the death penalty, see GEORGE P. FLETCHER, RETHINKING CRIMINAL LAW 336–340 (1978). On recent complexities, presented in a highly readable form, see DAVID VON DREHLE, AMONG THE LOWEST OF THE DEAD (1995).

25. Furman v. Georgia, 408 United States Reports 238 (1972).

26. This document is available in BASIC DOCUMENTS SUPPLEMENT TO INTERNATIONAL LAW: CASES AND MATERIALS 151–60 (Louis Henkin et al. eds., 3d ed. 1993).

27. U.S. CONST. art. I, § 7.

2

Law

When a legislature enacts a proposed law, the law is called a statute or statutory law. When a scientist validates a hypothesis, he or she confirms a scientific law. This correlation in the use of the word "law" holds across a large number of languages. This usage of the word "law" [*Gesetz* in (German), *loi* (French), *zakon* (Russian), *ley* (Spanish) or *ḥok* (Hebrew)] should make us sit up and take notice. Wherever you go in Europe or the Middle East, you will hear lawyers referring to the work product of their parliaments in the same idiom as physics teachers use to describe the law of gravity or the second law of thermodynamics. This is true, we should note, only for the word used to refer to the law laid down by an authoritative legislature. The notion of "higher law" as expressed in the terms like *Recht* and *droit* does not fit this pattern. There may, of course, be exceptions, but the correlation between the word for legislated law and scientific law is sufficiently strong that we must wonder about its implications.

Laws: Scientific and Human

Why should one think about human laws as though they were akin to scientific laws? Do we think that when Congress enacts a law, its action will be translated automatically into conforming behavior? Perhaps the question should be put the other way around: Do we expect falling objects to obey the law in the way that humans are expected to obey the criminal law? It seems that either there is some important point underlying the persistent use of the same word for human and scientific laws or, alternatively, we are dreadfully confused.

We are not confused. Nor are we fully conscious of the ways in which the popular model of scientific laws, lurking in the background, influences our thinking about law.[1] The idea of law stands, more than anything, for inevitability. When a law applies, things cannot be otherwise; they conform necessarily to the law. Scientific laws represent more than just an observed correlation between cause and effect. As the eighteenth-century German philosopher Immanuel Kant put it in developing his theory of causation, the very fact that we perceive causal relationships means that we bring to our observations an innate notion of necessary connection.[2] We see necessity in the spring sun's melting winter's ice and therefore we describe the relationship as a causal law. To speak about laws, then, is to speak about necessity.

One thing we know for sure, however, is that human laws are not necessarily obeyed. Legislatures can pass laws telling people how to behave, but there is no necessary response from the public at large. Sometimes people conform to changes in the statutory law; sometimes they continue to do what they want to, despite new decrees from the powers that be. This is particularly the case if the law seeks to change pleasurable habits, such as those connected to smoking, drinking, using drugs, or sex. Yet there is an element of inevitability or necessity in human laws as well as scientific laws. The necessity arises not in the response of those to whom the law is addressed, but in the response of state officials to violations of the law. Representatives of the state assume that violations of the law necessitate a response. The most familiar of these responses is criminal condemnation and punishment. But the range of possible responses includes compensation for injury and judicial injunction to compel compliance with the law.

One assumption unites the phenomena of scientific law, as common people perceive law in nature, and the laws by which society lives. The facts may diverge from the law. When a divergence of this sort occurs under scientific laws, the appropriate remedy is to reformulate the law. When, for example, the evidence became inescapable that the planets moved in elliptical orbits rather than in perfect circles, the response was to abandon Copernicus's model and adopt one that better fit the facts. When a similar divergence occurs in the realm of human conduct under human laws, we assume that the right thing to do is to change not the law, but rather to discipline the deviant conduct. This need to change conduct produces the practices of stigmatization, sanctioning, and punishment that some philosophers, called positivists, have taken to be the essence of a legal system. The positivist premise is that a legal system worth its name must use force to close the gap between norms and actual behavior.[3] The nineteenth-century German philosopher

G. W. F. Hegel wrote in metaphysical terms of the criminal's Wrong displacing Society's Right, with punishment of the criminal as the only means of reinstating Right over Wrong.[4] We would not so readily engage in this assumption, were it not for the association in our thinking between scientific and human laws. The idea of law carries with it the ideal of full compliance.

Economists preach a different ideal. In contrast to the ideal of *full* compliance with the law, the devotees of law and economics have introduced the competing standard of *optimal* compliance.[5] An earlier generation of scholars might have thought that the purpose of deterring undesirable behavior, such as accidents or crimes, should be to induce perfect or full compliance. Those influenced by the economic mode of thinking now realize that the sensible way to think about deterrence in tort (i.e., accident) law, for example, is to seek the cheapest combination of spending money to avoid accidents and spending money to compensate accident victims. Every dollar spent on accident prevention must be justified by a dollar saved in reducing accidents. The implication is that the system can achieve either too much or too little prevention, thus entailing too many or too few accidents. Only when the total cost of deterrence and compensation is minimized can we say that the level of accidents is optimal.

The same method of analysis is applicable when thinking about criminal violations. The traditional view is that the aim of the law is to eliminate all homicide, rape, and theft. The problem with this goal is that it would justify a level of expenditure on the police and on the courts— not to mention incursions into our civil liberties—that would, in fact, be worse than tolerating a low level of criminal behavior. As Herbert Packer argued, the costs of enforcing some drug laws might be much worse than the behavior occurring in violation of the law.[6] Yet it is difficult for the legal system to admit openly that it prefers some victims of crime to suffer because eliminating all crime would be too costly to society as a whole. There is something immoral about aiming for an "optimal" level of rape and child abuse. The proper aim of the legal system should be to eliminate all crimes of violence. Not everyone agrees.[7]

The implications of these ways of thinking about law and punishment come to the surface in the debate between full enforcement and discretionary theories of prosecution. The full enforcement program—suggestively known in Europe as the *Legalitätsprinzip* (legality principle)—is based on the premise that the state must act so as to realize the law in practice. The discretionary view—known as the *Opportunitätsprinzip* (opportunity principle)—reflects the economist's concern about investing resources to produce the most efficient result. The former view reflects the model of laws in natural science; the latter, the goals of efficiency and optimum allocation of resources, as taught by economics. We need not at this point prefer one school to the other; the question of which is more desirable will come up again. The important point to notice here is that the legality principle disregards the required level of investment to secure conformity with the law; it builds solely on the shared cultural assumption that deviations between laws and facts are intolerable. The legality principle requires, therefore, not optimal but total enforcement.

Others features of the legal system are informed by the analogy between human and scientific laws. We take it for granted that human laws should not incorporate arbitrary limitations. Unless there is some very good reason, we should not write laws that are applicable only to one group of people or that prohibit specified behavior on Monday and not on Tuesday. These are the requirements of universality (applying to everyone)[8] and generality (prevailing all the time) that we assume are essential attributes of well-formed laws. Why do we make this assumption? We could imagine rules of a game that had arbitrary elements built into them. If it is Tuesday, we might say, you get four strikes at the plate before you are counted out. We play chess to win, but we might decide that on April 1 we will play to lose. Games are meant to be fun, and adding arbitrary variations can add to the fun. Not so with legal systems. Arbitrariness in the definition of the laws violates our essential expectations in living under the rule of law.

Ronald Dworkin illustrates this point with the following thought experiment.[9] Suppose you, as a legislator, had to decide a controversy in which the public is deeply split, say, the conditions under which abortions should be permissible. You favor abortion on demand during the first three months of pregnancy, available to all women in the jurisdiction. Call this view position X. Your opponents would permit abortion only to save the life of the mother. Call this position Y. Positions X and Y are logically inconsistent. You are faced with three possible outcomes of the dispute: X for everyone, Y for everyone, or a checkerboard compromise in which X applied to an arbitrarily selected half of the population and Y applied to the rest. Say that thirteen letters of the alphabet are picked randomly from a hat and that women whose surnames begin with any one of those letters enjoy X; all others are bound by Y. How would you rank these outcomes in order of preference? Obviously, you would favor X as your first choice. But would your second choice be Y for everyone, the antithesis of your preferred position, or would you opt for the compromise represented by the checkerboard solution? The advantage of Y is that it is cast in the normal form of a law, that is, it is universal and general. The advantage of the checkerboard solution is that though not lawlike, it would at least grant the advantages of X to half the population.

There might be many sensible people who would favor a checkerboard solution over a total defeat. Utilitarians, favoring an action that increases overall human welfare, would see half a loaf as better than

none.[10] Economists would agree. A random sample of other philosophers reveals some support for this sort of compromise.[11] Yet Dworkin
thinks that the checkerboard solution is "unprincipled." His appealing
to "principle" is another way of stating the traditional requirements,
derived from the association of human and scientific laws, that laws
must be universal and general. Any legal system that would adopt an
arbitrary classification, he argues, lacks "integrity."[12]

In drafting their constitutions or legislating statutes, states do not
always insist on principled consistency. In its infamous three-fifths compromise, the American constitution holds that the population of each
state should "be determined by adding to the whole Number of free
Persons . . . , excluding Indians not taxed, three fifths of all other Persons."[13] The point often forgotten is that the South wanted slaves to
count fully in the census in Congress in order to increase their representation "of all other Persons." Relying on a fraction might have been
unprincipled, as was negotiating a cutoff date of 1808 for the importa-
tion of slaves. It might have been unprincipled for a united Germany to
permit unrestricted abortions for two years in the former provinces of the
German Democratic Republic, but this kind of settlement was a necessary condition for the fair recognition of the diverse policies that prevailed under the socialist regime. Compromises of this sort appear frequently in constitutions, treaties, and legislation. They represent the
most that people can agree upon at a particular moment of history.

Dworkin has a sound point so far as it addresses the decisions of
courts. It would be unacceptable for judges, among themselves, to negotiate a compromise that would permit each camp on the court to prevail
part of the time or for a section of the population. Checkerboard solutions would appear much too political to be acceptable in the legal
process. The reason, I submit, is that courts must maintain a commitment to deciding under law. And that phrase "under law" invokes the
criteria of universality and generality characteristic of scientific laws—at
least as these laws are popularly perceived.

Positivism

Scientific methodology informs legal thought not only in shaping our
sense of what laws are, but in supporting positivism as a school of legal
philosophy. Curiously, the relationship between legal and scientific positivism has received little attention, even though the similarity of the two is
patent and illuminating. Scientific positivists accept hypotheses as true in
the popular sense only if they meet agreed upon criteria of validation used
in mustering, confirming, and disconfirming evidence.[14] The principle of
nonfalsifiability holds that a proposition is scientifically meaningful only
if we can imagine evidence that would constitute its refutation. The
important point about positivist methodology is that claims must be

validated by a method open to all. Empirical evidence meets that requirement of universal accessibility, while the authority of tradition or a holy
book does not. Science based on the Bible or on Aristotle[15] is binding only
on those who accept these works as authorities.

Legal positivism shares the same commitment to an agreed-upon
method of validation. Like the scientific positivist, the legal positivist
cannot bear the thought of a proposition that is neither verifiable nor
falsifiable, but that, as it were, just floats in the body of law waiting to be
believed or disbelieved. Alleged rules of law require anchors. They must
be tied down to a legislative organ that enacts, repeals and modifies laws.
That legislative organ must, in turn, be able to trace its authority to a
constitution, which in turn must find its grounding either, in Hans Kelsen's version, in a "basic norm" of the system[16] or, in H.L.A. Hart's
idiom, in a "rule of recognition" that legitimates the constitution and
thus the entire legal system.[17] After all, why do we assume that fifty-five
men meeting in Philadelphia could write a constitution that would continue to bind the United States for generations and centuries after they
and those in the state ratifying conventions were dead. Underlying every
constitution is the simple fact that the people accept it; and they show
this continuing acceptance in their daily behavior of living, more or less,
by the rules of the legal system.

The critical assumption for legal positivists is that law cannot be
treated simply as a phenomenon that exists, as nature and the universe
exist. In law as well as in science, positivism requires an agreed-upon
method for deciding whether a particular proposition is valid under the
system, namely, whether it is a law. Legal positivists insist upon a
method for verifying and falsifying hypotheses about the contents of the
legal system. For any particular proposition of law, they want to be able
to determine whether it is valid or invalid, according to the internal rules
of the system. It is valid if it can be traced to an authoritative source,
which is itself validated by the basic norm of the system; it is invalid if it
is simply asserted without having an anchor in an authoritative source.

For purposes of further discussion, the simplest working definition
of positivism is this: Positivism holds that all law is enacted law.

Higher Law

Curiously, legal positivists de-emphasize the similarities between their
project and the tenets of scientific positivism. And they are not likely to
use my simple definition stated above. H.L.A. Hart takes the critical
feature of legal positivism to be the separation of law and morality.[18]
Hans Kelsen regards the advantage of positivism to be its focus on
norms and their internal structure, as opposed to all of the neighboring
disciplines—morality, theology, sociology, politics—that influence the
development of the legal system.[19] Yet for Hart, in particular, the separa-

tion of law and morals depends on a certain view of morality. If morality derived from an authoritative source, say, from the pronouncements of a moral guru, a positivist theory of law could easily accommodate a legal system that did not recognize a separation of law and morals. The rules of the system would consist of properly enacted laws that had not been rejected as immoral by the reigning guru. That is, all law *and morality* would be enacted law *and morality*. Hart regards this view of morality as rules subject to enactment to be conceptually impossible. Morality, he insists, is inherently controvertible; it cannot be rendered true by the declarations of a Wise One.[20] According to this widespread view, a church can no more declare what is moral than it can decide what is scientifically true. Morality simply exists, and it is there for us to debate and determine for ourselves.

As some people maintain that morality is beyond manipulation by the state, others hold the same to be true of the basic principles of our legal system. Those who think that law exists without cause hold a view comparable to "big bang" theories of the universe. In law as in cosmology, some questions may be out-of-bounds. Questions about origins lead us to postulate causes for the events we seek to explain, as the religious tradition posits God as the first cause of the universe's coming to be. I take the "big bang" theory to hold that questions about what caused the initial explosion are no more appropriate than inquiries about what unicorns eat for lunch.

The view that law simply exists, without cause, is sometimes called "natural law," but this term is fraught with misunderstanding and confusion.[21] The tendency is to think that if law is natural, it must be as obvious and as unyielding as the popular perception of the law of gravity. Better that we avoid the misleading associations of law and observable nature. The best way to formulate the alternative to positivism is to recognize that the basic principles of the law should be taken as given. They exist, as morality exists, without having been created by an authoritative lawgiver.

Antipositivists deny the proposition that "all law is enacted law." They claim that some principles of law simply exist and are perceived within a particular legal culture. As we have noted, this second, indwelling conception of law is expressed in the Continental European languages as *Recht* (German), *droit* (French), *pravo* (Russian), *derecho* (Spanish). English originally used the term "Right" as the analogue to *Recht*. This comes through clearly in the seventeenth-century English decision, Dr. Bonham's case, in which the great English judge Lord Coke (pronounced: Cook) declared a statute of Parliament void as a violation of "common right and reason."[22] The assumption guiding Coke's reasoning was that the court could perceive, without a written source to back it up, what "common right" requires. If the will of Parliament was at odds with the court's perception, then so much the worse for Parliament. A century and a half later, Chief Justice John Marshall of the U.S. Supreme Court used the same mode of reasoning to declare a statute unconstitutional in *Marbury v. Madison.*[23] In Marshall's thinking, the Supreme Court had to offer its best account of what the Constitution required, regardless of what the Congress had already decreed as its view of the basic charter. As Coke found a statute inconsistent with higher principles, so the U.S. Supreme Court embarked on its history of judicial review confident that some body of law, some principles stand above democratic politics.

It is hard to know why the term Right has atrophied in English usage. The idea survives in Continental European languages, but the proper terminology now eludes lawyers in the common law tradition. It may be that a long line of positivist legal thinkers, extending from Thomas Hobbes in the seventeenth century[24] to H.L.A. Hart in the twentieth century,[25] has influenced the language we use in discussing jurisprudence. Admittedly, the notion of Right survives in the idiom of individual and human rights. Recall Martin Luther King, Jr.'s invoking natural law to argue that segregation violates the basic rights of human beings.[26] In seeking to counter the orthodoxy of enacted law, theorists like Ronald Dworkin turn naturally to "taking rights seriously" as an opening wedge to nonpositive thinking about law.[27] Consider the debate between those who advocate a pregnant woman's right to an abortion and those who insist upon the fetus's right to life. Both sides of the debate treat these asserted rights as morally true. In this respect debates about personal or human rights fulfill the normative role of the abstract theory of Right in Continental European legal cultures.

One wonders precisely what we lack in English as a result of not distinguishing between the two senses of "law"—law as legislative will and Law (capitalized) as right reason. It is worth taking a glance, then, at the Continental European philosophical tradition elaborating the concept of Law or Right. As the German philosophers Immanuel Kant and G. W. F. Hegel theorized about law, there was only one theory of Right applicable to all cultures. The Right was conceptualized in the singular, for example, as in "justice is the same for all." There is no German justice as opposed to French justice (except when we are merely describing what the courts do). In the course of the last two centuries, however, we have begun to recognize that different perceptions of Law or Right evolve differently in distinct legal cultures. Today we think it is quite normal to study Italian Law and American Law separately as if they were unrelated collections of enacted rules rather than merely different perceptions of the same body of universal principles.

Within each legal system, there are, to be sure, different bodies of Law, and this is expressed by relying on the appropriate indigenous term for Right. Thus Germans and French refer to criminal law, respectively, as *Strafrecht* and *droit penal*; and to Constitutional Law as *Verfass-ungsrecht* and *droit constitutional*. Significantly, the codes that generate these bodies of Right are labelled statutes or *Gesetze*, for the codes, the finite set of words, enacted by the legislature are but acts of will. The body of law that is inferred from these words, the product of interpreting the bare words of the codes, is always considered a body of Law or Right. The transition from the words, to the statute, to the particular area of Law requires an infusion of interpretive sensibility. Legal minds bring the flesh of common sense to the bare bones willed into being by the legislature. The same point would be expressed in our tradition by think-ing about the difference between the Constitution—namely the original document signed in 1787—and the evolved body of Constitutional Law. The Constitution in the narrow sense is but a set of enacted words; the Constitution in the broader sense, or constitutional law, is a set of re-fined principles that would reflect the best understanding that the legal minds of a particular age bring to the naked words of their national charter.

The transition from a set of authoritative words to a body of binding principles, the transition from statute to Law, from *Gesetz* to *Recht*, is the task of legal studies. Cultivating this transition is what lawyers, judges, and legal scholars do. The transition is made, in part, by bringing to bear distinctions for classifying and interpreting the words of the enacted law. New rules are made to adhere to a traditional set of categories and principles. Yet the resulting body of law is more than the set of proposi-tions enacted by the legislature. That something more, the additional elements filling out the law, yields the depth and comprehensiveness of Law or Right as opposed to the isolated particularities of statutes. The additional elements consist in part in the set of concepts, definitions, principles, and teachings in which the code is received and embedded. Some of these principles, such as the criteria of criminal responsibility and the requirement of fair statutory warning, will engage us later. The important point is that these principles render criminal legislation coher-ent. They convert legislative will into norms that people can accept and live by.

Some conservative scholars, particularly in the field of constitutional law, claim to be fearful of these arguments of analogy and extrapola-tion. As expressed in Robert Bork's best-selling book, *The Tempting of America*,[28] the argument is that activist judges who elaborate the values and principles underlying the law are likely to import their own political views into the law. The remedy for this temptation is to stick closely to the words of the Constitution, of the relevant statute, or presumably to the historical rules of the common law. This view, called "originalism" or "strict construction" in the United States,[29] hardly makes sense in the European context, where it is assumed that a process of interpretation and analogy provides the necessary bridge from the words of enacted law to the Right as a body of binding principles. Paradoxically, Continental Europeans, who have codes at the foundation of their legal culture, recognize the authority of scholars and judges as necessary participants in the playing out of the cryptic and imprecise language of the codes. English and American conservatives, with a long tradition of judicial lawmaking behind them, often appear to be more fearful of judicial innovation than are their Continental European counterparts.[30]

Given the assumption that a body of law is more than the code or statute that generates it, the claims of positivism begin to dissolve. This is, in effect, the argument that Dworkin mounted against Hart's theory of law as a body of rules logically derived from a rule of recognition.[31] The principles that constitute particular bodies of law cannot be reduced to legislative acts of will. Yet from the recognition that criminal law invariably contains more than the sum of rules stated in the criminal code, one is tempted to make a more far-reaching claim that these principles are intrinsically just. It is true that participants in the legal culture only assert those principles that they take to be just, but it need not follow that their assertions are always right.

Nonetheless, the concept of Right stands for something more than conventional assertions about what constitutes the Right. The Right, as Radbruch put it, is the ideal of justice toward which the law strives.[32] Kant defined the Right as "the sum of conditions under which the choice of one can be united with the choice of another in accordance with a universal law of freedom."[33] Kant's conception of Right furnishes the intellectual foundation for John Rawls's first principle of justice, which provides—substituting "liberty" for "freedom"—that everyone should have "the most extensive basic liberty compatible with a similar liberty for others."[34] Significantly, these definitions share the features of universality and generality characteristic of positive laws, both human and scientific.

The ambiguity of "law" in English explains why it has become plausible to say that judges make law. We are tempted to use this expression to describe innovative decisions by judges that go beyond the strict letter of the statute or precedent they may be relying upon. The idea does not translate well into languages that distinguish between *Gesetz* and *Recht*, or statute and Right. The claim that "judges make law," could be interpreted in one of two ways. Perhaps the claim is that the concept of statutory law should be broadened to encompass the binding decisions of the courts. In this sense, judges enact the positive law. The alternative interpretation is that judicial decisions bear a compelling weight in our understanding of the Right. In this sense the opinions of the judges instruct us in the Right, and thus they "make" the Right. Neither of these interpretations, standing alone, would carry the day. Judges do not enact statutes, and their opinions are not always right. But together, melded in one ambiguous aphorism, these divergent versions of "judges make law" pass without critical examination.

The debate between the positivists and the nonpositivists has recurred over the last three hundred years. The issues seem always to be the same—Is all law enacted law?—but the political motives change. Positivism is usually associated with the defense of legislative as opposed to judicial authority. The English philosophers Thomas Hobbes (1588–1679) and Jeremy Bentham (1748–1832) sought to vindicate the authority of Parliament to legislate for the common good—without being curtailed by the supposedly given and unchangeable principles of the common law. At the outset of the debate, the antipositivist Sir Edward Coke (1552–1634) led the fight for the power of the courts to limit both legislative and executive authority.

In the mid-twentieth century, the debate took on new contours. Positivism provided a vehicle for de-politicizing legal analysis. Because positivism provides an account of the entire legal system rather than the justice of particular laws, regimes that were stable and predictable qualified as legal systems. It did not matter whether they lacked moral and democratic legitimacy. Nazi Germany, South Africa, and Communist governments in Eastern Europe could meet the supposedly neutral criteria of regular obedience to enacted rules, as developed in Hart's criteria of a legal system. Thus we could speak of law in the United States and in the former Soviet Union as though it were the same phenomenon. Dworkin's critique of positivism, beginning in the late 1960s, did not assail the supposed neutrality of a method that reduced democratic governments and dictatorships to a common denominator. His argument drew on the same pro-judicial impulse that informed Coke's arguments three centuries ago.

Of course, no one expected in the 1960s and 1970s that the most unjust regimes in the world—South Africa, the Soviet Union, the German Democratic Republic—would soon fall. Perhaps a positivist, nonmoral approach toward law served the interests of peaceful cooperation in the hostile world of the cold war. After all, one could think that in South Africa under apartheid, all law was enacted law. This meant that regardless of the immorality of the legal system, it was still a legal system. The South African judges even prided themselves on deploying their wits to counteract the worst effects of apartheid.[35] One might say the same for the functioning of the courts under the more or less reformed Communist systems of the 1980s. There is something fundamentally unsatisfying, however, about approaching law in a way that blurs the distinction between legal systems that survive and those that the people overthrow at the first opportunity.

Law as the Correct Path

In the West we cultivate the idea that the Right represents the realization of what is right and good in a legal system. But this approach is hardly shared by all the legal systems in history, or in the world today. An alternative approach is suggested in East Asian legal thinking, particularly in those systems that, like the Japanese legal culture, stress the law as a path, as the way. This idea is captured in the Japanese term for law, *Ho*, based on a radical connoting water (法). The original connection between "water" and "law" remains obscure. An appealing, though admittedly speculative, interpretation finds in the symbol of water the connotation of a waterway, a flowing stream, a way for the community to travel together in natural harmony.

A analogous idea emerges in some religious legal systems, particularly in the Jewish idea of *Halakhah*, a term for Law that derives from the root meaning "to go." The *Halakhah* captures the idea of a path that the community travels together in its effort to realize God's plan on earth. As written in Psalms 119: "Blessed are the undefiled in the way, who walk in the law of the lord." Significantly, neither traditional Japanese nor the language of the Talmud had a term for individual "rights." Rights separate the individual from the community; they express a capacity to stand apart from the collective path. Yet the basic idea for law in these cultures stresses the commonality and the cooperative nature of the legal experience.

The difference between the two approaches to law emerges boldly in the analysis of defensive violence. The Western approach toward legitimate self-defense stresses the wrongful nature of aggression.[36] An aggressive act against an innocent person violates the Right. The defensive response restores the Right by vindicating the freedom and autonomy of the threatened person. This Kantian way of thinking about legitimate defensive force has come to dominate Western thinking about justified force. Even the term "justification"—based on the root "jus" for law—elicits the symbolic restoration of the Law or the Right by resisting aggression.

The talmudic approach to defensive force starts not with abstractions like the theory of Right, but with the concrete duty of one person to rescue another in distress. The legitimation of force rests on our interdependence, on our obligation to intervene to shield others from disaster. Thus the talmudic sages interpreted the biblical maxim in Leviticus 19:16, *Do not stand idly by*, as a prohibition against passively standing by when one's neighbor suffers.[37] The duty to intervene to assist a victim of aggression is no different from a duty to aid someone attacked by wild animals or subject to a natural disaster. That the attack is wrongful, a violation of the Right, is beside the point. The duty to intervene derives from a neighbor's being in danger. Once established, this duty to intervene allows one to speak of an implied right to do that which duty requires.

The differing analyses of self-defense reflect competing approaches to the relevance of conflict and cooperation in the theory of law. The Western view that defensive force is justified in opposition to wrongful aggression reflects the more general view that the function of law is to resolve conflict, to provide an abstract medium that sorts out true claims from false. By beginning with the idea of protecting individual freedom, the Western notion of Right pits every individual against his neighbor. It is not surprising, then, that the liberal Western notion of Right would be hostile to a duty to rescue one's neighbor in distress. In an alternative idea of law, seemingly expressed in the Japanese and Jewish premise of a path traveled together, the fate of one's neighbor is critically important; the duty to rescue is assumed, for the neighbor is a partner in a common venture.

Thus there are three distinct sources for the idea of law. One is the analogy between scientific laws and human laws. A second is the notion of higher law that brings an element of moral rectitude to living under law, and the third is the ancient idea that law is the path on which the community travels as an organic unit. The first source lends certain formal criteria—such as regularity, generality, and universality—to the laws that govern social life. The second idea of higher law renders life under law an aspiration for all people everywhere. And the third, communal vision of law stresses the element of social solidarity that is induced in societies that live peaceably under law. In any given society, such as that of the United States, all three of these sources converge in generating a complex legal culture.

Notes

1. There is no reason to assume that the notion of scientific law is more basic than the idea of human law. *See* J. E. Ruby, *The Origins of Scientific Law*, 47 JOURNAL OF THE HISTORY OF IDEAS 341 (1986).

2. IMMANUEL KANT, CRITIQUE OF PURE REASON 172 (Norman Kemp-Smith trans., 1964, originally published 1781).

3. This was notably the position taken in JOHN AUSTIN, THE PROVINCE OF JURISPRUDENCE DETERMINED 21–25 (W. Rumble ed., 1951, originally published 1832).

4. G.W.F. HEGEL, PHILOSOPHY OF RIGHT 64–73 (T.M. Knox trans., 1952).

5. For an influential treatment of this theme, see GUIDO CALABRESI, THE COSTS OF ACCIDENTS: A LEGAL AND ECONOMIC ANALYSIS (1970).

6. HERBERT PACKER, LIMITS OF THE CRIMINAL SANCTION 337–42 (1968) (concluding that the costs of enforcement weighed against the attempt to ban the use of marijuana).

7. For more on the economic mode of thinking, see *infra* Chapter 10.

8. The notion of universality is not as simple as meets the eye. *See infra* the discussion of equality in Chapter 8.

9. *See* RONALD DWORKIN, LAW'S EMPIRE 178–84 (1986).

10. The principles of utilitarianism are explained *infra* in Chapter 9.

11. Without being in the camp either of the utilitarians or the economists, a distinguished legal philosopher, Joseph Raz, has indicated to me that he regards the checkerboard solution as a sensible second choice.

12. Dworkin, *supra* note 9, at 184. Revealing a rather common mistake, Dworkin refers to the checkerboard division as "Solomonic." *Id.* He forgot that Solomon did not actually favor or adopt a compromise solution in the dispute about who was really the mother of the disputed child.

13. U.S. Const. art. I, § 2.

14. On controversies regarding the use of "laws" in modern science, see E. Macmillan, *The Goals of Natural Science*, 58 Proceedings of the American Philosophical Association 37 (1984); Bas Van Fraassen, Laws and Symmetry 1–39 (1989). If theories of law are as complicated as this book argues, we can assume that theories of science are equally controverted.

15. The Greek philosopher Aristotle (384–322 B.C.E.) himself engaged in empirical scientific studies. When later writers simply cited Aristotle, they were relying on his authority rather than testing his hypotheses themselves.

16. Hans Kelsen, The Pure Theory of Law, ch. V, sec. 34 (Max Knight trans., 1967) (discussing the *Grundnorm* or "basic norm.").

17. H.L.A. Hart, The Concept of Law 94–99 (2d ed. 1994).

18. *Id.* at 155–84.

19. *See* Kelsen, *supra* note 16.

20. Hart, *supra* note 17, at 175–77.

21. For a modern version of Catholic natural law theory, see John Finnis, Natural Law and Natural Rights (1980). *See also* Thomas Acquinas, Summa Theological I & II, Quaestiones 90–97 (available in translation: The Treatise on Law (R.J. Henle, S.J. ed., 1993)).

22. 77 English Reports 638, 652 (C.P. 1610).

23. 5 United States Reports (1 Cranch) 137 (1803) (The Court declared a portion of §13 of the 1789 Judiciary Act unconstitutional because it purported to give the Supreme Court a power that the Constitution denied to the Court.).

24. *See* Thomas Hobbes, A Dialogue Between a Philosopher and a Student of the Common Laws of England (J. Cropsey ed., 1971) (1st ed. London 1681).

25. *See* Hart, *supra* note 17.

26. *See Letter from a Birmingham Jail*, in A Testament of Hope: The Essential Writings of Martin Luther King, Jr. (1986), also published at 26 University of California at Davis Law Review 835 (1993).

27. *See* Ronald Dworkin, Taking Rights Seriously (1977).

28. Robert Bork, The Tempting of America: The Political Seduction of the Law (1990).

29. Thomas Jefferson was one of the early advocates of what he called "rigorous construction." "Our peculiar security," he wrote, "is in the possession of a written Constitution. Let us not make it a blank paper by construction." The Political Writing of Thomas Jefferson: Representative Selections 144 (E. Dumbault ed., 1955).

30. For an elaboration of the ways in which the English tradition insists on constraining judges even more than the American practice, see Patrick S. Atiyah & Robert S. Summers, Form and Substance in Anglo-American Law: A Comparative Study in Legal Reasoning, Legal Theory, and Legal Institutions (1987).

31. *See* Dworkin's classic article, *The Model of Rules*, 35 University of Chicago Law Review 14 (1967), discussed in greater detail in Chapter 3.

32. Gustav Radbruch, Rechtsphilosophie 127 (6th ed. E. Wolf ed., 1963): *Recht [ist] die Wirklichkeit, die den Sinn hat, der Gerechtigkeit zu dienen.*

33. Immanuel Kant, The Metaphysics of Morals 56 (Mary Gregor trans., 1991).

34. John Rawls, A Theory of Justice 60 (1971).

35. *See* Stephen J. Ellmann, In a Time of Trouble: Law and Liberty in South Africa's State of Emergency 226–44 (1992).

36. For a classic account, see John Locke, Two Treatises of Government 278–82 (Peter Laslett ed., 1988).

37. Babylonian Talmud, Tractate Sanhedrin 72A. *See also* my article, *Punishment and Self-Defense,* 8 Law and Philosophy 201 (1989).

3

Rules and Discretion

Thinking about law in this century has focused largely on the role of rules in providing the foundation of a legal system. This preoccupation has seized the jurisprudential mind largely because the written materials of the law have progressively taken the shape of propositions that look like rules. We have the modern codes of the Continent as well as an imposing body of statutory law in the common-law jurisdictions. Law students in the United States—and presumably elsewhere—prepare for their examinations by mastering and memorizing rules. So far as anyone can tell, the law today is written in the form of rules.

Rules connote straight lines. The same Latin root *regula* generates the words for rule in Germanic as well as Romance languages. Decisions according to rules run in predictable, straight paths. Discretionary decisions invoke an image of unpredictable tangents. The discretionary line curves and weaves; its course depends on who is drawing it. The question presents itself, then: What is the relationship between law as following rules and the discretionary power to depart from the straight and narrow?

Kinds of Rules

Legal theorists have developed an extraordinary body of learning about rules, their structure, and the way we use them.[1] H. L. A. Hart develops an entire theory of law on the basis of the distinction between primary and secondary rules.[2] *Primary rules*, such as the rules of criminal and tort law, impose rights and duties directly on citizens; *secondary rules* provide the means of incorporation, contract making, legislation, and adjudication that generate the primary rights and duties. The best way to grasp this distinction is to think about the difference between the rights and duties generated by a contract and the rules about making contracts (requiring, e.g., an offer, acceptance, consideration, and perhaps a document testifying to the terms of the agreement). Suppose the contract is to purchase apples. The primary rule of the contract is that the seller must deliver a certain amount of apples of a certain kind and grade on a certain date and the buyer must pay a certain price. The secondary rules for making the contract resemble the steps in a recipe for baking a cake. If you follow the rules, step-by-step, the product in one case is a cake and, in the other, a contract.

Hart applies this distinction to explain the difference between primary rules enacted by a legislative body and the rules that establish a legislative body, define its competence, and specify the procedure for enacting a law. The secondary rules of legislation resemble the rules for making contracts. They empower people to change their legal relationships. A contract changes a legal relationship by generating new primary rights and duties. Legislation (e.g., the enactment of a criminal statute) also changes legal relationships by imposing new duties on individuals to conform their conduct to the statute. The French civil code noted this similarity between contracts and legislation by proclaiming that contracts "take the place of the [statutory] law among the parties to the agreement."[3]

Hart's distinction between two kinds of rules carries forward the effort by Wesley Hohfeld earlier in the century to clarify the different senses in which we use the term "right" in English.[4] Individuals acquire rights under contract, and they also have the right to make contracts. These two kinds of rights, Hohfeld claimed, are fundamentally different. The right under the contract is a right to claim a performance; the right to make a contract is the right to change one's legal relationship with another party, thus bringing into existence the right to claim a performance at a specific time. To make this distinction clear, Hohfeld proposed using the word "power" to connote the second kind of right, the right to change a legal relationship.

A simple triadic situation of conflict illustrates the illuminating power of these distinctions. Consider the case of Alex who enters into an agreement to sell his condo to Betty. Under this contract Alex has a duty to transfer ownership and possession of the condo to Betty, say, on the following June 1. And Betty has a right to compel Alex to engage in this act of turning over physical control as well as legal ownership of the condo. Now suppose that before the June 1 deadline, Charlie comes along and offers Alex more money for the apartment. Alex transfers legal title to Charlie by engaging in all the locally required formalities. The question is whether Charlie has become the owner of the condominium. The generally accepted answer is yes. Hohfeld would explain this complex relationship in the following way. By entering into a contract with Betty, Betty acquired a right that Alex transfer title in the condominium to her. Though Alex was under a duty to transfer title in the condo to Betty, he retained the power to transfer legal ownership to whomever he wished—even if doing so amounted to a breach of the contract with Betty. The result, therefore, is that Charlie becomes owner of the apartment and Alex must pay damages for breach of contract to Betty.

As this example illustrates, relevant distinctions sharpen our perception of legal phenomena. A legal system consists of diverse forms and structures. This diversity resists reduction to a single model for all laws. A few other distinctions are worthy of note.

Meir Dan-Cohen has elaborated an illuminating distinction between conduct rules and decision rules.[5] Conduct rules are directed to the citizenry; decision rules, to judges. Some primary rules instruct citizens that they must act or abstain from acting in certain ways; others instruct judges about how they should respond to legal violations. This is a useful distinction because, as Dan-Cohen argues, our tolerance for defects such as vagueness is more easily understood if we think of the rules as directed to judges trained in the system than to citizens who must base their conduct entirely on the language of the rule.

Another conceptual line of relevance to understanding the law runs between constitutive and regulatory rules. *Constitutive rules* define concepts that do not come into being unless the rules are followed; *regulatory rules* tell us how to work with entities that exist apart from the rule. The rules of games are constitutive. To move the knight in chess, you must follow the rules for moving the knight. If you move it the way you would move a castle, you have not transacted a bad move but rather have made no move at all. On the other hand, if you follow a recipe for a cake and forget to put in the sugar or the cinnamon, you still bake a cake, but it will be a bad cake. The recipe is a regulatory rule, at least as to many of the ingredients. I suppose if you forgot the flour and the baking soda, the result of your baking will be some kind of syrup that we would not call a cake.

This distinction has considerable relevance in legal theory. Consider a rule requiring that certain types of contracts be in writing. Is that rule constitutive or regulatory? Does it define for us when a contract comes into being? Or does it merely regulate the range of contracts that are subject to enforcement? Or what about the rule that contracts with prostitutes are void as against public policy [*contra bonos mores*]? Whether unenforceable contracts exist in these cases has considerable practical significance; if money changes hands pursuant to the contract, the question arises whether the recipient receives the money unjustifiably and must return it. In these two situations, most people, whether trained in law or not, would perceive a contract as having come into being; it could not be enforced, but it would a defense for the recipient against restoring funds received pursuant to the contract. A contract with a child below the age of capacity would be entirely different. The rule governing capacity is not regulatory but constitutive, which means that absent capacity, no contract comes into being. The person who takes the child's money has no justifiable basis for keeping it and must therefore give it back.

Hart's theory of positivism proceeds on the implicit assumption that all secondary rules are constitutive; they define whether a contract or will is made, a corporation comes into existence, a legislature enacts a law, or a court acts within its competence. The existence of merely regulatory secondary rules would threaten Hart's thesis, for they would imply that prior to the advent of the rules there was something—contracts, marriages, and property—there to regulate. We have an intuition that no matter what the law says, a deal is a deal, even when made with a prostitute. A marriage is a marriage, whether it satisfied the formal requirements of the law or not. These common sense judgments obviously spring from conventional social practices as well as from rudimentary ideas of fairness. As such, they are as immune to legal change and manipulation as are the concepts of action and blame that inform the criminal law. The legislature could scream at the top of its lungs: this is no contract! But the public would still feel that a deal with a prostitute or a drug dealer was a contract—though not enforceable.

The legislated law can be underinclusive in the sense that it defines certain deals as legal contracts and leaves out others from the scope of the enacted rules. The law can be overinclusive as well. The legislature could pass a statute holding that all couples who live together and share a common bedroom shall be regarded as married. This piece of official paper would not convince those who have not taken marital vows that they really are married. The legislature simply cannot manipulate the meanings of the basic legal concepts that shape our social lives. It is true that a properly constituted quorum may enact decision rules telling judges how to act; what the assembled men and women cannot do is pass laws that automatically change the way people think about contract, marriage, adultery, theft, and murder. The immutability of these basic concepts provides the second-century Roman jurist Gaius with a strong argument in favor of natural law, which means in this context simply that certain concepts are embedded in our social life.[6] The most the legal system can do is enact rules premised on these concepts—regulatory rather than constitutive rules.

Rules and Decisions

Despite this considerable sophistication about rules and the way they operate, we lack an adequate understanding of the way in which rules yield decisions in concrete cases. The two great vices of contemporary jurisprudence are to believe either that rules dictate results as do computer algorithms or that rules have no bearing at all on the adjudication of disputes. Either the rule produces a straight line or the resulting line is a random walk. Hart dubs the former vice *formalism* and the latter, *skepticism.*[7] According to the former extreme, decisions follow deductively from the rules; the judge as person, as a human being with feeling and a sense of Right, contributes nothing to the outcome of disputes. According to the opposite extreme, the creative impulse of the judge is all there is; the law itself contributes nothing.

Think of the law as a ray of light that passes through a drinking glass. The refraction of the light wave depends on how much water there is in the glass. The more water, the more the light is affected by its passing through the glass. The glass is in the role of the judge who receives and applies the law. How much the judge's personality contributes to the refraction of the law is the matter in dispute. Formalists contend that there is no water in the glass. The light—the ray of law—passes straight through the judge and defines the resulting decision. The skeptic holds that the glass is full, so full that the light can hardly be recognized after it passes through it. It is as though the full glass—the judge in the skeptic's mind—generates its own light. It becomes its own source of law.

It's hard to find reflective jurists who are formalists, who think that the glass is empty. Perhaps Montesquieu was one when he argued that the judge is no more than *la bouche de la loi,* "the mouthpiece of the law."[8] Curiously, the standard Communist line favored this limited conception of judging. Judges were supposed to apply the law—or any supervening Party directive—without considering the value questions raised by the statutory rule. Eastern European judicial opinions, even today, cite neither commentaries nor case law. They foster the pretense that the law somehow applies itself in the variegated circumstances of real life. This view is ridiculed in the American literature as "mechanical jurisprudence."

The formalist position invariably engenders the skeptical response of the disillusioned who have discovered that the God of rules is dead. If rules do not dictate results the way algorithms do, then they must be, in Karl Llewellyn's words, nothing but the "pretty playthings" of the law.[9] Oliver Wendell Holmes, Jr. captured this sentiment: "General propositions do not decide concrete cases."[10] These are slogans of the so-called realist school that came into prominence in the 1930s.[11] Contemporary critics rehearse this program as they speak of deconstructing legal doctrine and exhibiting the indeterminacy of the rules and of the system as a whole.[12] What, then, does the legal system actually accomplish? Skeptical leftists relish the thesis that the facade of law is but a mask for the exercise of political power. The source of light is an illusion. The glass, full of politically charged water, is all there is.

Neither the formalists nor the skeptics come close to the mark. Formalism cannot be right, for we know that judging requires sensitivity to the possibility of interpreting a rule broadly or narrowly, applying it as in analogous cases or recognizing an exception in view of the special circumstances of the case. Formalism trades on the analogy between the rules of games and the law. If the rules of baseball apply straightforwardly to the facts (assuming we know as a fact whether the player touched the base before the player on the opposing team tagged him out), then the same should be true of legal rules. Yet games are played under highly stylized, repetitive circumstances. There is no need to adjudicate novel cases of first impression. Radical skepticism, in turn, cannot be right, for it ignores the run-of-the-mill cases that are perfectly predictable under the conventional rules of the system. There must be an account of judging under law that reveals neither the naiveté of formalism nor the cynicism of those who think of judges as political advocates. A correct account would find the glass neither empty nor full.

Alas, we have no adequate theory to describe how full the glass might be. We know the judge receives the law and issues a decision. The law does not simply pass through him or her, without refraction. Yet we have no approach toward measuring the relative input of the law and of the judge's personality in the shaping of the law. We seem to be resigned to perpetual swings between the extreme positions holding that the glass is either completely empty or completely full.

Discretion in Hard Cases

Working out the relationship between rules and decisions has become the preoccupation of 20th-century American jurisprudence. Hart tried to solve the problem by distinguishing between the clear or core cases of a rule's application and the penumbra of "open texture" that surrounds the core. When a case arises in a rule's open texture, there is nothing that a judge can do but make "a choice" or "exercise discretion" in fashioning the best solution under the circumstances.[13] Hart seeks in this spatial metaphor to give both the formalists and the skeptics their due. The formalists reign supreme in the core of uncontroversial application; the skeptics have their day in the penumbral realm of open texture.

The operation of most legal rules illustrates the point. Hart relies heavily on the example of a municipal ordinance forbidding "taking vehicles into the city park." The problem here is deciding what is a vehicle. A motor-driven car or moped clearly is; baby carriages and roller skates are problematic. If someone drives a car into the park, a police officer need not pause and ponder the rule's meaning before issuing her a ticket. If someone is cited for pushing a baby carriage, the judge hearing the case will have to reflect upon the point of the statute before deciding whether the rule is violated.

Examples drawn from the daily work of the courts are even more gripping. Consider the problem posed in *School Board of Nassau County v. Arline*,[14] a recent decision by the U.S. Supreme Court. A school board in Florida dismissed a teacher infected with contagious tuberculosis. The school received federal funding and therefore the question arose whether the dismissal violated the Federal Rehabilitation Act of 1973, which, at the time of the decision, prohibited firing an "otherwise qualified handicapped individual."[15] It is very clear that the blind and deaf and those confined to wheelchairs are handicapped. But is someone infected with tuberculosis handicapped or just sick? The question has great significance in negotiating the question whether someone who is seropositive for AIDS (or someone stricken with the disease) should have qualified as handicapped and therefore received the antidiscrimination protection of the federal statute.

In the face of this ambiguity, how should the courts decide whether someone stricken with tuberculosis qualifies as handicapped? According to Hart's spatial conception of the problem, the case arises in the penumbra of the statute and therefore the judges should exercise their "discretion" or make a "choice" in resolving the case. The leftist critics would take this choice to be irreducibly political, presumably laden with implications for the rights of gays and other groups exposed to a high risk of AIDS. It is almost as though in passing from the realm of the easy to the hard cases, one falls off the plateau of the law into an abyss of political and legislative choices. There must be a better way to conceptualize the problem of deciding hard cases.

In thinking about judicial choice and discretion under the law, we are bedeviled by the language we use. In one sense, judges obviously bring to bear their wisdom or discretion when interpreting the law. But the claim that judges exercise discretion in deciding cases carries a stronger claim, reflecting a borrowing of the term from its original habitat in administrative decision making. Those entrusted with executing a program have the discretion to pick the means best suited to the program's ends. Agencies have discretion in developing programs to protect the environment, to insure safety in the air, and to collect taxes efficiently. Professors typically have discretion in planning their lectures and assigning texts to be read in class. Judges exercise discretion in managing their calendars. They must decide whether to grant continuances, when and how long to hold trial, whether to join or separate defendants, when to limit redundant testimony—and all these decisions are treated as exercises of discretion.

In their original habitat, discretionary decisions carried, and still carry, a specific legal consequence. Unlike decisions on the law, they are not subject to appellate reversal just because they are wrong. They are subject to reversal, as an *abuse* of discretion, only if they deviate substantially from normal and expected practice.[16]

In American legal thinking, discretion has been an imperialistic concept. Its field of application has invaded neighboring bodies of law and conferred upon them its conceptual cast. We now speak routinely about the Supreme Court's discretion in deciding whether to grant certiorari (whether the Court will hear the case). We also speak about a prosecutor's decision whether to charge someone as discretionary. In neither of these cases is reversal possible for abuse of discretion. Both decisions are managerial in nature. The Court regulates its calendar by selecting among the petitions for certiorari. The Court grants only 80 or 90 of the approximately 5,000 petitions it receives each year. Prosecutorial decisions, too, reflect the need to find the best means to realize the society's mixed and conflicting objectives in punishing criminals. This managerial feature of the decisions leads us to call them "discretionary," thereby assimilating them to standard cases of administrative decision making.

Perhaps the greatest linguistic incursion of discretion has been in the field of criminal justice. It is common as well to say that the police exercise discretion in deciding whom to arrest. Of course, in the elementary sense of exercising judgment in evaluating the evidence under the law, prosecutors and police on the beat obviously exercise discretion. So does everyone else who must decide whether roller skates are a vehicle or particular instances of risky motoring cross the line and become punishable as "reckless driving."

If this is all that is meant by discretion in the criminal process, however, it is unlikely that the precise word "discretion" would have been necessary. In Continental legal cultures it would be surprising to find literature relying on the administrative concept of *pouvoir discretionaire* (French) or *Ermessensfreiheit* (German) to capture Hart's point that in hard cases, in the open texture of the law, judges exercise "discretion" in reaching a decision. In the Russian literature, the term is virtually nonexistent—perhaps because administrative law under Communism was underdeveloped.

To be pondered, then, is the work the term discretion does as its usage extends into new areas. What is the point that observers of the legal process are trying to make as they find discretion at every turn? The weaker but valuable claim is that in making evaluations of fact and law, police, prosecutors, and judges not only perceive the world, but structure it as they see fit. They exercise a power that German sociologists illuminatingly call *Definitionsmacht*[17]—the power to define the world. That is, after prosecutors and judges collectively decide that a particular instance of risky driving is in fact reckless driving, it *becomes* reckless driving. In the legal process, arguably, the distinction is then lost between subject (what is in the mind of the decider) and object (what is "out there" to be decided). The power to decide becomes the power to define.

There is some truth to this claim simply because in many borderline situations the public defers to the judgments of authoritative officials. Yet there is no way in the world as we know it that the power to convict can actually make a person guilty. Convictions are substantively right or wrong depending on whether the suspect actually is guilty or not. It is the rule—and not the decision—that determines when someone is guilty. The insightful claim about *Definitionsmacht* holds in borderline situations with low stakes simply because the circumstances are so murky that the public cannot exercise effective supervision over its legal decision makers. As the stakes go up and the conflict becomes more visible, the issues become clearer and claims about the power to define become less compelling.

The second and much stronger sense in which we talk about prosecutorial and judicial discretion invokes the distinction made earlier between the *Legalitätsprinzip* and the *Opportunitätsprinzip*. The former stands for full enforcement of the criminal law; the latter, for discretionary enforcement. *Opportunität* is best translated here as expediency. Enforcement becomes expedient as prosecutors make judgments not only about whether they can secure a conviction but about whether they should allocate their resources in one campaign or another. Given their limited capacities, should they try to convict drug dealers, tax evaders, child abusers, wife batterers or petty embezzlers? These are policy decisions about how best to allocate the resources of the prosecution. A further level of expediency is expressed in the institution, common in the United States, of plea-bargaining or reducing charges for some suspects in order to minimize the expense of trial or to secure their testimony against more important suspects. While the principle of full enforcement might have to yield to judgments about how best to allocate limited resources, it need not, and does not, accommodate the prosecutor's tactical decision that some cases will fare better if particular defendants are favored with reduced charges.

The distinctions among these types of discretionary decision are often overlooked in debates about whether Continental systems of criminal prosecution are really discretionary, despite protestation of a commitment to the *Legalitätsprinzip*.[18] Yet there is an enormous gulf in principle between evaluating the facts and law and making resource allocation decisions, on the one hand, and deciding that some guilty people should receive lesser punishment or go free, on the other. The point of the legality principle is to ensure that only courts—and not prosecutors—decide when suspects should be treated as acquitted of the charges against them.

Let us return now to the question that initiated our inquiry. We need a label for the phenomenon of taking the term "discretion" out of its original habitat and using it to describe the process of deciding hard cases in the penumbra of a rule's meaning. Let us refer to this rhetorical move as a category shift. The roots of this category shift in discretion are unclear, but I hypothesize that the realists initiated the move in order to accentuate the power and the responsibility of judges to decide cases according to the best available arguments. Of course, no one would suggest that judges should simply make an arbitrary choice, that is, engage in the moral equivalent of flipping a coin. Discretion is not prerogative. A court's resolving a dispute at law is not equivalent to a governor's granting a prisoner's petition for clemency. Somehow, judicial decisions should both be under law and expressive of the judge's good judgment.

The category shift in describing the way courts decide cases dovetails with a parallel development about the values that should guide judicial decision making. At some uncertain point in the development of American legal thought, we began to distinguish between politics and policies, both of which derive from the same Greek roots *polis* and *politicus*. This is a rather unusual distinction, one difficult to express in European legal languages.[19] Politics is dirty; policies are clean. Politics is regarded as antithetical to law and the rule of law; policies are the goals that we seek to achieve within the law. The increasing emphasis on policies in modern jurisprudence expresses the value goals that courts should seek to maximize in deciding cases. Examples of these policies are deterrence in criminal law, risk distribution in the law of torts, and promoting trade in the law of commercial transactions. Economists have sought to unify all these policies under the policy objective of maximizing efficiency.

If judging is an instrumental practice designed to maximize the impact of decisions on policy objectives, then the concept of discretion seems to be the fitting way to describe the process of decision. As a policy-maximizing decision maker, a judge functions like an administrator charged with taking measures to implement a social program. However inexact it may be to use the term discretion to talk about interpreting rules of law, the usage has become commonplace. The usage expresses an emphasis in American thought on judicial power and responsibility and a conception of law that stresses the realization of policy objectives.

Thinking of judges as makers of policy flies in the face of some assumptions current at the time the Constitution was drafted. In response to a proposal at the 1787 Constitutional Convention to permit Supreme Court justices to advise the president on the merit of bills passed by Congress, Elbridge Gerry of Massachusetts said that it was "foreign" to the justices' office "to make them judges of the policy of public measures."[20] Nathaniel Gorham, also of Massachusetts, said that the justices "are not to be presumed to posses any peculiar knowledge of the mere policy of public measures."[21] Even today, as legal theorists have come to insist that judges exercise discretion, the perception of judges as policy administrators remains partial and conflicted. The term "discretion" may have caught on as a way to describe the process of decision, but trial judges do not enjoy the kind of autonomy that administrators have in the exercise of discretion. Administrators with discretion are subject to reversal on appeal only in extreme cases of bad judgment—where they "abused" their discretion. Trial judges are subject, more demandingly, to reversal any time they are wrong on the law in a way that matters to the outcome of the trial.

Discretion and Duty

There are, in sum, three basic strategies that one might follow in analyzing the relationship between rules and decisions. The skeptic treats the decision maker as free of the impact of rules and other restraints in the materials of the law; the formalist insists that the law determines the outcomes of cases, and Hart struggles to defend a middle strategy that divides the realm of rules between the domain of the skeptic and the domain of the formalist. Of these three positions, the most difficult to defend is that of the formalist. And that is precisely why Ronald Dworkin has made such a dramatic impression on American legal theory. He dared to defend the formalist position, not the simpleminded version scorned as mechanical jurisprudence, but a more sophisticated theory that denied the role of discretion in decision making and displayed sensitivity to deeper concerns of value.

Dworkin reconciled these seemingly inconsistent objectives in his classic article *The Model of Rules*, published in 1967.[22] The sensitivity to value is expressed in Dworkin's insistence that "principles, policies and other sorts of standards" not only bear upon decision making in the penumbra of open texture; these standards that bespeak value commitments are part of the law itself. Once we recognize the role of these principles and policies, Dworkin maintains, "we are suddenly aware of them all around us."[23] And it is true that courts could hardly function without invoking foundational criteria of justice such as the presumption of innocence, the principle of proportionality, *nulla poena sine lege* [no punishment without legislative definition of offenses], principles such as *volenti non fit injuria* [consent negates harm], and *nullus commodum capere potest de injuria sua propria* [no person should profit from his own wrong]. In addition, courts are moved by policy objectives such as deterrence, risk distribution, and promotion of commercial transactions. The important feature of these value-laden standards is that they apply in varying degrees. Their impact varies from case to case, context to context. Sometimes we take consent very seriously; other times we take consent less seriously and use different criteria to measure it. The implication of this "set of shifting, developing and interacting standards"[24] is to undermine Hart's thesis that a single master rule, called the rule of recognition, can generate sufficient criteria to assess when a particular standard is or is not part of the law. The gist of Dworkin's counterattack is that you can never tell whether a given standard will influence a legal debate until you are in the debate and one side or the other invokes the standard. There is no way of knowing today how important freedom of speech is in Russia until borderline cases arise in which advocates and courts will have to decide when free speech should yield to other values such as national security, the sensibilities of insulted ethnic minorities, the claims of those offended by obscenity, and the interests of businesses who wish to advertise harmful products. Conflicts of principle and policy are worked out in these concrete cases. No formula, no rule of recognition, can specify in advance the full range of criteria and desiderata that constitutes the law governing the conflict.

As far as it goes, Dworkin's thesis sounds like a vindication of those skeptical about the predictability and determinability of legal disputes. If there is no way of knowing the rule in advance of the argument, it sounds as though the champions of choice and discretion have won the day. Yet Dworkin's argument undercuts claims of pervasive discretion as well as the positivist insistence on a rule of recognition. His argument is that judges never exercise discretion except in the weak senses of bringing to bear their judgment in interpreting the law and rendering non-reviewable decisions.[25] What judges do *not* have is precisely the kind of discretion that realists (whom he dubs nominalists) said they have: they do not act as administrators or legislators or someone "simply not bound by the authority in question."[26] If the concept of discretion expanded to meet the jurisprudential claims of the realists, Dworkin's move is to drive the concept back to its original habitat.

The significant feature of Dworkin's critique of discretion is the way it differs from more conventional efforts to limit, check and, constrain the discretion of decision makers. Not all those who accept the ubiquitous nature of discretion in the legal process are skeptical about the possibility of controlling decision makers. It is quite common for legal scholars to talk about limiting discretion by developing more precise rules, better guidelines, and a defining practice in the case law.[27] This way of thinking about the restraining effect of the law starts with a particular conception of decisional leeway. The decision maker is viewed externally as restrained by a relatively narrow or wide channel leading to relatively few or many possible results. The way to control the decision maker is to narrow the channel by adding weights and words that narrow and limit the paths leading to decision.

An alternative approach to discretion requires us to think not about the external weight of the law, but about the internal sense of being bound by the law. Being bound is not the same as being subject to or subservient to the law.[28] Being bound connotes a duty, a commitment to decide on the basis of certain considerations. If judges are bound by *Recht* as well as *Gesetz*, Law as well as statutory law, they cannot decide solely on the basis of the law laid down. They must also consider the principles of Right that bind their deliberations.

The implicit claim in Dworkin's analysis is that a duty to find the correct result displaces discretion. He gives the example of a sergeant ordered to "take the five most experienced men" on a mission.[29] The claim is that the sergeant does not have discretion "because he is bound to reach an understanding, controversial or not, of what his orders . . . require, and to act on that understanding."[30] The same would be true of a boxing referee bound to decide which fighter has been the more aggressive. The open texture of the standard, the potential controversy about the decision, does not in itself render a decision discretionary. If the decision maker is duty bound to find the truth of the matter—either about who is the most experienced soldier or the more aggressive fighter—he or she has no discretion.

The general proposition underlying this claim is that however difficult an intellectual inquiry, the duty to find the truth renders an inquiry nondiscretionary. The verification of this claim turns on what we would say in describing the ordinary processes of inquiry when we believe there is a fact of the matter. We would not describe a scientist's or historian's empirical search for the truth as discretionary. Nor would we say that the jury has discretion to determine whether the defendant is guilty or innocent. Suppose that one juror admits to another, "I just cannot decide whether the prosecution has proved guilt beyond a reasonable doubt." It would be inappropriate to instruct her, "Just use your discretion" or to say, "The choice is yours." When there is a truth of the matter, as there is about guilt or innocence, the decision is not a matter of choice or discretion.

The problem is fathoming whether in legal discourse there is a fact or truth of the matter. Are claims about the law right or wrong in the same way that claims about the real world are true or false?[31] It is rather difficult to believe that they are, for the search for answers to legal questions takes us away from the world and into the materials of the law. The questions whether roller skates are a vehicle or being infected with the AIDS virus is a handicap are embedded in particular statutory enterprises, with their own histories, their own conventional purposes, and their own case law, all of which lend substance to their meaning. When questions of law cannot be answered without interpreting conventional legal materials, it becomes less certain whether there is always a truth of the matter. There may be cases in which the legal materials are conflicted or contradictory, in which no law on point surfaces, in which no legal solutions present themselves in a case of first impression. Where there is no clear way to derive an answer from the legal materials, then "discretion" and "choice" become more plausible terms to describe the power of decision.

Paradoxically, the claim of truth under the law may be the strongest when there are no relevant materials at all and the judge must decide under abstract principles of morality and justice. All we know is that two hunters negligently fired at the same time, and the victim was hit by a bullet from one of their rifles.[32] There is no way to prove the bullet came from one rifle or the other. It would be unjust to leave the victim uncompensated. Yet it would be also unjust to hold a hunter liable if he did not cause the harm. How do we solve the problem? There may be no answer under the law. But there might well be a right answer as a matter of morality and justice. Believing there is a right answer means that we must find it. Our duty to find the best solution as a matter of morality and justice means that we do not have the discretion simply to choose one result or another. We must ponder the problem until a compelling solution presents itself.

Discretion in Easy Cases

The intriguing corollary of Hart's position is that in routine cases that lie at the core of legal rules, judges do not exercise discretion. In taking this stand, Hart distinguishes his jurisprudence clearly from the position of the realists and the contemporary exponents of indeterminacy in the law. In some areas of the law's governing our lives, the rules do seem to entail results in concrete cases. Driving a car into the park is an undisputed violation of the ordinance; a blind person is unquestionably handicapped. The prohibitions against rape, theft, homicide, and other criminal actions readily call to mind paradigm cases in which the prohibitions are violated.

Now why should this be so? Does it depend on the language of the rule to be applied? Witnesses may know nothing about the definition of crimes, yet they perceive a crime occurring. But these may be special cases of the law that draw directly on a shared understanding of what constitute the basic crimes in society. When the legal rule contains a slight element of artificiality—when it is, as lawyers say, *malum prohibitum* rather than *malum in se*[33]—then some attention must be paid to the language of the rule. A rule based on "vehicle" obviously differs from one that turns on the words "dangerous device" or "polluting engine." Yet the legislature could have chosen any of these expressions to cover the case of driving a car in the city park. The expression chosen obviously has an impact in the borderline cases (bicycles and roller skates might be dangerous devices, but surely not polluting engines), and presumably the range of clear cases will vary with the language of the rule. The problem remains one of understanding the nature of clear cases in which judges exercise no discretion.

What could it mean for judges not to have a choice, not to have discretion? If there were rules in law as precise as those that govern baseball or chess, then it would make sense to say that there was no choice but to apply the rule to the perceived facts. Yet legal rules always admit of exceptions. Even clear rules, with high moral content, such as those enumerated in the Ten Commandments, admit of exceptions. Self-defense is a justification for homicide. Necessity is a justification for theft. Duress would be an excuse for adultery and bearing false witness. Saving life justifies breaking the Sabbath. There are no rules of law that are exempt from the logical possibility of a special circumstance blocking application of the law. If a police car enters the park in hot pursuit of a dangerous criminal, the entry would presumably be justified in the interests of law enforcement. At the very least, judges must consider whether special circumstances of this sort are present; if they are not, the rule applies as written. It seems, however, that the very process of deciding whether special circumstances are present requires an act of judgment and evaluation that could be seen as a choice or a discretionary judgment.

We could put the issue this way. Hart has in mind the normal case in which no exceptional circumstances are present. In that type of case, the rule is applied as a matter of routine, as a deductive syllogism leading to a unique result. Yet the very process of classifying the case as normal as opposed to abnormal (where there are possible claims of justification or excuse) requires a value choice. Thus the role of choice and discretion cannot be totally eliminated even in the simplest and most routine case.

This way of putting the problem reminds one of a thesis developed some years ago by philosopher John R. Searle in an attempt to bridge the gulf between statements of fact (statements of what is) and claims of value (what ought to be).[34] His argument from "is" to "ought" begins with a factual statement: Elizabeth said, "I promise to return your book by the end of the week." From this it follows that Elizabeth made a promise to return the book and further that she placed herself under an obligation to perform the promise. This in turn yields the conclusion that, other things being equal, Elizabeth ought to return the book by the end of the week.

Of course, all sorts of things might come up that would prevent Elizabeth from returning the book. Her husband or children might be sick and she would have to stay home to take care of them. She might be called on a sudden mission on the other side of the world. The possibilities are endless; they are captured under the clause: *ceteris paribus,* "other things being equal." The "other-things-being-equal" condition represents an attempt to distinguish between normal and abnormal cases. In the normal and routine cases, "other things" are perceived as equal; in the abnormal situation, something has intervened to make them unequal, to generate a justification or excuse for not performing the promise. Searle's assumption was that perceiving the case to be normal did not in itself inject an evaluative judgment into the syllogism; it did not sneak an "ought" into the series of factual inferences.

This is the point at which many of Searle's critics attacked his argument. To perceive that a situation is "normal" is, the counterargument goes, to make a judgment. This judgment has an evaluative dimension; it is tantamount to saying that nothing in the situation "ought" to block the normal inference from making a promise to the duty to perform on a particular occasion. This critique of Searle's argument provides a good model for understanding the debate about judges' exercising choice or discretion in the normal and routine cases. Judges who decide that the case is simply a routine affair—not requiring special consideration—also make a judgment. The decision is discretionary in the sense that it could easily go the other way. Of course, if they decide the case is abnormal and different, they will engage in more evaluative work to find the right decision, but there is still evaluative work implied by the act of classifying the case as routine and normal.

On behalf of Searle's position, one could respond by questioning whether merely perceiving a state of affairs as normal is to make a decision at all. Is there an actual experience of "deciding" that goes along with perceiving a state of affairs as normal? Not necessarily. Consider this example. Every judge in the United States—even the humblest traffic court judge—has the power to declare every statute and every ordinance unconstitutional. Yet the question of constitutionality is in fact addressed in but a small percentage of the cases. Does it follow that judges are always implicitly deciding the constitutionality of every statute that they apply? In one sense, yes; in another sense, no.

It would be a mistake to say that judges actually ponder and decide the constitutionality of every statute they apply. In the routine case of speeding, traffic court judges never even think about whether the statute is constitutional. There is nothing in the case to trigger their interest in the question. It is only in the abnormal case, characterized by special facts, that one is prompted to think seriously about the issue of constitutionality. Yet one could argue that every conviction for speeding logically presupposes a judgment that the relevant provision of the vehicle code is constitutional. After all, the judge would not apply the statute unless he or she assumed that it was valid under the state and federal charters.

Thus there are two senses of "deciding" at work in the discussion. One sense points to an actual experience of deciding. The inquiry is about what actually happens in the throes of decision. The other sense is logical. The inquiry is about the propositions implicitly assumed as the background of the decision: the distinction holds true in thinking about Hart's views on exercising discretion in core cases and Searle's claim on reasoning from *is* to *ought*. As a matter of observable experience, judges do not decide the question of constitutionality in routine cases, they do not exercise discretion in deciding core cases of a statute's application and we do not make evaluative judgments when we hold people, in normal cases, to their promises. Yet from the logical point of view, the opposite is true in all three instances. As a logical matter, judges do decide the constitutionality of all statutes they apply, they exercise discretion or choice in assuming that exceptions do not apply, and we make an evaluative judgment when we assume that "other things are equal."

It is no easy matter, then, to give a definitive account of the relationship between rules and legal decisions, for in the end the argument hinges on the meaning of the word "decision." It is not clear what we think, for we persist in maintaining an ambiguity in our language about the nature of decision making. This is but another instance of a philosophical problem that takes on sharper relief when we begin to examine the discourse we are using in pondering the problem.

Notes

1. *See, e.g.*, Frederick Schauer, Playing by the Rules (1991); William Twining & David Miers, How to Do Things with Rules: A Primer of Interpretation (1982).

2. H.L.A. Hart, The Concept of Law 79–99 (2d ed. 1994).

3. Code Civil § 1134: *Les conventions légalment formées tiennent lieu de loi á ceux qui les ont faites.*

4. Wesley Hohfeld, *Some Fundamental Legal Conceptions as Applied in Judicial Reasoning*, 23 Yale Law Journal 16 (1913).

5. Meir Dan-Cohen, *Decision Rules and Conduct Rules: On Acoustic Separation in Criminal Law*, 97 Harvard Law Review 625 (1984).

6. 3 Gaius, Institutes Sec. 194, 1 F. De Zuleta, The Institutes of Gaius 217 (1946). (A statute can not "turn into a thief one who is not a thief at all, or into an adulterer or homicide one who is neither the one nor the other.")

7. Hart, *supra* note 2, at 124–41.

8. Montesquieu, The Spirit of the Laws 149 (T. Nugent trans., 1949).

9. Karl Llewellyn, The Bramble Bush 14 (1930).

10. Lochner v. New York, 198 United States Reports 45, 76 (1905) (Holmes, dissenting).

11. *See, e.g.*, Jerome Frank, Law and the Modern Mind (1930); Karl Llewellyn, *Some Realism About Realism: Responding to Dean Pound*, 44 Harvard Law Review 1222 (1931).

12. *See* Chapter 1, note 17.

13. Hart, *supra* note 2, at 135.

14. 480 United States Reports 273 (1987).

15. The statute was superseded by the Americans With Disabilities Act of 1990. The word "disability" replaced the use of the word "handicapped."

16. *See* Geders v. United States, 425 United States Reports 80, 86–87 (1977) (discussing role of judge as "governor of the trial" whose determinations can be overruled only for "abuse of discretion" (Citation omitted)).

17. *See* J. FEEST & E. BLANKENBURG, DIE DEFINITIONSMACHT DER POLIZEI: STRATEGIEN DER STRAFVERFOLGUNG UND SOZIALE SELEKTION (1972).

18. *See* Abraham Goldstein and Martin Marcus, *The Myth of Judicial Supervision in Three "Inquisitorial" Systems: France, Italy and Germany*, 87 YALE LAW JOURNAL 240 (1977)(arguing that discretion is exercised in each of the French, German, Italian systems for reasons similar to those prevailing in the United States).

19. The notion of "policy" is expressed in German, for example, by combining the word for law with the word for politics, generating the oxymoron *rechtspolitische*. Dutch has coined the term *beleid* meaning goal, which enjoys a usage similar to "policy." The term in modern Hebrew *m'diniut*, deriving from the root for state, was coined as the equivalent of policy.

20. JAMES MADISON, NOTES OF DEBATES IN THE FEDERAL CONVENTION OF 1787 REPORTED BY JAMES MADISON 61 (A. Koch ed., 1984).

21. *Id.* at 337.

22. Ronald Dworkin, *The Model of Rules*, 35 UNIVERSITY OF CHICAGO LAW REVIEW 14 (1967).

23. *Id.* at 29.

24. *Id.* at 41.

25. *Id.* at 32–33.

26. *Id.* at 33.

27. *See*, in particular, 2 KENNETH C. DAVIS, ADMINISTRATIVE LAW TREATISE sec. 8:1–8:12 (2d ed. 1979).

28. The tradition of higher Law is reflected in the German GRUNDGESETZ [Constitution] article 20 (3), which provides that the courts, *die Rechtsprechung*, are bound by *Recht und Gesetz*. This provision coexists, paradoxically, with article 97 descending from earlier German constitutions, which provides that the judges are subject only to the statutory law (*nur dem Gesetz unterworfen*). The juxtaposition of these two provisions—one holding that judges are bound by the *Recht* as well as *Gesetz* and the other stipulating that judges are subject only to the *Gesetz*—raises a puzzle. Is this simply an inconsistency in the text? Or could the postwar constitutional drafters also have provided that judges are "subject" to the Right as well as to the statutory law?

29. *See* Dworkin, *supra* note 22, at 33.

30. *Id.* at 37.

31. Claiming that there is a "real world" and that we can make truthful claims about it may seem naive to many philosophers. So be it.

32. This problem came up in Summers v. Tice, 33 California Reports 2d 80, 199 Pacific Reports 2d 1 (1948).

33. *Malum in se* refers to something that is "evil in itself" whether legally prohibited or not. *Malum prohibitum* is evil made so by the will of the legislature.

34. John Searle, *How to Derive "Ought" from "Is,"* 73 PHILOSOPHICAL REVIEW 43 (1964).

4

Discourse

Discussion of the rule of the law seems to center on what judges do. The Hungarian case study reveals the importance of prosecutorial decisions and even the nonjudicial resolution of a labor dispute as key tests for the emergence of a *Rechtsstaat*. For Western thinkers, the romantic, engaging moment is the judge confronted by a difficult situation in the borderland of the rules. This is the "High Noon" of the law: the solitary figure put to the test. He or she must decide what to do. Of course, there are materials of the law—statutes, precedents, commentaries—but none of these determines the outcome of the difficult case. This is the proverbial hard case that requires judicial imagination. Dworkin devises an ideal judge Hercules who, when faced with this case, must balance all the law and every possible theory of political legitimation and find the right outcome.[1]

It is almost as though we thought of law as a peculiar kind of mechanics. We know that it is not the kind of mechanics that Newton reduced to a few simple formulas. Yet there must be some mechanism, we believe, between the input of the law and the output of the courts. There must be some formula for figuring how full the glass of judgment must be to produce the refraction we call a judicial decision. The input consists of all the written materials we conventionally call the law— rules, principles, policies, statutes, precedents. The output specifies who wins and who loses the disputes. The assumption of those preoccupied

with the process of decision is that some analogue to Newtonian mechanics, some golden mean between formalism and skepticism, will tell
us how the input produces the output.[2]

This focus on the mechanics of decisions slights the most common
feature of participating in a legal system, namely, the experience of
constant communication. As lawyers and as citizens, we rarely confront
the use of coercive state power—bailiffs laying hands on us, jailers slam-
ming shut steel doors, or sheriffs seizing our property. What we do
experience as participants in the legal order is incessant argument, verbal
thrusts, ripostes, and parries. We receive warnings and traffic tickets
from police officers, notices from the IRS, occasional letters from credit
agencies telling us to pay up. We argue back to the police officers and
traffic judges by quoting words in statute books and case reports. We
respond to the IRS by invoking the language of tax regulations. We tell
our creditors that if they understood the subtleties of contract law, they
would realize that we did not really owe the sum alleged. All of this is
talk. It is interaction, and sometimes play, in a highly restricted mode of
discourse.

Admittedly, the possible invocation of coercive state power has a
bearing on the discourse. The participants in the discourse are undoubtedly mindful of the risk of going to court. But take away the apparatus of
state power, and you still have legal argumentation—as we know from
international law and from other legal systems, such as modern Jewish
law outside of Israel, that function without tools of enforcement. Even
where the threat of violence looms in the background, official decisions
should be understood as but a continuation of the conversation. Decisions are not self-enforcing. A court issues an eviction notice. You are
supposed to leave your rented apartment. But the order to leave does not
mean that you are out in the streets. Getting the eviction notice enforced
requires additional interaction and argument. By and large, compliance
with legal decisions comes about as a result of their persuasive power.
The Supreme Court has bailiffs to keep order in the Court, but it has no
army to enforce its decisions, no power except the prestige of its decisions.

Of course, there are times when the state must deploy its executive power. And when it does, it seeks, by the use of verbal cues,
to appear legitimate. The distinction between a police arrest and a criminal kidnapping lies in the signs and rituals that label police intervention
as acting under "the color of law." Without the signs of uniforms,
badges, pieces of papers called tickets and warrants—police officers
would appear to us as roughnecks encroaching upon our freedom. A
simple ritual, such as police officers reading suspects their *Miranda*
rights,[3] reinforces, by discourse, the legitimacy of the state's use of
force.[4]

Divergent Styles

The legal system, I am suggesting, should be seen as an engine that generates incessant verbal interaction. The rules of the discourse are clearly understood by those who participate in it. You are entitled to make certain kinds of arguments and not others. You can refer to statutes and cases and regulations, you can make arguments of morality, fairness, and justice, but you cannot invoke poems, novels, art history— or the racing form or any number of items assumed to be irrelevant to serious law talk. These customs of legal discourse change over time. In Blackstone's time, the Bible was a persuasive authority. But when Justice Burger invoked "Judeo-Christian moral and ethical standards" to justify the Court's holding that punishing sodomy was compatible with the Constitution,[5] critics responded that the reference was improper.[6] A few decades ago lawyers shied away from explicitly economic arguments in the law. Now the supposed science of economics generates arguments that count as compelling.[7]

In speaking about law, lawyers and judges engage in a range of speech acts. Sometimes they *describe* the state of the law, as, for example, when a lawyer writes an opinion letter to advise a client about his options under the law. Sometimes lawyers *assert* what the law is, as when they go into court and claim that their client has a right to collect money from the defendant or vice versa. Sometimes citizens *declare* what the law is, as when they are sitting in parliament and vote collectively to enact a statute.

The reigning theory of law determines how much we perceive the actors in the legal culture as describing, asserting, or declaring when they utter propositions of law. The best guide to these differing perceptions is the extent to which the legal culture has positivist (all-law-is-enacted-law) or antipositivist (law-as-principle) leanings.[8] Those who believe that the Law consists of principles see most legal propositions as assertions of what this ideal requires. Those with more positivist leanings will eliminate the category of assertion and divide the world of legal propositions into declarations of law and descriptions of the law so declared. From the positivist perspective, the claims that lawyers make in court are not assertions about what the law is but rather arguments about what the law ought to be.[9]

Most Europeans treat judicial decisions as assertions of what the Law really is. This corresponds to Blackstone's view that cases are merely evidence of the higher law. In the more conventional Anglo-American view of *stare decisis*, as it emerged in the nineteenth century, the courts declare what the law is. And because their decisions are the law, they constitute precedents binding on judges and litigants who come after. There are also different perceptions among Continental

Europeans and lawyers in the Anglo-American tradition about what scholars do when they write articles or books. Europeans would describe scholarly work as assertions about the content of the Law as principle. Anglo-American lawyers treat scholarly works as secondary authority— as descriptions and inferences about the law as it is defined by the primary sources of statutes and cases. There are, then, these variations in our perceptions of what legal actors do. How their speech acts are understood depends on the lens of legal theory through which they are perceived.

There are also considerable differences, from country to country, in the style of legal discourse. The American scholarly literature has recently evidenced an extraordinary openness to new styles of legal argument, including autobiographical reflection and fiction.[10] These stylistic innovations have not yet had an impact on the writing of judicial opinions.

One of the striking features of legal argument in English is our pervasive reliance on the term "reasonable." We routinely refer to reasonable time, reasonable delay, reasonable reliance, and reasonable care. In criminal law, we talk ubiquitously of reasonable provocation, reasonable mistake, reasonable force, and reasonable risk. Within these idioms pulse the sensibilities of the reasonable person. Without this hypothetical figure at the center of legal debate, we would be hard pressed to mount an argument about responsibility or liability.

As anglophone lawyers negotiate in the language of reasonableness, French, German, and Russian lawyers argue in a different idiom. Their languages do deploy a concept of reason, and their terms for "reason"— *raison, Vernuft*, and *razumnost'*—readily yield corresponding adjectives. Yet these parallels to our term "reasonable" do not figure prominently in legal speech on the Continent. The French civil code uses the term *raisonnable* precisely once; the German and Soviet civil codes do not use the term at all. The criminal codes—the natural habitat of the reasonable person—are barren of these derivatives of reason. In the civil codes, we see a variety of standards of care: in France, the conduct expected of a *bon père de famille*; in West Germany, the "care necessary in the particular transaction." Other countries use a variety of expressions. The adjectives describing a faultless mistake in Continental languages do not translate as "reasonable" but as "invincible," "unavoidable," and "non-negligent." All these emanations of the reasonable person find diverse translations in Continental legal discourse, a distinct word for every context.

As one would expect, every legal language exhibits some kind of conceptual bent just as peculiar as the common law's affection for the term *reasonableness*. In German legal discourse, for example, we find a number of terms—not readily translatable—that figure almost as prominently in legal German as *reasonableness* does in legal English. Consider the terms *Treu und Glauben* (good faith and fair dealing),[11] *Recht* (objective right),[12] *Rechtsmissbrauch* (abuse of personal rights),[13] *Zumutbarkeit* (fair expectability).[14] For German legal stylists, these terms are just as significant in crafting points of law into acceptable arguments as is the term "reasonableness" for English-speaking lawyers.

Whether arguments are cast in one idiom or in another, it is worth inquiring: What is the point of all this talk? The question is disarming, for it is not clear that there is a single or precise point. Of course, the dominant motive may be to induce a judge or opposing counsel to respond in a particular way. Yet sometimes the inner dynamic of the discourse is to seek an understanding of an event, injury, or crime that has unnerved the society. Our feelings about environmental damage are expressed in and, in turn, shaped by the way we describe and attach legal labels to the *Valdez* oil spill. Our sense of urban violence is informed by the legal filters we use to capture Bernhard Goetz's shooting four young black men in the subway. Whether the point is to persuade an opposing lawyer, a judge, or some other official, or whether we address our legal remarks to colleagues or to the public at large, we engage in discourse to reach a consensus about what the law is.[15]

This way of thinking about law is prefigured in H. L. A. Hart's distinction between external and internal points of view toward a legal system.[16] The external point represents the customary perspective stressing rules, violations, and enforcement. The internal point of view captures—for the first time, so far as I know—the role of discourse in legal life. In the internal point of view, we use the formulas of the legal systems as gambits in discourse about our behavior and the behavior of others. We use the rules, principles, and policies of the law in order to criticize the behavior of others and to justify our own actions in the face of criticism. The background assumption is that unlawful behavior is worthy of criticism; lawful behavior is immune from legal attack.

Materials of the Law

We should see the production of statutes, precedents, and commentaries not as the final words of the law but as the opening thrust of legal discourse. Passing a statute is but the beginning of a conversation. Congress tells us that we cannot discriminate against those who are handicapped. But then the argument begins about the meaning of the key provision. If a dispute develops about firing a teacher stricken with tuberculosis, then we have lawyers on both sides making claims about what the statute should mean. They may go back to the legislative history behind the statute, particularly to the committee reports, to find out what various legislators thought they were doing when they prohibited discrimination against the handicapped. If and when a dispute reaches the appellate courts, we see an extraordinary outpouring of words in the

form of briefs, oral argument, and finally the opinion of the court supporting one interpretation or another.

Different styles and strategies apply in invoking the three sources of
law in modern legal systems—statutes, cases, and scholarly commentary. *Statutes* are acts of legislative will. The transition from legislative
will to binding law is more subtle and complicated than conventionally
assumed. All that flows from the legislative pen is a statute. It could be a
restatement of the common law, or it could represent a radical change
that flouts the customs of the community. For this raw statute to become
Law, something more is required. Lawyers, judges, and scholars must be
willing to defer to the supposed wisdom of the legislature to decide what
is Right and binding as Law.

That legislatures have achieved this presumptive wisdom in modern
legal cultures is nothing short of remarkable. In the early stages of English law, the power of Parliament to intervene and change the accrued
customs of time was cloaked in ambiguity. It was commonplace in medi-
eval statutes to begin with an apologetic preamble stating that because
the common law was controverted, it was necessary for Parliament to
intervene. Today we just assume that legislatures can change the Law at
will. It is as though the community of citizens as well as the professional
community of lawyers simply agreed to defer to elected officials as oracles of the Law. Occasionally one encounters the kind of irreverent
reaction that Nozick dared: "Is there really someone who, searching for
a group of wise and sensitive persons to regulate him for his own good,
would choose that group of people who constitute the membership of
both houses of Congress?"[17] Generally, however, the convention is that
within the limits of their jurisdiction, what they say is law! If we are
arguing about what the law is, a statute on point settles the matter.

Alas, in a concrete case, it is never entirely clear whether a statute is
precisely on point. The statutory gambit invites further discourse about
what the statute means and whether it applies. This is called the process
of *interpreting* the statute. Interpretation typically means that one set of
words takes the place of another. The interpretation replaces the seemingly obscure words that require interpretation. A definition or articu-
lated theory of "handicap" functions in place of the word "handicap" as
used in the federal antidiscrimination statute. Since, however, interpretations are rendered in words and words are rarely if ever transparent, the words in interpretation will themselves require interpretation.
Thus the discourse is advanced but never comes to an end.

The language game of statutory interpretation fluctuates between
two extremes, the pole of will and the pole of reason. Statute as legislative will is expressed in debates about what the legislature really
intended—in their collective heart and mind—when they passed the
statute. What they really meant is relevant, however, only so far as one
views that statute as a command, with the implication that we as citizens

must obey the command as the commander, that is, the legislature, wished it to be obeyed. This is the argument of original intent and it is most commonly found today in theories of the judicial process that claim to be suspicious of judicial power to interpret either statutes or the Constitution.[18] The only way to bind the courts to the statutory mast is to insist that judges rely on the plain meaning of the words and if that meaning is not obvious, they should seek to understand what the legislative or the constitutional drafters meant when they used the language. If the words of the Eighth Amendment prohibiting "cruel and unusual punishment" are ambiguous, we know at least the drafters did not intended to label the death penalty—which they sought to maintain—as "cruel and unusual."[19]

The other pole in the argument begins with the recognition that legislative or constitutional will is never sufficient to bind other people as law. The act of will must meet the test of reason. Thus the words of the statute must negotiate the path from *Gesetz* to *Recht*, from statute to binding Law. The statutory language should be interpreted, therefore, not as those particular legislators intended it, but as reasonable legislators would have intended the language to be understood. The words should be understood, as Dworkin puts it, in their "best light overall."[20] This mode of interpretative discourse takes the words of the statute or the Constitution as the text of departure, as the beginning of the argument. The best interpretation is the one that takes ambiguous words like the prohibition against "cruel and unusual punishment" and renders them in a way that makes sense to us today. That rendering might imply that the death penalty does indeed violate the constitutional prohibition.

Not only does discourse of interpretation fluctuate between will and reason, between statute as command and statute as perception of the Right, but we engage in an ongoing metadebate about which of these views is correct. The metadebate is hardly new, as the following tale from the Talmud illustrates.[21] The rabbis were debating whether a particular stove, the Oven of Aknai, was made according to the law as revealed to Moses on Mount Sinai. In this context, think of the law that God reveals at Sinai as analogous to any other statute, God is the lawgiver, the Bible the enacted law. Rabbi Eliezer took a position and he "brought forth every imaginable argument, but they [the other rabbis] did not accept them." Finally, Rabbi Eliezer sought to prove that the divine will [i.e., original intent] was on his side.

> Said he to them: "If the law (*halakhah*) agrees with me, let this carob-tree prove it!" Thereupon the carob tree was torn a hundred cubits out of its place—others affirm, four hundred cubits. "No proof can be brought from a carob-tree," they retorted.

At this point, Rabbi Eliezer invokes other supernatural signs, such as inducing a stream to flow backwards and the walls of the room to collapse, but the other rabbis rejected what they saw as irrelevant to the legal debate.[22] Rabbi Eliezer grows desperate in the argument and seeks a direct verbal cue from the lawgiver:

> Again he said to them: "If the law (*halakhah*) agrees with me, let it be proved from Heaven!" Whereupon a Heavenly Voice cried out: "Why do ye dispute with R. Eliezer, seeing that in all matters the law (*halakhah*) agrees with him." But R. Joshua arose and exclaimed, "*It is not in Heaven.*" . . . We pay no attention to the Heavenly Voice, because Thou hast long since written in the Torah at Mount Sinai. *After the majority must one incline.*[23]

Leaving aside the prescription of majority rule for a moment, the surprising message of this talmudic text is that God, as the supreme legislator, does not have the final word on what He meant at the time of giving the Law at Mount Sinai. God gave the law (it is no longer in Heaven) and thereafter it is up to the rabbis to figure out what it means. That they should resolve disputes by majority vote does not absolve them from the burden of discourse. Their primary task is to articulate arguments for and against particular constructions of what God could or should have meant at Mount Sinai. The Talmud lovingly records these arguments, and those who study Talmud today rehearse these logical moves as a celebration of an inspired rabbinical mind.

We intuitively share the assumption of the rabbis who ruled out intervention by the divine lawgiver. Suppose the drafters of a constitution in one of the new democracies in Eastern Europe or Latin American observe the newly established constitutional court interpret the document in a novel way. They meet as a group to denounce the court's decisions as a violation of their "original intent." Their intervention would be just as inappropriate as the Heavenly Voice's declaring that the law was on the side of Rabbi Eliezer. The point is that once the lawgiver lays down the canonical set of words that constitute the statutory or revealed law, the lawgiver must retreat from the field of discourse. The only way that it, the lawgiver, can reenter the arena is not by clarifying its original intent, but by initiating an amendment to the statute or the law that grounds the legal debate.

The paradox is that if we were really interested in original intent, we would listen attentively to the drafting committee's retroactive clarification of its original intent, for after all, who should know better than they what they meant? Yet the rabbis are not willing to consider God's intervention favoring the better interpretation of the text revealed at Mount Sinai. And we would regard it as inappropriate for a constitution-drafting committee to dictate to a constitutional court how it should interpret the society's basic charter. The resolution of this paradox may be a bit arbitrary. Original intent may be relevant, but the debate is limited to evidence of intent available at the time the law is laid down. Later signs of original intent are excluded as irrelevant.

The revealing assumption behind this exclusion is that although we are interested in what the lawgiver meant, we are more concerned about structuring discourse after the law is enacted so that it is free of the lawgiver's control. The statutory (or biblical) words, once they are laid down, provide the frame for ongoing efforts to fathom what the law should be. But the discourse is in the hands of those charged with cultivating and refining the law. (For the rabbis, it was no longer in Heaven.) For us, in a secular legal system, the canonical words, once spoken, are no longer in the hands of the legislature or the constitution-drafting committee.

The language of "legislative intent" is sufficiently pliable to bridge the gap between the conflicting schools of statutory interpretation. Those who tend to see statutes as the sovereign's orders use the term narrowly to mean what the sovereign really intended. Those who think about the interpretation that puts the statute in its best light can shift subtly to the broader term "statutory purpose" or focus on what a reasonable legislature would have intended with the words actually used.[24]

The second conventional source of law, *judicial decisions*—to be precise, opinions written by appellate courts—are treated differently from statutes. Yet we do not read opinions in search of the judges' intentions. Why not? Once decided, an appellate decision becomes a source of law not by virtue of the judges' will, but by the persuasive power of the opinions justifying the decision.[25] Judges interpret past decisions as expressions of a consistent and coherent system of principles. Whether a decision becomes an influential precedent depends on the wisdom of the decision and the rhetorical elegance of the opinions supporting the decision. The decisions of Justices Cardozo, Brandeis, and Holmes live on, not because these men had any special authority as judges, but because they reached wise decisions under the law, persuasively explained in the language of the tradition.

The essential difference between statutes and cases, then, is that if a case deviates from traditional principles of law, it will be quickly forgotten. It will become, as Justice Frankfurter predicted of one decision by the Supreme Court, "a derelict on the waters of the law."[26] Even if statutes deviate from tradition, even if they explicitly repeal a law that made sense, they cannot be ignored. By common consent of the lawyers who live under statutory rule, legislatures can do what they want with the law—within the bounds of the Constitution. The job of lawyers and judges is to listen to the voice of democratic authority.

In the last two hundred years there has been a movement in Anglo-American law to make case law more like statutory law. In the mid-eighteenth century, in the writings of Blackstone, judicial decisions are treated as evidence of the law, not as the law itself. This is the way Continental European lawyers think about case law today. The English positivist movement of the nineteenth century generated the idea that judicial decisions were not just evidence of the law, but conclusive on the law. Thus emerged the idea of stare decisis—the principle that precedents must be followed as binding law. The citing of a precedent on point could settle an argument.

This ideal led to a way of reading appellate opinions that resembled the reading of statutes. The problem was winnowing down the lengthy exposition of the judge to the *holding* of the case and distinguishing the holding from dicta—the chaff of the opinion that could be discarded. The holding was supposedly the decision of the court as pitched to the particular facts of the case. Once a lawyer got hold of the holding, he had a club like a statute. He could use it to win his argument. In a more naive time people might have thought that the doctrine of holding and dicta gave us the mechanism to explain how the input of precedent could explain the output of decisions.

Critical minds eventually noticed, however, that there was no sure-fire way of figuring out the holding of a case.[27] The holding—as well as the relevant facts—could be stated narrowly or broadly. If Coca-Cola was held liable for damage caused by an exploding coke bottle, there was no certain way of knowing whether the holding was limited to Coca-Cola, other colas, other soft drinks, other drinks, other glass containers, containers in general, explosions caused by internal pressure, caused by defects in the container, caused by mishandling the container—just to illustrate a few folds in the accordion-like nature of judicial decisions.

The old lore about holdings and dicta is still taught in many law schools, but it is almost impossible to find courts who take the distinction seriously. Today courts read cases with considerable imagination and adapt them to new circumstances if the move seems right to them. As evidenced by the Supreme Court, even newer precedents are readily overruled if they are not in conformity with the general principles that guide the Court's thinking. Also, as we shall see later, in many situations conflicting and contradictory lines of cases survive side by side and wait to be invoked as "precedent", should the decision go one way or the other.

This is not an argument for cynicism about the impact of appellate opinions as persuasive gambits in the discourse of the law. Carefully crafted opinions have an extraordinary rhetorical force. They make their way into the casebooks that educate novitiates in the profession. They are written up and analyzed in law review articles. They become the centerpieces of the ongoing debate about what the Law really is. Yet it would be a mistake to think of precedents as levers that stabilize the law and determine the outcome of future cases. This happens occasionally, but only when the precedents clearly make sense as expressions of the underlying principles that inform the thinking of the legal profession.

The terms "evidence of the law" and "source of law," as we have used them here, invite reflection. What is the sense of "law" that finds expression in these terms of art? Is it the law laid down as positive law (*Gesetz, loi, ley*) or is it Law intrinsically binding as right principle (*Recht, droit, derecho*)?[28] Blackstone thought of the law in the latter sense, as higher Law, as the dictate of reason, and therefore he took the experience manifested in a single case as evidence of the principled reason that moves judges to their decisions. This is the same sense of law that informs the term "source of law" in its conventional understanding.[29] The sources are the materials that enable us to formulate a claim of Law. The sources of Law stimulate the discourse. Citing them, analyzing them, disputing them—these responses to the statutes and cases generate the mainline of legal debate.

In this sense of evidence and sources of Law, *scholarly writings* should be included as material that provides insights into the true nature of the Law as binding principle. The tendency in Anglo-American circles, however, is to treat scholarly commentary as "secondary" authority on the law. Articles and books should be cited only so far as they correctly summarize the primary sources of law, namely, statutes and precedents. Continental European lawyers are more generous toward their scholars; they treat commentaries and articles as sources of wisdom about the Law, not just as descriptive materials about what the actors with power—the legislatures and the courts—are doing. This deferential attitude toward scholarly writing as a source of Law may indeed be the single most distinctive feature of European, Latin American, and Japanese civil law systems as opposed to the Anglo-American common law.[30]

Categories and Degrees

Once the phenomenon of law as discourse comes into focus, we can better understand the different modes of speaking in the legal culture. As underscored by the leading German legal theorist Niklas Luhmann, the concepts used in legal discourse have a striking either/or quality.[31] Lawful is contrasted with unlawful; guilt with innocence; obligation with freedom, permission with prohibition. In affirming one of these pairs, lawyers deny the opposite. Property, tort, contract—these basic concepts are also distinguished from their opposites. There is no gray zone at the borders of these concepts. There is no such thing as a little bit of contract, tort, or property. There is no partial consent in the law, no actions that are lawful "to a degree." The law operates on the assumption that actions are either right or wrong, in or out, protected or unprotected.

The black-and-white utterances of the law resemble the pointed imperatives of the Ten Commandments. Consider these implied commands in legal discourse:

> It is my property: stay off!
> You are bound by contract: do it!
> You committed a tort: pay up!
> He committed a crime: punish him!

Other oppositions carry similarly precise messages. The line between the voluntary and the involuntary carries implications for criminal responsibility. Labeling conduct as aggression entails the legitimacy of defensive force in response. The edifice of the law is built on these dichotomies that bear messages of "do's" and "don't's."

Legal discourse does not always display this sharp edge. The tendency to rely on the notion of discretion, as discussed in Chapter 3, reveals a tendency to move toward a gray limbo suspended between the opposition of "lawful" and "unlawful." Discretionary decisions come in degrees of effectiveness. They serve their policy goals more or less. This is the instrumental fashion of administrative thought.

It is worth thinking, also, about institutional deference as a matter of assigning different weights to legal claims on the basis of the context and the speaker's authority. Actors of differing influence interact in the legal cultures. Judges, lawyers, advocates in courts, legislators, police officers —they may all speak the same language and utter the same propositions, but their words carry different weights. Recognizing the superior position of another speaker is called *deference*. By common understanding, the statutory utterances of legislatures are entitled to special respect and deference in the debate about what the law is; well-established, oft-cited precedents in the courts warrant the same kind of attention. Scholarly articles and treatises enjoy varying degrees of respect, dependent often on the status and reputation of the writer. This deference or respect means that in a dialogue about the law, added persuasive power accrues to the side that enjoys deference.

Deference is, of course, a matter of degree. It does not lend itself to hard and fast rules. To master the art of deference, one must be socialized into a particular legal system. Americans are particularly sensitive to issues of deference. We stress the customary deference of trial judges to the opinions of the jury; the deference of courts to administrative agencies; and the deference of the U.S. Supreme Court to the legislative arm of government. In all these situations the deferring party ranks the opinions of those deferred to above its own perception of the Law. These acts of deference reflect a subtle dance of accommodation among the agents of power in the American legal system. There are no rules but rather an ongoing search, expressed in the discourse of the law, for coordination, mutual respect, and recognition of influence.

The notion of deference may be an idea peculiar to Anglo-American legal systems, with our complex structures of power. The jury system, the federal structure, the subtle relationship between courts and administrative agencies, the authority of the Supreme Court to nullify state and federal legislation—these are all American phenomena. It would be difficult to find another legal system exhibiting relationships of legal power as subtle and nuanced as those in the United States. It is not surprising, then, that it is almost impossible to render the concept of deference in the legal lexicon of other systems. French has a cognate, infrequently used term, but in German, Russian, and Hebrew, one searches in vain for the apt translation.

Discourse and the Rule of Law

Some insights emerge from shifting our focus from the way rules shape decisions to the way the participants in the legal culture talk and argue about what they are doing. The danger of this approach is that we lose sight of the values that should properly shape the outcome of legal decisions. The peaks and valleys of conflicting values suffer the flattening effect of reducing all arguments to the single plateau of verbal interaction. When all we hear is talk, we lose our sensitivity to the higher issues at stake. As a corrective to the exaggeration that law is just a form of discourse, we turn in the next seven chapters to ultimate considerations that both shape the discourse and, as values, guide judicial decisions.

Before leaving the subject of discourse, however, we should note the aspiration of many who believe that in dialogue and principled argument we are able to communicate respect for the reason and the humanity of those with whom we speak. The ideal of the legal culture is that we engage in this form of respectful argument with our adversaries. Indeed the rule of law may be no more than a form of stylized argument based on mutual respect and limited by the conventional restraints of the legal culture. When courts reason in this way, and when advocates can approach their task with this ideal in mind, the law achieves its finest moment.

Notes

1. Ronald Dworkin, Taking Rights Seriously 105–130 (1977).

2. Dworkin carries forward the analogy with mechanical forces by employing the notion of gravitational force to explain the persuasive power of leading precedents. *See* Ronald Dworkin, *Hard Cases*, 88 Harvard Law Review 1057, 1089 (1975).

3. As spelled out in Miranda v. Arizona, 384 United States Reports 436 (1966).

4. On the role of rituals in criminal trials, see Laurence Tribe, *Trial by Mathematics: Precision and Ritual in the Legal Process*, 84 Harvard Law Review 1329, 1391–92 (1971).

5. Bowers v. Hardwick, 478 United States Reports 186, 196 (Burger, J. concurring) (1985).

6. Note that Justice Blackmum chided the State of Georgia for invoking *Leviticus* on behalf of its statute prohibiting sodomy. Bowers v. Hardwick, 478 United States Reports at 211 (Blackmun, J., dissenting).

7. For more on economic analysis in the law, see *infra* Chapter 10.

8. This definition of positivism is compatible with the view expressed earlier that positivists stress the necessity of sanctions to enforce conformity with the law. *See supra* pp. 29–30.

9. This is another way of approaching the debate between the positivists and their critics. For further elaboration, see George P. Fletcher, *Two Modes of Legal Thought*, 90 YALE LAW JOURNAL 970 (1981).

10. *See, e.g.*, PATRICIA WILLIAMS, THE ALCHEMY OF RACE AND RIGHTS (1991); ALAN DERSHOWITZ, CHUTZPAH (1991); NORVAL MORRIS, THE BROTHEL BOY AND OTHER PARABLES OF THE LAW (1992); DERRICK BELL, FACES FROM THE BOTTOM OF THE WELL (1992).

11. *See* BGB § 242 (establishing the general principle that obligors must fulfill their obligations according to the dictates of *Treu und Glauben*). This provision has become the source of a general jurisprudence of equity and reciprocal fairness in the execution of contractual relationships.

12. *See supra* pp. 34–37.

13. Eörsi, *Rechtsmissbrauch und funktionsmässige Rechtsausübung im Westen Und Osten,* 6 ZEITSCHRIFT FÜR RECHTSVERGLEICHUNG 30, 39–40 (1965); H.C. Gutteridge, *Abuse of Rights*, 5 CAMBRIDGE LAW JOURNAL 22 (1935).

14. *See* StGB § 35(1) (a wrongful act will be excused on grounds of necessity or duress only if abstention from that act is not "fairly expectable" under the circumstances).

15. More generally on the role of discourse in the law, see the work of Chaim Perelman: JUSTICE (1967); THE NEW RHETORIC: A TREATISE ON ARGUMENTATION (1969); *Symposium in Memory of Chaim Perelman*, 5 LAW AND PHILOSOPHY 279 (1986).

16. H.L.A. HART, THE CONCEPT OF LAW 89–91 (2d ed. 1994).

17. ROBERT NOZICK, ANARCHY, STATE, AND UTOPIA 114 (1974).

18. ROBERT H. BORK, THE TEMPTING OF AMERICA: THE POLITICAL SEDUCTION OF THE LAW 143–160 (1990) (referring to "original understanding").

19. The textual argument for this conclusion is that the drafters adopted the Fifth and the Eighth Amendments at the same time. The former implicitly permits the taking of life if the requirements of "due process" are satisfied.

20. RONALD DWORKIN, LAW'S EMPIRE 338 (1986).

21. BABYLONIAN TALMUD, *Baba Mezia* 59a–b.

22. *Id.* The deleted portion of the text reads:

> Again he said to them: "If the *halakhah* agrees with me, let the stream of water prove it!" Whereupon the stream of water flowed backwards. "No proof can be brought from a stream of water," they rejoined. Again he urged: "If the *halakhah* agrees with me, let the walls of the schoolhouse prove it, whereupon the walls inclined to fall. But R. Joshua rebuked them [the walls], saying: "When scholars are engaged in a legal (*halakhic*) dispute, what have ye to interfere?" Hence they did not fall, in honor of R. Joshua, nor did they resume the upright, in honor of R. Eliezer; and they are still standing thus inclined.

23. The text continues:

> R. Nathan met Elijah [the messenger of God-G.P.F.] and asked him: What did the Holy One, Blessed be He, do in that hour?—He laughed [with joy] he replied, saying: "My sons have defeated me. My sons have defeated me." *Id.*

24. Note the nominal difference between talmudic and secular interpretation. The rabbis do not discuss God's purpose at all. And if they did, they would not interpret the revealed words by speculating about what a "reasonable God" actually meant by the words actually used.

25. See the comment by Alexander Hamilton: "The judiciary . . . may truly be said to have neither force nor will but merely judgment." THE FEDERALIST No. 78, 465 (C. Rossiter ed., 1961).

26. Lambert v. California, 355 United States Reports 232 (Frankfurter J., dissenting)(1957).

27. For the classical approach, see Arthur Goodhart, *Determining the Ratio Decidendi of a Case*, 40 YALE LAW JOURNAL 161 (1930). For a more contemporary analysis, see Kent Greenawalt, *Reflections on Holding and Dictum*, 39 JOURNAL OF LEGAL EDUCATION 431 (1989).

28. For further elaboration of these concepts, see *supra* pp. 34–37 above. Recall the convention there introduced of using Law with a capital L to refer to law in the sense of Right. I have attempted to adhere to this distinction when the context requires it.

29. There is another sense of "source of law" that appears in positivist writings, notably in HART, *supra* note 16, at 95, 97, 101, 106, 264–267.

30. Note the approach of The Statute of the International Court of Justice, Article 38(1)(d), which lists as a fourth source of international law: "Judicial decisions and the teachings of the most highly qualified publicists of the various nations."

31. I rely, in particular, on NIKLAS LUHMANN, RECHTSSYSTEM UND RECHTSDOGMATIK (1973).

II

ULTIMATE VALUES

5

Justice

The concept of justice is singular and universal in a way that the concepts of law and Right can no longer claim, if they ever could. Law has become located in national cultures, but justice stands above all culture. It is an Archimedean point beyond history and local practices. Some people may think that justice, too, is reducible to the conventions that happen to crystallize at particular moments of time. Of course, different cultures may reflect divergent perceptions or visions of justice. Yet we retain the sense that one standard of justice applies to all people at all times. If this were not true, one would be hard pressed to criticize the unjust practices of other societies. Northern abolitionists could not have criticized Southern slaveholders, for whom slavery was a conventionally acceptable institution. Nor would it make sense for feminists to attack the subjugation of voluntarily obedient women in Islamic cultures. That we regard this criticism as coherent and often correct testifies to our commitment to a universal ideal of justice, however difficult it might be to fill out the details of the ideal in particular cases.

The notion of universal justice is found, in biblical sources, to be binding on God as well. When God and Abraham debate whether God should destroy Sodom and Gomorrah, Abraham insists that God should not "destroy the righteous with the wicked."[1] When God appears to be unmoved by this argument, Abraham challenges Him: "Will not the judge of all the universe do justice?"[2] And God responds that if he finds fifty just people, He will not destroy the cities. Having reached this major concession of principle, Abraham begins to argue about the details, and eventually pushes God to the position of being willing to spare the cities for the sake of ten innocents. The entire debate proceeds on the assumption that even God is bound by the principle that it is unjust to punish the innocent.

Four Kinds of Justice

We still classify problems of justice in the categories that Aristotle bequeathed to us.[3] The architectonic distinction runs between distributive and corrective justice. Closely related are the additional categories of retributive and commutative justice. *Distributive justice* addresses the basic organization of all things, good and bad, in setting up society. Corrective justice addresses the problem of temporary dislocations in this basic organization. The inquiry into distributive justice begins on the assumption that a central authority has control over all things, good and bad, that can be possessed. The act of distribution is designed to realize a just relationship among two or more claimants. For example, the principle that everyone should get an equal share is a common guide to distributive justice. There are always at least three parties involved: the central authority plus two or more claimants for the things that the central authority may distribute.

Corrective justice responds to a disturbance in this initially just distribution. The imbalance is signaled by a victim's suffering harm at the hands of another. There are only two relevant parties, the victim and the party bringing about the harm. The aim of corrective justice is to recreate the just distribution that existed prior to the disturbance. A good deal of the law, as we shall see, is encased in the mold of corrective justice, or something like it.

Retributive justice addresses the same phenomenon of harm caused by another that lies at the core of corrective justice. These instances of harming are called, for example, rape, battery, homicide, arson, and mayhem. The retributive response is to inflict a form of suffering, called punishment, on the offender. While private individuals sue for compensation as a form of corrective justice, the state takes the initiative in identifying offenders and prosecuting them for crime. Some philosophers claim that punishment equalizes the relationship between offender and victim by forcing the offender to suffer as the victim has suffered.[4] If this is true, then punishment has a function resembling remedies designed to achieve corrective justice.

Punishment also has a distributive dimension. Because the state is responsible for distributing the burdens of fines and imprisonment (not to mention the death penalty), it is critical that the state not discriminate in selecting some people and not others to suffer for their crimes. This is why the leading philosopher of retributive punishment, Immanuel Kant, stressed the imperative of maintaining equality among offenders. It is patently unjust, in Kant's view, to punish some offenders less because they are willing to cooperate in some way with the state. Kant would turn over in his Königsberg grave if he knew about the modern American practice of plea bargaining, under which the prosecution makes special deals with certain suspects in return for their providing evidence against other suspects. Kant was so firm in his commitment to equality among offenders that he regarded any deviation from equality or the sake of practical advantage as illustrative of the principle: "if justice goes, there is no longer any value in men's living on earth."[5]

Commutative justice addresses the inequality that might result from exchanging goods. The just exchange maintains the equality of the parties.

All four of these forms of justice—distributive, corrective, retributive, and commutative—are substantive as opposed to procedural. They all speak to the result rather than the process by which the result is achieved. A distinct form of justice addresses itself to the question of how this result is realized. The central term in the discussion of *procedural justice* is "fairness."

Our notions of fairness and fair play draw heavily on the analogies from competitive sports and gaming that pervade idiomatic English. Fair procedures are those in which both sides have an equal opportunity of winning. The playing field is level; the dice are not loaded, the deck not stacked. Fairness consists in playing by the rules that are fair to both sides. Neither side hits below the belt. No one hides the ball. Idioms like these inform the way Americans think about procedural justice.

Remarkably, the concept of fairness does not readily translate into other languages. While the concept of justice appears, it seems, in all cultures, it is virtually impossible to find a suitable translation for fairness in European or Semitic languages. As a result, the term is transplanted directly in some languages, such as German and Hebrew, and absent in others, such as French, that are resistant to adopting loan words that carry unique meanings. Why has Anglo-American culture cultivated this distinctive concept of fairness? It may be that our culture, more than others, is permeated by a sporting ethic. Our reliance on sporting metaphors in everyday speech certainly provides a clue to what we regard as important.

In its pure form, a fair procedure is all that is needed to generate a just result. Systems of perfect procedural justice are illustrated by flipping a coin to resolve a dispute or the venerable method for fairly dividing a piece of cake, namely, letting one person cut and the other person choose his preferred slice. These are procedures that do not admit of mistakes; no one can complain about the outcome as unjust. By contrast, imperfect systems of procedural justice aim at a just result and do admit of mistakes. The outstanding example is our system of trial. We try to make the procedures as fair as possible to both sides, but even the best designed system occasionally yields mistaken results.

The difference between procedural and substantive justice is illustrated by the following story. Two friends, one named Shark, the other named Minnow, dispute the division of a piece of cake. Shark cuts it and takes the bigger piece. Minnow complains. The following dialogue ensues:

Shark: What are you complaining about? If I had given you the choice, which piece would you have taken?
Minnow: I would have been a good sport and taken the smaller piece.
Shark: Well, that's the one you got. So why complain?

Minnow's humble point is that process matters. It makes a difference how she ends up with the smaller share. The result that would occur under fair procedures might be just (Minnow gets the smaller piece if she so chooses), but it is not just under unfair procedures (someone assigns the smaller share to her). The similarity of results cannot vindicate Shark's seizing upon an unfair procedure for resolving the dispute.

The connection between fair procedures and substantive justice underlies the most significant attempt in this century to develop a theory of distributive justice, namely, John Rawls's theory described by the catch phrase "justice as fairness."[6] If the procedures for choosing principles of justice are fair, Rawls maintains, the outcome will be just. This is one of three types of procedural justice that Rawls explains as follows:[7]

> 1. *Imperfect procedural justice*: The procedures are fair, but the result is not always just. The best example is criminal trials. Sometimes those guilty in fact are acquitted, and the innocent, convicted.
>
> 2. *Perfect procedural justice*: The procedures are fair, and the result could logically be unjust but it never is. An example might be the way pious Catholics view the Pope's speaking ex cathedra on faith and morals. He always gets it right.
>
> 3. *Pure procedural justice*: The procedures are fair, and the result, by definition, is always right.

The critical difference is between the latter two, perfect and pure procedural justice. The former presupposes an independent standard for deciding whether the outcome is just or unjust. For pure procedural justice, there is no independent standard. The procedure determines that, by definition, the outcome will be just. The-one-cuts-the-other-chooses procedure for allocating pieces of cake is an example. The procedure makes the outcome just. Flipping a coin is another example. And Rawls's theory of justice is a third.

Rawls thinks of his enterprise as establishing the principles of justice that will define the basic structure of society. The procedures for choosing these principles will be fair if those voting on them have no conception whether they personally will benefit from the particular principles. They must vote regardless of their personal interest. They must proceed, therefore, under a veil of ignorance about the characteristics that could lead them to prosper or suffer under one principle or another. They may not know whether they will be patrician or plebeian, strong or weak, male or female, religious or atheist, talented or untalented. They must vote, as it were, as idealized beings abstracted from the concrete circumstances that enable people to use some systems of rules to oppress others. This state of ignorance, Rawls calls "the original position," a position separated from reality by a "veil of ignorance."

Voting under these restraints, Rawls reasons, rational individuals would choose two principles of justice. The first principle closely resembles Kant's definition of Right: "Each person is to have an equal right to the most extensive basic liberty compatible with a similar liberty for others.[8] This is another way of expressing Kant's principle that each person should enjoy maximum freedom so that "the choice of one can be united with the choice of another in accordance with a universal law of freedom."[9] With regard to the allocation of freedom, then, the guiding criteria are strict equality and the maximum possible liberty for each person. This is precisely the principle that rational people, all with an equal vote, would choose behind a veil of ignorance. No one would have a self-interested reason to choose any principle but maximum liberty for all.

This first principle, as noted, expresses a commitment about the just foundations of society. Strictly speaking, it is a principle for a just and egalitarian social organization, but it is not distributive in nature. The liberties at stake are not assets that can be lumped together and possessed by a centralized authority. When a tyrant deprives someone of liberty, the resulting sum of liberty is negative; one person loses without a compensating gain by the other side. It is in the nature of freedom and particular liberties that they cannot be added together and possessed by a central authority charged with finding a just mode of dividing the total quantity among possible claimants.

Distributive Justice

Rawls reserves consideration of the distribution of "social and economic" goods—the kinds of goods that can be quantified and transferred from one person to another—for his second principle of justice. If Rawls's first principle is egalitarian and libertarian in nature, his conclusions in working out the criteria for distributive justice are far more socialistic and communitarian than any modest Marxist has ever claimed. Understanding Rawls's reasoning in this area requires first that we reflect on the range of goods that might be distributed in the society as a whole. We must free our imaginations to consider all the goods that might bear on how well individuals prosper socially and economically.

First, obviously, resources matter. Money and wealth make a difference in circumscribing the range of opportunities that individuals enjoy. Second, access to education and other society-wide developmental experiences shape individual personalities and determine life prospects. These are factors that generate inequalities in society and the question is how much inequality, as a matter of distributive justice, we can tolerate. This can hardly be answered unless we consider other sources of inequality as well.

As a third factor shaping a person's life prospects, the crucible of home and family may even be more important than material resources. The culture of the dinner table can often be more significant than raw capital in raising a person's long-range opportunities. Fourth, the individual's inherited talents and intelligence generate undeniable inequalities of potential. And finally, the individual's own effort, his or her own inner drive to take advantage of opportunities that present themselves, may be the ultimate factor determining the inequalities we observe around us. Let us refer to these five sources of inequality as those of resources, education, family, talent, and effort.

Political philosophers have developed two radically divergent strategies toward these five sources of inequality. One approach, characteristic of libertarians such as Friedrich Hayek[10] and Robert Nozick,[11] is to start from the last two, *talent* and *effort*, and note that inequalities in this arena are simply given, as a fact of nature. We cannot even ask the question, they would insist, whether it is just that some people are born more intelligent than others or some people have a greater innate drive than others. If the talented and the hardworking produce more and become richer, they need not apologize for having greater opportunities in life; on the contrary, their talent and effort mean that they have made a greater contribution than others in the society and therefore that they deserve a better life.

The libertarian argument starts, therefore, from a recognition that inequalities at the level of talent and effort are inescapable. If that is the case, then we cannot be too disquieted by family inequalities that give some people a head start in life. And if we can accept that, it is but a short step to accept the idea that rich families are entitled to have better schools for their children. And if all that is common ground, as it is in the United States today, then, of course, one need not be concerned about the injustice of vast inequalities and disparities in material resources. Thus from the undeniable inequalities of talent and effort, the libertarian makes his way, step by step, toward tolerating disparities in material resources.

Rawls takes the opposite path. He begins at the opposite end of the spectrum by applying the veil of ignorance to the distribution of material resources. What would be the fairest division if none of us knew who would be able to make the most effective use of the available resources? Given the voting procedure of one person one vote, the starting point would obviously be equal division of the society's resources. Yet that need not be the final resting point of our deliberations behind the veil of ignorance, for we might reason that in the real world some people might make better presidents and some people better fire fighters and therefore we should encourage people to use their talents in our collective interest. This is the line of reasoning that leads Rawls to the second principle of justice: "Social and economic equalities are to be arranged so that they are both (a) reasonably expected to be to everyone's advantage, and (b) attached to positions and offices open to all."[12]

This sounds like a plausible principle so far as it applies to material resources and educational opportunities. Some people are entitled to more schooling because their becoming surgeons, for example, is to everyone's advantage and, in principle, the position is open to all. For the same reason, higher wages for some are justified so far as their added income induces them to undertake risky and demanding vocations that serve the society's interests. Differences and inequalities are justifiable, therefore, only so far as they meet the twin conditions: "(a) reasonably expected to be to everyone's advantage, and (b) attached to positions and offices open to all."

The problem is how great a domain this principle, called the *difference principle*, should cover? There is little problem about resources and education. But what about the opportunities implicit in family life? Why should some people have the advantage of intellectual and artistic parents and others suffer boors at the dinner table? That is a very good question, Rawls would respond, and indeed he would consider this inequality unjust. Behind the veil of ignorance rational people would not gamble. They would not choose to allow some people to win the family lottery that would give them a head start over everybody else. And if the family poses a problem of justice, then it is but a small step to recognize the injustice of some people being born with greater talents than others. Unjust as it is to allow some people to win the family lottery, so is it wrong to allow them to win the talent lottery. Of course, you cannot exactly prevent some people from being born more gifted than others. But if that happens, the just response would be to insist on compensation from the more to the less talented. Thus Rawls completes the opposing circuit that begins by applying the difference principle to the distribution of resources and ends by insisting that the same principle apply to the distribution of natural talents. The last step of differential effort remains to be considered, but, curiously, Rawls does not think that effort in itself justifies greater rewards to those who try harder. Differential rewards can be justified only so far as they further the interests of us all.[13]

The view that individuals have no natural rights to the talents they are born with seems counterintuitive. The best way to account for Rawls's position may be that reality in his argument consists not in concrete people born in specific circumstances with defined talents. Reality, for Rawls, exists behind the veil of ignorance. The dimension of the person that counts is the abstract universal self, the rational impartial being that can make decisions without knowing whether he or she is patrician or plebeian, strong or weak, religious or atheist, talented or untalented. When this abstract universal comes to occupy a position in the real world, the concrete attributes in which it is clothed come to seem arbitrary. And if intelligence and talent are but an arbitrary shell that the abstract self happens to enjoy, then there is as much injustice in having disproportionate intelligence as there is in possessing disproportionate wealth.

It is not surprising that the most notable critics of Rawls's system fasten on the role he assigns to the abstract universal self that makes decisions behind the veil of ignorance. Robert Nozick attacks from the libertarian right by denying that the universal rational self has any bearing at all on the just distribution of wealth,[14] and Michael Sandel comes at Rawls from the communitarian left by insisting that the self can never achieve the detached rational universality that both Rawls and (before him) Kant ascribe to it.[15] The self is always situated in, and constituted by, a historical community and though this claim has no necessary implications for Rawls's theory of distributive justice, it calls into question Rawls's methodology.[16]

Let us restate the two basic strategies. Some people (usually called libertarians or conservatives) begin with the inescapable inequalities that derive from differences in personal effort and talent, which lead them to tolerate inequalities in opportunity in family life and educational opportunity, and finally, to accept the resulting inequality of material resources. Others (usually called liberals or socialists) start at the other end of the spectrum and posit that inequalities of material resources are unjust, unless rendered acceptable under a principle such as Rawls's second principle of justice. From the unjust distribution of material resources, it is but a series of small steps to argue that other inequalities are unjust, including those that result from education, family, talent—and, finally, from individual effort. We have yet to find the right solution to this ongoing conflict of philosophical argument and democratic politics.

Although few question the first principle's enthroning the liberal idea of maximum equal liberty, controversy continues to encircle the second principle's solution to the problem of distributing social and economic goods. The questions of distributive justice remains at the top of our philosophical and political agenda.

Corrective Justice

Assuming we can solve the problem of distributive justice, we can turn to the implications that arise when some local incident disturbs the global solution represented by a just distribution of wealth and opportunity. The task of corrective justice is to correct this local disturbance and to return to the status quo ante. To think more about corrective justice in context, let us consider a typical dispute in the field of tort law.

Suppose that a hotel runs a swimming pool for the use of its guests. The depth varies from three to nine feet. It is customary in the community to provide a lifeguard for the protection of those who use the pool. The hotel management decides that in view of the small number of people who use the pool, it would be wasteful to put a lifeguard on duty. A child uses the unattended pool and drowns. Her parents sue the hotel management for negligently causing the death of their child. The argument would be that a reasonable hotel owner would have provided the lifeguard. Not to do so was negligent, and the hotel's negligence produced the death.

The hotel owner could defend himself by showing that in fact under a sensible analysis of the competing costs and benefits, it was perfectly reasonably *not* to provide a lifeguard to protect the occasional guest who would use the pool. For the sake of an occasional swimmer, it would have been wasteful to have a lifeguard on duty all day (and night). Alternatively, he could argue that the parents themselves were responsible for the death. They should have kept an eye on their child, their failure to do so was negligent and the true cause of death.

The important point to note about these arguments is that they invoke only the behavior of the defendant and the plaintiff. Absent is the impact of the decision on liability on the society as a whole. Will liability make this and other hotel owners more careful in the future? Should we induce them to spend more money on safety measures at swimming pools? Or should we emphasize the responsibility of those who use the pool or let their children play near it. These arguments, based as they are on the predicted impact of the decision, are outside the framework of corrective justice. The parties are private individuals and the considerations that bear on the outcome of the dispute are private. At least those who insist that accident law is private law take this position.

What does corrective justice imply in this case? If the defendant had indeed *wronged* the plaintiffs by negligently causing the child's death, then he can correct that wrong by paying them a sum of money to console them for their loss. Of course, there is no way to "compensate" for the loss of a child; no amount of money will equalize the situation. Yet an apology seems to be too little—at least in modern America. A sizeable damage award could at least generate financial security for the family and ease the pain of other problems. Intervention by a court is not essential to an agreement to rectify the loss. The plaintiff need only approach the hotel owner and demand compensation for the wrong. If the case is sound, the owner might well recognize his duty to make compensation, and his motive could well be grounded in his sense of justice as well as his fear of the costs of litigation.

Is it really true that compensation corrects the wrong? If the hotel owner pays the bereaved parents two million dollars, then they are consoled but he is out a large amount of money. He might now be insolvent and unable to continue operating the hotel. A large damage award then creates a new victim, the newly poor defendant. To see whether this result is compatible with Aristotle's conception of corrective justice, let us begin with his words: "[J]ustice in transactions between man and man is a sort of equality indeed and injustice a sort of inequality. . . . [Therefore] the judge tries to equalize things by means of the penalty, taking away from the gain of the assailant."[17]

The model for this form of injustice is the taking of another person's property. The gain to the defendant is then equal to the victim's loss, and equality is restored by requiring the defendant either to return the object taken or to pay its equivalent. This formula is more difficult to apply in cases of negligent conduct producing personal injuries. Aristotle assumed, it seems, that the negligent defendant gains from acting carelessly and that the victim suffers a proportionate amount. And this is true in the case of the drowning, for the hotel owner saved money by not having to hire a lifeguard and he could pass this savings onto the guests by proportionately lowering the hotel's prices. The function of the damage award is to take from the gain of the defendant by compensating the victim for her loss, thereby restoring the equality that is characteristic of "justice in transactions between man and man."

True, the hotel owner gains by saving money. In other torts, particularly the cases of negligent driving, it is more difficult to identify the benefit to the defendant. Monetary gain does not always attend driving with bad brakes or even in driving past the speed limit. In many instances of careless conduct, the most the defendant gains is the psychic advantage of ignoring the risks implicit in his conduct or enjoying an activity like fast driving that entails risks to others. Yet even assuming that negligent action always entails some benefit to the actor (otherwise there would be no motive for being careless), there is no reason to accept Aristotle's assumption that the loss to the victim is equal to the defendant's gain. And when gains and the loss come in different quantities, there is no apparent way to apply Aristotle's idea of a monetary transfer that will restore equality between the parties.[18]

Aristotle's conception of tortious conduct seems to be based on a model of intentional deprivation or transfer from the victim to the wrongdoer. Yet even intentional deprivations entail risks that can issue in inequalities between the defendant's gain and the victim's loss. An illuminating example, often invoked in American discussions of tort law, is an old precedent based on a dispute between a dockowner and a shipowner.[19] The shipowner was moored to the former's dock. When a dangerous storm came up, he decided that it was too dangerous to set out to sea. He kept the ship moored to the dock during the storm, thus causing the ship, under pressure from the elements, to collide repeatedly against the dock. The resulting damage was $500. The gain of the ship-owner was much greater, for he saved his entire ship, worth, say, $10,000. In view of the costs and benefits of keeping the ship moored at the dock—slight damage to the dock compared with saving the ship—there was nothing unreasonable or negligent about the defendant's con-duct. In fact, other cases make it clear that under these circumstances, the dockowner would not be entitled to expel the ship in an effort to protect his dock.

One reason the case is so widely discussed in the American literature is that even though the shipowner was doing the right thing and indeed had a right to stay moored to the dock, the court held the shipowner liable for the $500 damage to the dock. The reasoning seems to resound in corrective justice. The shipowner benefitted himself at the expense of the dockowner, and therefore he should disgorge his gain and compen-sate the dockowner for his loss.

Suppose, however, the cost/benefit calculus were transposed. The shipowner avoids a $500 loss but totally destroys the dock and small boats also moored, resulting in damage to others of $10,000. This is clearly negligent conduct; if the shipowner should pay in the first case when he was not at fault, a fortiori, he should pay in this case when he is negligent. Yet how much should he pay? Should he merely transfer his gain (i.e., loss avoided) of $500 to the dockowner. Or should he pay the $10,000 bill for damage to others? Or should there be some compromise between the defendant's gain and the victim's loss? The important point is that no matter how much he pays, the transfer of wealth will not restore equality between the parties. Either the defendant or the plaintiff will be poorer than he would have been had the storm never occurred. If the shipowner pays $500, he will break even and the dockowner will be out $9,500. If the shipowner pays the full amount of the damage, he will suffer a net loss of $9,500. Splitting the difference—that is requiring payment of $4,750—means that both parties will be out of pocket in equal amounts, but the victim's damage will only be partially compen-sated.

Corrective justice seemingly requires two things: the "corrective" component of compensating the victim for his loss, and the "justice" of returning the parties to the equality that prevailed prior to the accident or harmful incident. This is possible, as I have noted, in cases where the defendant appropriates to himself a quantifiable asset belonging to the plaintiff. But it seems hardly possible in cases of accidents where there is no reason to assume that the gain to the defendant equals the loss to the victim. In the latter cases, we must choose between correction and justice. We can require the defendant to compensate the victim and thus bear the loss himself, or we can restore equality between the parties by forcing them to split the sum total of the gain to the defendant and the loss to the plaintiff. The only way to achieve both is to share Aristotle's unrealistic assumption that the defendant's gain is equal to the plaintiff's loss.

Since Aristotle's writing some 2400 years ago, the way people think about risks and accidents has undergone a major transformation. We now recognize the element of risk-taking resulting in accidents, and we insist that however the risk materializes the wrongdoer must pay the entire harm. If we are now aware, as premoderns were not, of the role of risk in the occurrence of accidents, the shift betokens a more general reconceptualization of legal relationships. In the field of contracts, say, for the sale of goods, Aristotle assumed that the exchange of goods preserved equality between the parties. In the relevant passage: "The number of shoes exchanged for a house must therefore correspond to the ratio of builder to shoemaker. For if this be not so, there will be no exchange and no intercourse. And this proportion will not be effected unless the goods are somehow equal."[20]

Because the exchange preserved equality, Aristotle perceived a distinctive form of justice in trading goods. He called it commutative justice or justice in exchange. The assumption was that "the goods are somehow equal." Today economists make precisely the opposite assumption: There will be no exchange and no intercourse unless both parties, viewing the transaction subjectively, gain from the trade. The builder must value a quantity of shoes more than his house, and the shoemaker must value the house more than a quantity of shoes. Each side is driven by the expectation of advantage. If the two bundles of commodities were equal, there would be no motive for the trade. The problem for economic theorists is to figure out how to compare one person's subjective gain with another person's subjective gain. There is no reason to assume, however, that gain is equal for both sides.

As there has been a transformation in our thinking about trading, a parallel shift has occurred in the theory of tort liability. In neither field do we continue to share Aristotle's assumption that private law preserves equality between the parties. We now recognize that in every accident, the victim suffers a loss without there always being a corresponding gain on the part of the injurer. The loss is, as the economists say, a "sunk cost." It cannot be erased by imposing liability on the party who caused the injury. The most we can do is shift the loss. And this is the way American lawyers now describe the objective of tort litigation.

It is rare today to argue that tort law is about restoring equality between the parties.[21] Tort law nonetheless does raise serious problems of justice.[22] One of the perennial problems is whether the wealth of the parties—or their access to insurance—should matter in determining liability. Considering the background of the parties raises a distinct issue of equality in litigation. Should we assume that the parties are equally situated prior to the accident? Aristotle was convinced that this is what a just legal system required: "The law looks only to the distinctive character of the injury and treats the parties as equal, [and seeks to determine] if one is in the wrong and the other is being wronged, and if one inflicted injury and the other has received it."[23]

The point is that litigation is blind to the relative wealth, power, and life history of the parties. This is why the figure of justice is typically portrayed as blindfolded. The Bible in *Leviticus* 19:15 underscores this feature of judgment: "Ye shall do no unrighteousness in judgment; thou shalt not respect the person of the poor; nor favor the person of the mighty."

The narrow focus of private litigation, the purposeful blinding of justice to issues of wealth and power, is under constant attack in contemporary jurisprudence. The argument is that the notion of a just initial distribution is a myth, and therefore litigation should seek to help those who are generally treated badly in society. Every judgment should be an occasion to correct pervasive inequalities of wealth. It follows that tort litigation should be converted into an ad hoc mechanism to achieve, finally, a just distribution of wealth. Therefore, the poor should win and the rich should lose.

The narrow compass of corrective justice is under attack from another source. While the criteria of distributive justice invite us to broaden the inquiry to consider the wealth of the parties, another wing of critics claims that tort law should serve not just private justice but the welfare of the society as a whole. Disputes about accidents, it is argued, are public matters—occasions for promoting social programs such as deterring accidents, spreading the costs of injury, and guaranteeing compensation for victims not covered by social insurance. These social goals arguably promote liability (or sometimes, nonliability) where the criteria of the law might be ambiguous. To argue today in favor of purely private disputes, of cases in which there is no public interest, is to ignore the utility of lawsuits as levers for social change. American lawyers now believe that a responsible judge is one who considers not only the imperative of doing justice between the parties, but the impact of the decision on the future welfare of society.[24]

It is no easy task to maintain the narrow focus that Aristotle urged for corrective justice and that is stressed in the biblical injunction not to consider persons (i.e., personal criteria) in judgment. The double-sided challenge for corrective justice is warding off both—broadening the inquiry to include criteria of distributive justice and judging in the interests of social welfare. Holding to the traditionally narrow focus of litigation is no easy task when the conceptual foundations of corrective justice seem to have been lost in the course of historical evolution.

The narrow focus might be justified on grounds of privacy. You, personally, would probably not want courts engaging in a free-ranging inquiry about your merits and demerits as a person. The better reason for favoring a limited focus on the transaction triggering the lawsuit is that this is what the litigation promises to be about. The accident brings the parties into court. In the long run, it makes more sense to rest one's fate on the analysis of the accident as the basis of the decision. If distributive justice were the standard, the rich and generally wicked would always lose. It would make no difference how careful they were in the particular case. In the interest, then, of integrity and a decision that makes sense in view of the basis for the litigation, a rational litigant would let his or her fate ride on the narrow focus of corrective justice.

This point is readily illustrated by a thought experiment. Imagine that the parties could choose their judge and jury, and the candidates for their choice had to state, honestly, which criteria they would use in judgment. No one could qualify who did not have the consent of both sides to the dispute. Some candidates would say that they would rely on the relative poverty of the parties; this would obviously not be acceptable to the wealthier side. Some would say that they would decide on the basis of the advantage that would accrue to the rest of society from one decision or the other. Both sides would resent this orientation, for they think of the dispute as their own; the decision maker should focus on them. They would no more pick a judge who focused on the welfare of society than they, if sick, would consult a physician who promised to use experimental therapy that would, in the long run, be useful to future patients. The only grounds for decision left would be events that occurred between the parties, the transaction that stimulated the dispute. The just resolution of the dispute must be found, therefore, in this narrow focus on the transaction generating the dispute. This thought experiment leads one to Aristotle's conception of corrective justice, and this may explain the lasting appeal of Aristotle's teachings and why they have survived repeated challenges in recent years.

Aristotle's account of justice comes close to the reigning view today, but with one important and easily forgotten supplement. Today we are likely to think of justice simply as a goal of correct action, as conformity with some ideal. Aristotle, following Plato in *The Republic*, perceives justice as a human virtue, a quality that leads to the flourishing of the individual. The just person achieves harmony of the soul.[25] The just man or woman not only does justice to others, but demands that justice be done to him or her.[26] He or she finds the mean between service to others and preoccupation with self. The just person is neither altruist nor egoist. He follows another piece of ancient wisdom captured in the saying of Rabbi Hillel:

> If I am not for myself, who will be for me?
> If I am only for myself, what am I?

The just person, then, has a healthy sense of personal desert, of what is coming to him or her. Yet this self-centered notion of desert seems to have fallen by the wayside in our survey of distributive, corrective, retributive, and commutative justice. It is time, then, that we turn to desert as a distinctive source of claims of just treatment.

In the course of this inquiry into distributive and corrective justice, we have overlooked an influential ground for claiming that one owns, or should own, something, namely: "I have earned it and therefore I deserve it." As we see in the next chapter, many of the issues of justice considered in this chapter take on a different coloring when viewed through the lens of desert.

Notes

1. *Genesis* 18:23.

2. *Id.* at 18:26.

3. ARISTOTLE, THE NICOMACHEAN ETHICS 1129–1134 (D. Ross trans., 1925).

4. *See* Herbert Morris, *Punishment and Persons*, in HERBERT MORRIS, ON GUILT AND INNOCENCE 31 (1976).

5. IMMANUEL KANT, THE METAPHYSICS OF MORALS 141 (Mary Gregor trans., 1991).

6. *See* JOHN RAWLS, A THEORY OF JUSTICE 11 (1971).

7. *Id.* at 85–86.

8. *Id.* at 60.

9. KANT, *supra* note 5, at 56.

10. FRIEDRICH A. HAYEK, THE CONSTITUTION OF LIBERTY 85–102 (1960).

11. ROBERT NOZICK, ANARCHY, STATE, AND UTOPIA 149–64, 232–46 (1974).

12. RAWLS, *supra* note 6, at 60–61.

13. I leave aside the refined dispute about the meaning of the phrase "everyone's advantage."

14. NOZICK, *supra* note 11, at 183–231.

15. *See* MICHAEL SANDEL, LIBERALISM AND THE LIMITS OF JUSTICE (1982).

16. For an analogous critique, see GEORGE P. FLETCHER, LOYALTY: AN ESSAY ON THE MORALITY OF RELATIONSHIPS (1993).

17. ARISTOTLE, *supra* note 3, at 1132a.

18. One approach would be to split the difference. Suppose the gain to the defendant is 5 units and the loss to the plaintiff is 10 units. The best application of Aristotle's principle would be to require the tortfeasor to pay 7.5 units to the victim.

19. *See* Vincent v. Lake Erie Transportation Company, 109 Minnesota Reports 456, 124 Northwestern Reports 221 (1910).

20. ARISTOTLE, *supra* note 3, at 1132b.

21. *See* Ernest Weinrib, *The Gains and Losses of Corrective Justice*, 44 DUKE LAW JOURNAL 277 (1994).

22. For recent efforts to develop theories of corrective justice, see JULES COLEMAN, RISKS AND WRONGS (1993); ERNEST WEINRIB, THE IDEA OF PRIVATE LAW (1995).

23. ARISTOTLE, *supra* note 3, at 1132a.

24. For a thorough exposition of the view that the collective interest is the only relevant determinant of justice, see *infra* Chapter 9.

25. PLATO, THE REPUBLIC, Book IV, 443d–e.

26. ARISTOTLE, *supra* note 3, at 1133b–1134a.

6

Desert

Different languages have amusingly different ways of talking about "earning" or "making" money. The French talk about "winning" it (*gagner l'argent*); Germans, about "deserving it" (*Geld verdienen*); Russians, about "working for it" (*zarabotat dyengi*); Israelis, about "turning a profit" (*lharviah kesef*); and Hungarians, about "searching for it" (*penzt keresni*). On a matter as basic and universal as going to work and receiving a salary, we encounter these striking cultural differences. This, I would suggest, is our common experience of "desert." If we give of our time and effort, we deserve an appropriate return for our labor.

Curiously, many of these languages have no single term for "desert." In colloquial Hebrew and Hungarian, the idea of desert is expressed by a phrase that means "coming to me." Getting what I deserve is rendered as "getting what's coming to me." This is a perfectly respectable locution in English as well, but in French and English, as one impious theory holds, we like the term "desert" because we associate it with the lemon meringue pie we get at the end of the meal. Sometimes, redundantly, we speak of "just deserts," which is not something you say to the waiter, but a term meant to underscore that what you've got coming to you conforms to criteria of justice.

In this context one hopes that linguistic diversity does not camouflage a very simple message. The Bible is replete with stories of good and bad fortune allocated on the basis of good and bad conduct. Indeed one might say desert—punishment for those who abandon God—is the preoccupation of the prophets, and whether individuals actually receive what they deserve in life becomes the agonizing theme of the Book of Job. We do not need a word in biblical Hebrew meaning "desert" in order to make this the central question of God's relationship to humankind. Having a single word to refer to the concept is useful, but not obligatory.[1]

The striking feature of desert, as we have seen in the preceding discussion, is that it comes in both positive and negative forms. We earn money and we earn punishment. We are both praised and blamed for our actions. When rewards and penalties are just, we say that we deserve them. This symmetry is an illuminating feature of our moral lives, for it provides a structure for inquiring about the foundations of desert and whether the same criteria apply in both the positive and negative context. What, then, are the preconditions for saying that we deserve either reward or punishment? And how do we know how much reward and how much punishment are just?

The Conditions of Desert

The first condition of desert is that you *do* something or that something be *done* to you. To deserve punishment, one must have at least acted in the external world and, we can assume for the time being, this action must have had an impact on other people. The action must bring about a state of affairs that other people wish either to condemn, reward, or punish. There is no punishment for thoughts alone—at least in secular legal systems.

The same principle applies, by and large, to positive desert. We praise people for what they do, for what they make of their own lives, and for the contributions they make to others. We do not reward them simply for having the right thoughts. Yet being the object of wrongdoing can generate positive desert, though without praise. The victims of accidents and other torts deserve compensation under the law. The damages are not paid as a reward, but they are nonetheless "coming to the victim." One of the more hotly debated topics today is whether the victims of crime deserve the gratification they may receive by witnessing the punishment of the person who wronged them.[2] Though the criminal may deserve punishment, it is difficult to maintain that the victim deserves anything on the positive side.[3]

We have considerable experience evaluating the negative forms of conduct that lead to criminal punishment. The relevant factors are the value of the interest attacked and the attitude—or state of mind—of the offender. Accordingly, mass murder is worse than killing one person; homicide more heinous than rape; rape worse than battery. Crimes against the person are generally more grievous than crimes against property; stealing a lot is worse than stealing a little. Killing intentionally is worse than causing death accidentally. These value judgments ranking crimes are common to the world's legal systems.

On the positive side, there is considerably more controversy about valuing the good we do for others. The moral debate between Capitalism and Communism turned (and still turns, in principle) on whether the market is a sound measure of what people deserve for their labor. The market knows no limits to its generosity and shows no mercy to those it rejects. A basketball player can make millions; a magnificent poet can go unsung. The market registers people's relative appreciation for what they buy (as affected, of course, by the available supply). So far as consumers are good judges of value, the market is the best possible vehicle for determining the rewards of those who produce. Yet there are many areas where the market fails to function properly, either because the state is the sole employer, say, of judges and jailers, or because some groups, such as lawyers and doctors, exercise a monopolistic control over pricing for their services.

Those who criticize the market argue that productive labor has an intrinsic value.[4] Its ingredients include, among other things, the effort and skill required, creativity, and the beauty of the final product. These criteria lend themselves to considerable debate and sometimes to abuse. But no more, it would seem, than our collective judgments about the negative side of desert, namely assessing just penalties for various crimes. Yet where the market is available, it is often defended as impersonal and objective.

As mentioned earlier, an offender's attitude, or state of mind, is critical in measuring his deserved blame and punishment. Those who kill intentionally are thought to be worse than those who kill recklessly or negligently. The assumption seems to be that intentional actors invest more of themselves in the crime and therefore become more clearly identified with the evil they do. Also, the relative voluntariness of the action might be important; if at the time of the homicide, the offender suffers from partial insanity—called "diminished responsibility" in the law—the degree of his culpability is reduced. If the act is less than fully voluntary, the actor is less than fully responsible for the outcome.

These points are taken for granted in the criminal law, but intriguingly, their analogues do not seem to apply in the field of positive desert, particularly as measured by the market. Let's imagine that the inventor of velcro thought his sticky cloth would make a better mousetrap; mice would get stuck on it, spelling their end. He gets a patent (because as the inventor he deserves one!) and puts it on the market. Consumers seize on it and convert it into an all-purpose fastener, sales and royalties from which make him a billionaire. Under the principles of capitalism, he deserves the money whether he intended or thought he was doing nothing more than building a better mousetrap.

The same principle seems to hold for discovering minerals in the earth. Many prospectors for gold and oil put in considerable time and labor and find nothing. But if I stumble upon a vein of gold in an area open to prospecting, the discovery is mine, simply because I am the one who, through minimal effort, first reduces it to knowledge and control. It is better that there be more inventions and more valuable minerals known to us, and therefore those who bring about these appreciated events apparently deserve to receive the value of their contribution.

This, then, represents an asymmetry between positive and negative desert. In the case of the latter, we measure deserved punishment to a considerable degree by the actor's knowledge, personal investment, and control over the outcome. These factors seem not to matter for receiving rewards in the fields of discovery, invention, and marketing. The criterion of positive desert seems to be how much the product of our actions is valued by others.

Yet one reason to think that intention matters, even in the case of positive desert, is the evolution of our thinking about attempts. Attempted crimes are signaled by trying and failing to harm someone, say, by shooting and missing. Though the criminal law initially insisted on actual harm,[5] legal systems around the world began about two centuries ago to punish criminal attempts. The person who tries and fails deserves punishment simply because he has committed himself to doing evil and has tried to execute his plan. At first blush it seems that we do not reward attempts to do good that fail, yet pedagogic principles of recent years seem to reward effort as well as accomplishment. The pupil who tries hard deserves recognition whether she succeeds or not. This shift from result to effort represents a recognition that attitude matters for positive desert; there is no positive effort worthy of reward without consciously and intentionally setting one's sights on a goal. Thus it seems that our attitudes toward positive desert may be in flux.

Another intriguing point of comparison is complicity, that is, assisting someone in doing good or evil. The traditional rule of the criminal law is that those who aid and abet crimes are responsible only if they actually contribute to the success of the crime. Let us suppose that trying to assist bank robbers in their escape, a collaborator parks her car so as to hinder the police from pursuing them on a particular escape route. It turns out that the robbers take a different escape route and therefore the blocking of the street is irrelevant to the success or failure of the crime. Though there is considerable debate about this point in the law today, the traditional rule was that the friendly motorist would not be liable for trying, but failing, to assist the bank robbers.[6]

In the field of positive desert, however, success of the primary venture does not seem to matter in assessing the merit and the desert of the person who tries to make it succeed. Suppose that a young man is willing to sacrifice his education so that his older sister can finish medical school. It seems that as so far as rewards are possible in this world or the next, the young man deserves something for his sacrifice—particularly if he really wanted to stay in school himself. But suppose that the sister takes the money and then turns to sex, drugs, and rock and roll. She never finishes medical school. If the brother had tried to do evil and failed, he would still deserve blame. But if he tries to do good and fails, it is not clear that he merits positive desert for his well-intentioned sacrifice.

It is not surprising that we are relatively more certain about the conditions for negative than for positive desert. Negative desert has been pondered for centuries in working out the rules that govern the sentencing of convicted criminals. Positive desert finds no precise institutional counterpart. Because there is no area of the law concerned with measuring appropriate rewards, we are left to rely on our accumulated moral sensibilities about who deserves more and who deserves less. Positive desert reflects judgments that crystallize in our social life, but which are not laid down as legal rules.

Challenging Desert

Precisely because the institutions of negative and positive desert are so deeply ingrained in our moral and legal culture, they repeatedly draw philosophical challenges. The question always is: How is it possible that some people should earn more than others—either more praise or more blame? Desert upsets the pattern of equality. Therefore those committed to equality as a principle of justice are often disquieted by a theory that dictates inequality of rewards and penalties.

Before considering the two primary objections to desert, it is important to grasp why desert entails inequality. Desert is a principle pitched, above all, to individual actions. Some people do more than others, both good and bad. Some people work harder than others. Some people are born stronger, swifter, more intelligent, and more artistically gifted than others. They are better able to produce things that others appreciate. On the negative side, some people are more inclined to be aggressive and less restrained than others in their violent and acquisitive impulses. Why some people choose to do good and others to do evil is one of the greater mysteries of the human condition. We need not solve the problem here except to note that each person acts distinctively in ways that matter for the receipt of rewards and penalties. The individuality of deserved consequences renders equal distribution impossible.

The first recurrent challenge to the principle of desert focuses traditionally on criminal punishment. No one deserves punishment, the argument goes, for no one is responsible for his or her actions, whether normal or deviant, law-abiding or criminal. No one is responsible because we all act in ways that are determined by our genetic inheritance, our psychological development, our environment, or some combination of these forces. Even if we think that we are the architects of our individual lives, we are deluded. We are simply unaware of the deep computer programs that run us as though we were machines. It just happens that the program is designed to make us think that we are acting freely.

This is the classic position of strict or hard determinism. There are some softer forms of determinism that are compatible with individual responsibility. Immanuel Kant himself, the great exponent of freedom as well as responsibility, held that no event can occur in the physical world without being caused.[7] Explaining our actions as caused does not undercut responsibility. But reducing human action to the playing out of a computer program would, it seems, mean that no person could ever do other than he or she did do, and therefore there would be no basis for saying that they, as individuals, deserved praise or blame, rewards or punishment, for their nominal actions. Not even the philosopher who advanced determinism would deserve praise for her clever argument.

Of course, even if hard determinism were true, we could carry on with practices of praising and blaming each other. We could award gold medals at the Olympics and impose prison terms on shoplifters. But some people might wonder whether these practices were a sham. We would be like atheists praying as if there were a God.

The most serious consequence of determinism is that we lose the sense of human interaction, either in reasoned argument or in love. When we engage in reasoned discussion with others, we are sustained by the sense that our partner listens to us and we listen to her. When she responds, she responds to *my* argument, and when I respond, my firm conviction is that I am responding to *her* thinking. Neither of us is simply acting out an inner program. If we thought we were, I am not sure we would have the patience to listen to each other and engage each other's vision of the world. What is true of reasoned discourse is also true of loving interaction. If the gesture of love is not really from her to me, or from me to her, if in both cases, the act springs from a hidden program, it loses the quality of expressing devotion from one person to another. In short, determinism undermines the notion of human agency, and without human agency, without the sense that we are the author of our thoughts and sentiments, our actions lose their quality as responses to the unexpected actions of others.

The first argument against desert, then, denies that there are actions that are grounded in individual assertion. The quality of individual assertion is something called "free will," but this term, too, is fraught with difficulty and is better avoided. All that is needed is a way of perceiving human actions as the individualized expression of human agents, rather than as the mechanical response to encoded signals. The second argument against desert focuses primarily on whether those who achieve more in their lives deserve the fruit of their labor. As discussed in the previous chapter, Rawls challenges positive desert, it seems, not by asserting determinism but by denying our moral title to the qualities of intelligence and talent, and to the efforts that enable us to succeed. All of these individualized qualities, he claims, are "arbitrary from a moral point of view." They are arbitrary relative to the universal self, the rational self, which engages in discourse about justice behind the veil of ignorance. We do not deserve the product of our labor because, as Rawls reasons, we have no individual claim to the conditions that enable us to succeed.

It follows from Rawls's system that as we cannot justly be rewarded for our actions, we cannot be justly punished for our crimes. If we have no claim to our positive qualities, it would surely be unjust to be saddled with our negative dispositions. For Rawls, the only sensible way to approach punishment becomes the converse of his second principle of justice, which permits differential rewards as an incentive to those with talent to make a contribution that is beneficial to all. Recall that Rawls's second principle of justice reads as follows: "Social and economic inequalities [i.e., benefits] are to be arranged so that they are both (a) reasonably expected to be to everyone's advantage, and (b) attached to positions and offices open to all." As adapted to burdens rather than benefits, the principle would read: "Social and economic burdens [e.g., threats of punishment] are to be arranged so that they are both (a) reasonably expected to be to everyone's advantage, and (b) attached to acts and omissions that anyone can avoid."

The point of punishment under the Rawlsian system turns out to be indistinguishable from the rationale of punishment as a deterrent to future crimes. This is not surprising, for as Rawls would use rewards to stimulate social contributions, he should use the threat of punishment to deter socially pernicious actions. Yet Rawls purports to be writing in the Kantian tradition. The version of Kant that emerges is one that abandons the cardinal Kantian moral principle: "Never treat anyone merely as a means, but as an end in himself." Using rewards and punishments as a way of stimulating socially useful behavior is the classic mode of treating people as a means to an end.

It is worth noting that both determinists and Rawlsians, with different arguments and motives, deny the significance of individuals as autonomous agents. For determinists, individual action is suppressed in the playing out of a scheme fixed in advance. For Rawls, human actions lose their moral status as the expressions of individuals, for actors cannot claim as their own the talents and conditions that enable them to act creatively.

Desert and Legal Entitlements

If Rawls takes the rational universal self to be the centerpiece of his theory of justice, the argument of desert starts with the individual as he actually is, embodied in flesh, endowed with certain dispositions, engaged in projects of his own choosing. This is the individualized concrete self as opposed to an abstract self that turns out to be the same for all of humanity. The concrete self acts in the world—sometimes rationally, sometimes irrationally—sometimes creating good, sometimes doing evil. The theory of desert is a response to these actions of individuals. In order for the theory to make sense, there need be no abstract or universal self that backs up the person as he or she appears to us.

Taking the actions of the concrete self as his starting point, Robert Nozick responds to Rawls with a sustained critique of theories of justice that ignore desert and individual entitlement. Nozick focuses on three types of human interaction that can affect entitlement to property.[8] People acquire property initially by creating it, by discovering it, or by occupying it with due regard for the equal rights of others. This is entitlement by acquisition, grounded on a theory of desert. Those who take the initiative—who labor, create, discover—deserve the bounty of their assertion. Once in possession of property, individuals can transfer it by barter, trade, and gift and thus vest property rights in others. Finally, if a property holder suffers wrongful injury at the hands of another, he is entitled to compensation as rectification of the injury. These three modes of entitlement enable Nozick to imagine a possible evolution of a system of property holdings that would be just. So long as all property is initially acquired justly, transferred justly, and all wrongs are rectified, then the resulting system of holdings should be just.

These three fields of creating entitlement trace the contours of three recognized fields of law—property, contract, and tort. The law of property specifies how individuals acquire original ownership; the law of contract enables them to transfer that ownership to others; and the law of tort specifies the conditions under which those who injure another must make compensation. Each area of law bears a different relation to the theory of desert.

The law of acquiring property, as we have noted, is based, in part, on deserving the fruits of one's labor. But it would be a mistake to think that there is nothing more to the criteria of original acquisition. Individuals can acquire vast holdings with little effort, as in the case of the individual who stumbles upon the gold mine or in that of an explorer who claims and acquires an island by planting a flag. The customs and conventions of original acquisition tilt the balance toward acquiring more rather than less. This suggests that it is in the social interest for things to be owned individually rather than left unowned or in common ownership. Economists have pressed the argument (and they are probably right) that private ownership encourages the careful husbanding of resources. Common ownership encourages each person with access to take as much as possible, as quickly as possible.

Contracts permit the reallocation of goods to those who value them most. In the modern economic theory of buying and selling, we assume that each person acquires a subjectively better position as a result of trading. The car is worth more than the money to the car buyer; and the money is worth more than the car to the seller. Otherwise, if they are fully informed of their alternatives and they are not under pressure, they will not trade. It is hard to see the justice in trading, except that both are made subjectively better off. The only sense in which each deserves her improved position is that she has enabled her partner to be better off as well.

More acute problems of justice arise from gift giving and inheritance, which are variations on the institution of contracting. The recipient of a gift or bequest has typically done nothing to deserve the sudden increase in wealth. Perhaps in some cases the recipient has related to the donor in a particularly supportive or loving way, and for this behavior deserves the windfall. But gifts depend solely on the will of the donor; there need be no inquiry about whether the beneficiary deserves it.

One wonders then how, in Nozick's system, one can justify the transfer of wealth by gift and inheritance. It may be the case that the donor should have the right to give away his property. If she may destroy it, she should be able to give it away. It does not follow, however, that the recipient should have the right to keep his unexpected and undeserved gain. It seems that the recipient's rights derive from those of the original holder. But looking at it this way does not solve the problem of desert and justice.

The rectification of wrongs in the tort system raises problems of desert on both sides of the dispute. Innocent people who suffer injuries to their persons or property deserve to be made whole. But there is no reason why equally innocent actors who cause the injury should pay. The positive desert of the victim must be matched by a negative desert on the side of the wrongdoer. This way of thinking has led to the quest for a justification for "shifting the loss" from the victim to the alleged tortfeasor. The fault standard became popular in the first half of this century as the rationale for holding injurers liable. The person who is at fault, because he was negligent and injured another, deserves, in the negative sense, to pay. The victim deserves, in the positive sense, to collect. The case of the shipowner and dockowner, discussed in the last chapter, offers another view of why some people deserve to pay and others deserve to collect.[9] The shipowner profited from the dockowner's loss. Not requiring payment would be tantamount to a licence to exploit. It was critical that the dockowner was not permitted to defend his property from invasion and harm. His being forced to sacrifice his property rights generated a basis for saying that he deserved compensation for the resulting harm.

Proportionality and Excuses

The notion of desert provides the foundation for many commonly used ideas of the law. Without the principle of proportional punishment— making the punishment fit the crime—it would be hard to understand retributive justice. In fact, this principle prescribes a relationship, a correlation, between the offender's desert and the severity of punishment. This relationship is illuminated in the formula proposed by Robert Nozick.[10] R (the quantity of deserved punishment) is a function of r (the degree of responsibility) times W (quantitative level of wrongdoing). Or:

$$R = r \cdot W.$$

The variable r varies from 0 to 1, from zero to full responsibility for wrongdoing. The variable W or *wrongdoing* varies from the trivial to the catastrophic. The measure of wrongdoing, by and large, is the impact of the criminal conduct on the victim. Homicide is worse than rape, which is worse than battery, which is worse than larceny of large sums, which is in turn worse than larceny of smaller sums. Of course, there are some delicate questions raised by rankings of this sort. Where, for example, does one put crimes like treason that are committed not in harming a victim but in breaching a duty of loyalty to the government?[11] Resolving questions of ranking is essential to working out a rational and consistent system of sentencing.

The variation of r from zero to one expresses a number of widely held intuitions in criminal law. For example, negligent homicide is typically punished less severely than intentional homicide. This reduction in penalty expresses a judgment that the negligent killer is less than fully responsible for the death; the intentional killer is, in contrast, fully responsible. Provoking someone into killing, say with racial insults, light physical blows or, in some states, sexual infidelity, typically reduces the crime of murder to manslaughter. The same reduction is available when mental illness partially reduces the offender's "capacity" to conform his conduct to the law's demands. So far as these mitigations of murder are justified, the assumption is that provocation reduces the degree of the offender's responsibility and therefore, to a like degree, reduces his or her deserved punishment.[12]

The illuminating instruction offered by the formula $R = r \cdot W$ is that it restates and explains the function of the distinction between justification and excuse. This distinction, rooted in the common law, had been long forgotten, but it has recently enjoyed revival and gradual acceptance as a standard feature of Anglo-American criminal law. Claims of justification, such as self-defense and lesser evils, address the problem of wrongdoing. A valid and proven claim of justification reduces W to zero and therefore provides a complete defense against deserved punishment. Claims of excuse address the offender's degree of responsibility for proven wrongdoing. Excuses reduce the r to zero or at least to a negligible amount below the threshold required for liability.

Excuses are directed specifically to the question of involuntary action. The common assumption since Aristotle is that an action might be involuntary for one of two reasons: either it is subject to coercion or it is carried out in ignorance of the relevant facts. Coercion, in turn, might be either external or internal. The standard cases of external coercion are duress and personal necessity. The proverbial mode of duress is a gun pointed at the head as the ultimate persuader to do (or not do) something . . . and right now! Here is an offer she cannot refuse. Either she opens the safe or she dies. The clearest case of coerced action, therefore, is but a short step from physical coercion, from the case of actually forcing the hand of another. Yet she can always say "no" and be shot. Her "will" is engaged by the act of submission to the gunman. Because she is acting rather than just being acted upon, we need an argument why we should excuse her.

The best explanation is that involuntary action is treated as the moral equivalent of no action at all. And in the absence of action, voluntary action, there is no basis for imposing responsibility. Yet it is not so clear what one means by "involuntary" action. The judgment of involuntariness invariably entails a comparison of the threat and the action that the allegedly coerced party must undertake in response to the threat. As the threat becomes less severe and the action becomes more harmful, the judgment of involuntariness loses its grounding. Sooner or later, we reach the point at which we conclude that the actor should have resisted the threat. If she must kill in order to avoid damage to her car, she hardly acts involuntarily. The threat of property damage is one she should resist, particularly if the only way of avoiding the threatened harm is to kill an innocent person.

The boundary between voluntary and involuntary behavior lies some place between two extremes: It is excusable to open a safe to robbers in order to avoid being killed (low harm, high threat), and inexcusable to sacrifice an innocent person in order to avoid property damage (high harm, low threat). The way the line is drawn depends on our sense of what we can fairly expect of each other under circumstances of pressure. Different cultures will draw this line at different places. Some cultures are indulgent toward those who must act under severe pressure; others are more exacting and refuse, for example, to excuse the killing of an innocent person, no matter how severe the threat of harm to the coerced party. The point to remember about excuses is that the question is always focused on the actor's having done something wrong. Excusing is a matter of recognizing that ordinary mortals cannot always do the right thing. Yet a severe and puritanical culture might well demand that individuals sacrifice themselves rather than identify themselves with evil.

The question of involuntariness invariably raises an issue of fairness to the individual caught in a difficult matrix of conflicting forces. The problem is when and under what circumstances we can fairly expect of people that they suffer rather than do the wrong thing. The Germans capture this issue under the term *Zumutbarkeit,* which hardly translates into English except indirectly as the question of what we can fairly expect of others under conditions of stress.

Apart from duress, English and American courts have been loathe to recognize excuses based on external coercion, in particular, external coercion generated by natural circumstances. In the famous case of *The Queen v. Dudley and Stephens,*[13] the English Queen's Bench held that starvation on the high seas could not excuse homicide and cannibalism. Perhaps acts under duress are more easily excused, than the personal necessity present in *Dudley and Stephens.* In a gun-to-the-head case, someone is always responsible for the crime, namely, the threatening party. In the case of killing one person to save many others from a natural disaster, excusing the killing means that no one bears the stigma of the crime. In principle, however, it should not matter whether someone is available to answer for the wrongful deed. Those who act under pressure of immediate starvation are no different from those who act with a gun to their heads.

The internal analogue to external pressure is mental illness. It is common to think of mental illness as a kind of compulsion that interferes with the actor's freedom in the same way that external coercion undermines the possibility of voluntary action. Whatever the field of law, the actor's insanity becomes relevant in assessing responsibility. The insane make no contracts, their wills are invalid and, with some exceptions, their wrongful actions entail no personal responsibility.[14] Yet as we noted above, we need not necessarily think of insanity as a weight that bears down on the actor's freedom of choice. An alternative approach treats mental illness and insanity as conditions that go to the foundation of the actor's capacity for rational thought.[15]

According to Aristotle, actions can be involuntary either if they are the product of coercion or if they are carried out in ignorance.[16] The actor cannot be said to choose his action unless he knows what he is doing. The problem with the theory of ignorance and mistake is that no one ever knows everything about the circumstances and the consequences of action. What did Bernhard Goetz know when he drew his gun and began to shoot at the four black youths on the subway? He knew the elementary facts, but he was ignorant about important features of the confrontation. There was no way for him to know what would have happened had he not drawn his hidden revolver. Yet we would have to say that Goetz acted voluntarily despite his ignorance of factors that mattered to his fate.

In a contract case, neither the buyer nor the seller knows which way the market is going to move. And the ignorance does not make them less responsible for choosing to buy and sell at a certain price. Yet if the two parties are mistaken about the object they are talking about—such as which thing is being sold or which ship the crops will arrive on—the dissensus precludes the formation of a binding contract.[17]

The knowledge that people have about their actions is always a matter of degree. No one ever knows everything about the circumstances and consequences of action. Thus there is no conceptually clear standard for deciding when ignorance and mistake should negate the voluntariness of the action. There are, however, some standard cases on which jurists, both here and abroad, readily agree.

In a homicide case, for example, the defendant cannot be guilty of intentional homicide, if he thinks he is shooting at a tree and it turns out to be a human being. She cannot be guilty of stealing a fur coat if she thinks the coat she is taking belongs to her. These are clear cases. There is much controversy, in criminal law, about the relevance of mistakes in heterosexual rape cases, either a mistake about the age of the girl in a prosecution for statutory rape or a mistake about consent between adults.[18] In these cases the suspect knows that he is engaging in intercourse, and that is all many courts require. The difference between a mistake about who owns the umbrella and a mistake about consent to sex, they would say, is that the former negates the intent required for the crime and the latter does not. The intent required for theft is to deprive the *owner* of his property; if you think the coat you are taking belongs to you, you do not intend to harm the *owner* of the coat (because you think you are the owner). But the intent required for rape is merely the intent to have intercourse; a mistake about the age or consent of the woman leaves this intent intact.

This, alas, is a circular argument. The problem always is deciding what the required intent should be. Some courts have indeed held that the intent required for rape is the intent to have sex against the woman's will, in which they conclude that a mistake about consent does negate the required intent.[19] The better solution to this problem would be to leave aside the issue of intent and to concentrate on the conditions under which a mistake should constitute an excuse. In criminal as well as tort cases, mistakes should excuse wrongdoing whenever they negate the personal culpability or fault of the suspect. If the suspect is not aware of the resistance offered by the woman with whom he seeks intercourse, he could well be culpable or at fault. He could be negligent for not paying closer attention to her way of saying no. The proper test then is not simply whether he is mistaken about consent, but whether he is reasonably or non-negligently mistaken. If he is reasonably mistaken, however, he is not to blame for his transgression and he should not be held liable.

As in the analysis of coercion, we arrive finally at the point at which the judgment of involuntariness and desert merges with our intuitions of fairness. The problem always is what we can fairly expect of each other in resisting pressure and in paying attention to signals implicit in the circumstances under which we act. When we do not meet the common standard we set for each other, we are at fault and cannot invoke an excuse that would negate our responsibility. We deserve the punishment prescribed for the offense.

Notes

1. In modern Hebrew, "deserves to" is conveyed by the passive form *raui l–X*, which means something like: the person is "seen to be connected" to X.

2. In GEORGE P. FLETCHER, WITH JUSTICE FOR SOME: VICTIMS' RIGHTS IN CRIMINAL TRIALS (Addison-Wesley 1995), I generally support a range of victims' rights but specially criticize the role of "victims' impact statements" in sentencing hearings. *See id.* at 198–201.

3. For a refined analysis of the categories of desert, see Joel Feinberg, *Justice and Personal Desert*, in JOEL FEINBERG, DOING AND DESERVING 55 (1970).

4. For the classic statement of this view, see Karl Marx, *Economic and Philosophical Manuscripts*, in KARL MARX: EARLY WRITINGS (T.B. Bottomore trans., 1964).

5. One exception to this rule is punishment for treason. *See* GEORGE P. FLETCHER, RETHINKING CRIMINAL LAW 208–211 (1978).

6. For discussion of this point, see *id.* at 679-81.

7. IMMANUEL KANT, CRITIQUE OF PURE REASON 409–415, 464–479 (N. Kemp-Smith trans., 1964).

8. *See* ROBERT NOZICK, ANARCHY, STATE, AND UTOPIA 150–82 (1974).

9. See the discussion *supra* in Chapter 5 at pp. 89-90.

10. NOZICK, *supra* note 8, at 60–63 (The original formula was $R = r \cdot H$, where H stands for harm).

11. See the discussion of treason *infra* at p. 174.

12. For an analysis of the controversy surrounding this reduction of the crime of manslaughter, see FLETCHER, *supra* note 2, at 16–21.

13. 14 Queen's Bench Division 273 (1884).

14. One exception is the liability for intentional torts. *See* McGuire v. Almy, 297 Massachusetts Reports 323, 8 Northeast Reports 2d 760 (1937).

15. *See* MICHAEL MOORE, LAW AND PSYCHIATRY: RETHINKING THE RELATIONSHIP (1984); H. FINGARETTE & A. HASSE, MENTAL DISABILITIES AND CRIMINAL RESPONSIBILITY (1979).

16. ARISTOTLE, NICOMACHEAN ETHICS 1110–1111b2 (D. Ross trans., 1925).

17. *See* E. ALLAN FARNSWORTH, CONTRACTS 677–700 (1990).

18. See the discussion of consent *infra* in Chapter 7.

19. Director of Public Prosecutions v. Morgan, 2 All England Reports 347 (England 1975).

7

Consent

No idea testifies more powerfully to individuals as a source of value than the principle of consent. When individuals consent to undergo medical operations, to engage in sexual intercourse, to open their homes to police searches, or to testify against themselves in court, they convert what otherwise would be an invasion of their person or their rights into a harmless or justified activity. The existence of a doctrine of consent testifies, therefore, to the existence of personal rights. Individuals possess (one might say 'own') rights to their bodily integrity, to their physical privacy, to their property, and to their freedom from state intrusion. They can waive these rights and sometimes transfer them to others, as in the case of property rights. Waiver and transfer are specific instances of consent.

Consent resembles desert as a concept that dignifies individuals by giving them control over their lives and fortunes. Desert justifies individuals' claims to the fruit of their labor. It also requires that individuals be punished for their wrongdoing. Consent affects our relations with others by vesting in them the power to act toward us in ways that would otherwise be wrong and prohibited. That one may consent to an operation, to sexual relations, or to the loss of privacy and liberty introduces the possibility of idiosyncratic relations with others. Some will say "yes" and others will say "no" under exactly the same circumstances.

One could imagine a world with a minimal role for consent. Medical criteria of probable benefit would determine the permissibility of operations.[1] Marital status would determine the permissibility of sexual relations. The legally defined authority of the police would be the exclusive basis for determining whether they could search your home. A suspect could not choose to confess his guilt; the state would have to prove guilt without the suspect's participation. This would be a world in which individuals counted for less. They would be regarded, to a lesser extent, as a source of legitimation. The test for whether something done to them was right or wrong would not be what they *wanted* but what was good for them or for the state.

Yet it is hard to imagine the total elimination of consent. A culture that recognizes personhood, where individuals are distinct entities, must recognize, it seems, consent as it bears on the institutions of property and sexual access. Without the distinction between mine and thine, the notion of a person has little meaning.[2] The institution of property leads immediately to the notion of consent. For property is transferred by consent, and it is used and occupied with the consent of the owner. Similarly, the power to control access to one's body hardly makes sense without the power to say "yes" or "no" on the basis of totally personal and possibly irrational criteria.

Consent is a powerful tool of moral and political justification. Democratic decision making is said to express the consent of the governed. Those who consent can no longer complain. They are not injured if they agree to what happens to them. *Volenti non fit injuria*: Consent negates the injury. This idea is so seductive that it is often stretched to cover cases where there is no real consent but either hypothetical consent or implied consent. The social contract tradition in political philosophy reasons that for the sake of securing their rights and insuring their security from aggression, individuals consented at some mythical moment of time to the powers of the state. In the writings of Thomas Hobbes, John Locke, and Immanuel Kant, however, the social contract is a purely hypothetical construct that draws on the moral power of actual consent. No one supposes that people actually sat down and said to each other: "O.K., let us set up the state and give it the power to preserve the peace." Hypothetical consent, as we shall see later,[3] provides an argument for justifying existing political institutions.

In cases of implied consent, an individual is taken or deemed to have consented to one thing as a result of choosing to do another. Motorists who enter a state other than where they live are taken to have consented to service of process, that is, to be subject to suit, if they have an accident and return home.[4] At one time, American women who married foreigners were taken to have abandoned, by consent, their American citizenship.[5] The argument is sometimes made that by committing a crime, the offender consents to his punishment.[6] These are all cases of fictitious consent; the consent that matters (being sued, abandoning citizenship, being punished) is inferred artificially from another event that is chosen (driving in the state, marrying a foreigner, committing a crime).

One wonders why consent has this power. How does it work? What is its moral foundation? To approach this issue, think about these various contexts in which consent may be allowed or disallowed.

A. *Assisting in Suicide.* A suffering patient gives permission to another to put him out of his misery, either a depression or a terminal illness. Though the point is hotly debated today, killing another is not ordinarily justified on the grounds of his or her consent. The traditional reason, inspired by the religious roots of criminal homicide, is that our lives are not ours to give away.[7] Also, practical considerations enter the argument, for this is the one case in which the consenting person is not available after the deed to confirm or disconfirm having given consent. Videotaped declarations might be available in some cases, but the risk of abuse remains great.

B. *Sadomasochistic Beatings; Medical Operations.* It is worth noting that the argument that our lives belong to God could as well apply in the field of consenting to violence to the body, either in the form of submitting to the sadist's whip or to the surgeon's knife. There has been considerable debate about whether sadomasochists may consent to dangerous beatings.[8] There has been less debate in the secular world about cosmetic medical operations (face lifts, nose jobs, etc.); some religious people still hold to the view that our bodies are not ours to change in nontherapeutic ways.

C. *Sexual Taboos.* Most sexual prohibitions "between consenting adults in private" have fallen, but we are not about to give up the barrier against incest, however defined in the modern composite family; and we still have problems defining who is an adult who can give valid consent. The taboo against incest is too deep for casual justification, but we can reflect profitably on why children or young teenagers cannot given valid consent to sexual intercourse. Two revealing reasons present themselves. First, it is thought that young people below a certain age (18, 16, 14, 10?) cannot rationally consent to sexual relations. They can give their spending money to shopkeepers, but they, particularly females, may not give their bodies to others. They don't quite know what they are doing, and therefore their consent cannot be considered well-founded.

The second reason trades on the factor of domination that issues between adults and children, either between older males and younger females or vice versa. Domination means that the older party exercises a degree of influence over the younger partner that undermines the consent. Influence can derive not only from age but from any situation—employment, medical, educational—in which one party is in a position of authority over the other. This is an important point that we will return to later: under conditions of domination, consent cannot be considered valid.

D. *Waiving Constitutional Rights.* To express the defendant's control over his own fate in a criminal trial, our legal system allows the defendant to waive various rights recognized in the Constitution. She can waive, consensually, her right to a trial (plea bargaining), her right to be represented by counsel, her right not to take the stand and testify, and several procedural rights that make a difference at trial. She can also waive her right not to be subject to search and seizure of personal effects and her right not to be interrogated in the absence of counsel. European systems do not allow the defendant to waive his trial or, in many cases, representation by counsel. The more restrictions there are on waiving rights, the more responsibility the state, as opposed to the individual, takes to insure a just outcome in the trial.

E. *Changes in Legal Status.* Though contracts and commercial transactions bear an element of promising for the future, they can be interpreted—by analogy to marriages—as consensual changes of legal status. True, the classic cases of consent listed above are those in which the consenting party has something and by expressing consent to another, gives it up. Commercial contracts represent the creation of new relationships where none existed before.

Consent functions in different ways in these different contexts. Sometimes consent undermines a possible allegation of harm. If the owner consents to the taking of his property, he suffers no harm when it is taken. This could hardly be said of consent to sadomasochistic beatings, where there is definitely physical harm despite the consent. The same is probably true of waiving constitutional rights, such as the right that the police not search your home without a warrant. In some situations, then, consent negates the actual harm; in some, it negates only the right to complain about the harm.

Domination, Equality, and Consent

Consent is not valid for either of its functions (undermining the harm, negating the right to complain) unless it is freely and intelligently given. The consenting party must know the relevant facts and act without being under pressure. This model of free and informed consent has an extraordinary attraction. The ideal is one in which the person as he truly is expresses himself. When the consent comes from a person's existential roots, it reveals the uniquely personal stand of that person on the issue at hand.

This ideal has many precursors in the history of philosophy. In one version or another, philosophers have sought the true person within, the person who expresses himself essentially, unaffected by any form of domination. Kant had an image of moral behavior, based purely on reason, unaffected by the domination of sensual impulses.[9] John Locke argued that it was irrational to try to coerce someone to follow the true religion, for salvation could only come from the free person within.[10] Roberto Unger has recently invoked the same model of thinking by defining the good as that which individuals choose under conditions of nondomination.[11] Economists have adapted the same model of the truly free and informed actor in building their models of the perfect market.

Unfortunately, it seems, the notion of the truly informed and free actor is a myth. First, it is impossible to be omniscient about the consequences of our actions. Risks and uncertainties attend everything we do. Assessing those risks is always a guess. Further, the notion of acting freely, without influence, is also unattainable. We always act in context. The cues of approval and disapproval from friends and family invariably affect our actions. Even those who think they reject society's values still stand in a relationship to those values and thus act by reaction.

That perfect consent is impossible in the real world does not mean that there are not cases of more or less influence, more or less domination. The dimension of knowing the relevant facts seems the easiest to analyze; the more information the better, provided the person asked to consent is able to assimilate the material. Before a medical operation, doctors and nurses inform patients of the risks involved, but they cannot ask the patient to spend a week in the medical library before giving a response. The more difficult dimension to fathom is the subtle ways people influence each other in their interactions. This is the dimension of potential domination.

Of course, there can be more and less interpersonal influence or domination. The problem is perceiving when acts of influence cross the line and render consent invalid. Consider the inducement of paying money in return for consent. This does not render a contract of employment suspect; receiving money is what working is about. But suppose a police officer offers money to a suspect to induce him to confess. There is no doubt that this level of inducement, and even lesser acts of influence, would render the confession involuntary. Why should offering money undermine consent in one context and not in another?

In plea-bargaining negotiations, there is nothing untoward about a prosecutor offering a lower charge or sentence in order to convince the defendant to plead guilty.[12] Yet he could not achieve the same end by offering a monetary payment to the recalcitrant defendant. If a police officer comes to your door in uniform and asks to look around, he need not advise you of your right to refuse entry. But if he arrests you he must read you your *Miranda* rights before eliciting a statement that would be admissible in court. These are curious inconsistencies. Sometimes the influence is acceptable and sometimes it is not. There does not seem to be any precise way of measuring influence and domination and deciding when they invalidate the consent of the person affected.

The ideal of free and informed consent expresses Isaiah Berlin's conception of negative liberty.[13] It is the liberty that springs from being left alone, from not being subject to the domination or coercion of others. Positive liberty, which Berlin railed against as a concept exploited by dictators, holds that people act freely only when they are doing the right thing.[14] The prime example is Kant's notion of the moral law. Only when legislating the moral law and subjecting oneself to it is the individual autonomous and free.[15]

It would seem that doing the right thing, if induced by external pressure, would never be consensual. But this is not necessarily true. Our evaluation of the conduct at stake sometimes influences our assessment of whether it is freely chosen. A good example presents itself in the Jewish tradition. A man must voluntarily grant a divorce to his wife; he must freely consent to the rabbinical decision ending the marriage. Yet if he refuses to grant the divorce and the rabbis find that his conduct is unreasonable, they may apply coercive means, such as locking him up, in order to get him to consent. The justification for forcing him to consent is that though it is right that there be a divorce, the rabbis do not have the power to circumvent his power to say "yes" or "no."

There are many cases in political life where we accept implicit domination in the name of a good cause. There is no doubt that General MacArthur and his American staff exercised considerable influence over the Japanese transition to democracy after the Second World War. The same is true of the Allies's influence over the Germans in the wake of the Third Reich or the North's sway over the South in the aftermath of the American Civil War. Covert domination provides the mode of cooperation between victor and vanquished. Yet it would be difficult to say that the Japanese and Germans did *not* consent to their new mode of democratic government or that the South did *not* consent to the new national order created by the Civil War.[16] Sometimes the right result warrants some compromise in the process leading to decision.

The same is true of negative results. The reason we do not let children consent to sexual intercourse is that we regard these acts as questionable for children. If sex were no more serious an event than going swimming, we would let children do what they wanted to do. Also, when testators act bizarrely, leaving bequests contrary to all expectations, courts are more likely to scrutinize their actions for signs of undue influence. The negative result of unexpected action induces suspicion that the action was not rational, not free and informed.

That no one can lose his or her rights without consent testifies to the equality of all persons—at least of all adults. Yet there are many versions of consent and therefore of equality. One version stresses the purely formal equality of opportunity. This formal mode of equality ignores the role of material resources in enabling people to give their consent freely, without constraint and domination of others. It is satirized in Anatole France's well-known reference to "the majestic equality of the laws, which forbid rich and poor alike to sleep under the bridges."[17]

Versions of equality that take into account material resources come in many variations. Some theorists insist on equality of material resources, namely, the same number of chips for each player. Others stress the equality of welfare or of the psychological appreciation of the goods distributed. The point of all these theories of equality is that there must be some material backing to the equal opportunity to consent or not. It is not enough that everyone is free to say "yes" or "no."

No Means No

No one can be regarded as a person unless he or she can say both "yes" and "no," effectively, about the things that matter most. This explains why the politics of consent have become so important to feminists fighting for the equality of women. Free love, birth control, and abortion have asserted themselves from time to time as feminist issues, for women have often perceived the path to full citizenship as lying in their right to say "yes" to sex without bearing greater repercussions for the act than do men. In recent years, the right to say "no" to sex has loomed even larger in the women's movement. The "no means no" movement stands for the proposition that what a women says explicitly should weigh more heavily than the supposed implicit communication of coyness. The opponents of the feminist position seem to be those who find wisdom in the line of Lord Byron, "Whispering 'I will ne'er consent,' [she] consented" or those who tell the old joke about the difference between diplomats and ladies. The punch line informs us that if a diplomat says "no" to anything, he is not a diplomat; if a lady says "yes" to everything, she is not a lady.

The critical cases of ambiguous consent are those in which a woman engages in conduct that in many or most cases would indicate probable consent. Most men would think that if a woman voluntarily undresses in front of him, she is interested in sex. Fewer would assume that just because she comes to his room at 2:00 A.M., ostensibly for a conversation, her presence betokens consent. Requiring a verbal affirmation is a way of ruling out these contextual signs of consent as sufficient to indicate willing cooperation. Feminists insist that in modern America, we do have "world enough and time" to clarify the situation and female "coyness [is] no crime."[18] It may go too far to insist, as did the Antioch

College code of sexual manners, that students secure "affirmative consent" from each other for each stage of sexual exploration. But the moral point is important. Do not assume consent just from the context of interaction.

Demanding clarity as the basis of consent expresses a concern about the risk of error. The assumption is that sex on a date, without full and willing consent, is a grave misfortune. It is equivalent, in the minds of many, to forcible rape by a stranger in a dark alley. Yet date rape is inherently difficult either to prove or disprove. The only witness is the alleged victim, and often there are no bruises or other traces of violent aggression. If the crime is so serious and the evidence so easily disputed, perhaps the traditional rule of the common law was right: The state should not prosecute rape unless there is some independent evidence to corroborate, that is, to confirm, the complaint.

The corroboration requirement has come under sharp attack because it seems to discriminate against women as victims of rape. In other criminal cases corroboration is not necessary. One of the leading writers in this field, Susan Estrich, questions whether corroboration should be required in rape cases if it is not required in prosecutions for theft between acquaintances.[19] We are willing to believe witnesses who say that they said "no" to a defendant's taking away goods belonging to the victim. And therefore, we should be equally receptive, she argues, to uncorroborated testimony (i.e., testimony not backed up by other evidence) that the victim said "no" to sexual intimacy. Yet there are so many differences between these two fields of life that the analogy is hardly compelling.

There is no great misfortune in property's becoming misappropriated. If there is a misunderstanding between owner and someone who takes her property, he can find a solution that leaves her unharmed. He can give it back. He can pay compensation equivalent to the market value of the lost goods. Not so with nonconsensual sex. If there is a misunderstanding here, if she thinks that she has said "no," and he hears "yes," and she gives in to his importunity, there is no way to erase the falsely intimate connection. Property transactions do not go to the core of personality, and they are reversible without a trace. But sex carries the potential for deep emotional bonding, and when this potential is abused in dissonance, the victim suffers a scarring in her inner life. The only filter between bonding and scarring, between love and rape, is the thin wedge of consent.

Precisely because nonconsensual sex represents an irreversible harm, the crime and the punishment are so serious. If the crime represents a grave deprivation of the victim's rights, there is an understandable impulse to convict in borderline cases, and therefore there should be proper safeguards against easy convictions. To find the proper analogy to consent in date rape cases, we have to turn to transactions that bear more severe consequences than do disputes about property.

Consider a possible analogy to cases of terminally ill patients who consent to have a physician terminate their lives. Doctor-assisted suicide is now illegal in all fifty states, but it has many supporters, and it crops up from time to time as a popular ballot initiative. (In 1994 Oregon narrowly approved a proposal that allows physicians to prescribe fatal dosages of drugs.) Those who favor the practice see the decision to end one's own life, with a physician's help, as an assertion of human autonomy and dignity. "Whose life is it, anyway?" captured this moral point in the title of a hit play. Opponents distrust the role of consent over so grave a matter and tend to see the doctor's assistance as criminal homicide. If and when this practice is institutionalized, we can be sure that a physician's testimony about the patient's verbal consent will not be enough to ward off a criminal conviction. This is a matter obviously weighty and irreversible. There will be procedures, signed documents, guarantees, checks-and-balances. If a physician asserted the consent of a deceased patient, she would not be believed unless she could demonstrate, with reliable evidence, that proper procedures were followed. This would suggest that the burden should be on a man claiming consent from his sexual partner to demonstrate that he followed proper procedures in securing consent to sexual intercourse. Perhaps we have reached the stage in which consent in writing should become the norm.

We confront a classic problem of analogical reasoning in the law. We have a problematic situation, namely, alleged consent to sexual intercourse between young adults without witnesses. And we have two relatively clear cases. Consent in property transactions is easily proved; consent to physician-assisted suicide is subject to rigorous standards of proof. The problem of analogical reasoning is to determine which of two relatively clear cases the problematic case more closely resembles. Does it resemble the case of consent to the taking of property? Or does it more closely resemble consent to physician-assisted suicide? Consent to sexual intercourse seems more grave a matter than consent to property transfers, and less grave than consent to the termination of one's own life. Yet the physician evaluating the patient's wishes is a neutral decision maker. A man deciding whether to engage in sex is hardly neutral; he is, as it were, a judge in his own case. This suggests that we should be tougher on men claiming consent than on physicians alleging consent to suicide.

This mode of reasoning, the response might be, grossly exaggerates the danger of miscalculation between the sexes. If there is a misunderstanding between men and women about their respective wishes in bed, this mishap might simply be the price, at least one feminist argues, that women must pay for sexual freedom.[20] The proper analogy proves to be elusive. Property transactions are too trivial and yet the unauthorized taking of sexual pleasure hardly appears to be akin to the unauthorized taking of human life. One reason that the matter is so difficult is that there are in fact two competing risks at stake. One is risk of undesired sexual intercourse. The other is the risk of convicting innocent men for allegedly engaging in date rape. The more the legal system seeks to minimize the first risk by convicting more easily, the more the courts increase the latter risk of convicting the innocent. This is one of the tensions in the legal system that explains the necessity of ongoing debate about what justice requires.

Rational, Hypothetical Consent

Consent, as I have presented the concept in this chapter, is an expression of the individual's desires and commitments. The source of consent is a real person, with idiosyncracies and irrationalities. Contracts gain their binding force, it seems, from two distinct individuals coming together and entering into an agreement, each with a different objective and with a different advantage to be gained from the contract. Linking these distinct objectives in a common venture gives contract its appeal as an instrument of social stability.

Yet there is another idea of contract that plays a role in political philosophy. Rawls thinks of his principles of justice as principles negotiated in an original position, behind a veil of ignorance, and binding as a social contract. The key feature of this negotiating situation is that it is not real people at odds over terms, but abstract rational beings who are ignorant about whether in the real world they would be male or female, rich or poor, strong or weak, intelligent or inept, whether, in short, they possess any of the characteristics that can generate injustice in the world. In the darkness of their ignorance, these abstract rational beings have nothing serious to disagree about. They readily accept principles of justice that accord each person in the real world a maximum possible amount of liberty and guarantee a floor of social and economic benefits in the interests of all. Yet it is a mistake to think of this univocal agreement as a contract linking two or more parties with divergent interests. It is nothing more than the expression of what a single rational person would choose under the conditions prescribed by the veil of ignorance.[21]

It is not clear whether it even makes sense to talk about an abstract rational being consenting to specific principles of justice. These doubts arise in thinking about one of the puzzles in Rawls's logic, namely, his ruling out risk taking in the original position. What if having one slave would make a thousand people better off, and quantitatively more so than the slave would suffer? Utilitarians see this result as acceptable, for it yields a net social advantage. Yet slavery or any condition of unequal liberty would violate Rawls's first principle of justice, which guarantees maximum liberty to everyone. Yet why should a rational person behind the veil of ignorance, who does not know whether he will be a slave or master in the real world or not, accede to the principle of equal liberty?

The problem is posed in the following apocryphal story. A rich man speaks to his slave and asks her whether she is satisfied with her condition. "No," she says, "I regard slavery as unjust. I should be liberated at once." The master responds: "Let me explain why your situation is just. You have heard of Rawls's original position. We were both there together, and we decided, as rational risk takers, that it would be better that one person in our society turn out to be a slave. We all took a chance, and I'm sorry. I won and you lost."

If this story does not get a laugh, at least it explains why risk taking in the original position is incoherent. Risk taking carries with it a theory of desert. If you take a chance and you win, you deserve your winnings.[22] Yet when imaginary dice are rolled in Rawls's original position, there can be no outcome in the real world. No real person's lot can be justified on the ground that some rational being took a risk in his or her name. Risk taking is not an option in the original position because the conditions for desert are absent. We can speak of deserved winnings and losses only when real people roll the dice.

The same is true about consent. It makes no more sense to attribute consent (or any other form of voluntary acceptance) to an abstract being than it does to think of an abstract being as deserving the fruits of its actions. Both *consent* and *desert*, as I have argued in these last two chapters, are attributable to concrete people, acting in the real world, motivated by good reasons and bad. Subtract the action, leave aside the deep motivations that make consent and desert personal and individual, and you deprive the concepts of their hinges. They cannot turn on rational thought alone.

The principles of desert and consent, as we have explored them in the last two chapters, stress the importance of individual efforts and idiosyncratic decision making. The focus on individuals and why they are different might lead us to forget the value of equality that leads Kant and Rawls to search for the common denominator of all humanity in rational action. Behind the original position, in the world of pure reason, all humans are of equal value. Thus we are reminded of the tension between individuality and equality. In the next chapter we explore the ways in which this tension plays itself out in legal thought.

Notes

1. This, I am told, is the position toward medical operations expressed in talmudic law.

2. Note that Kant begins his study of legal principles in "The Philosophy of

Law" with an analysis of "mine" and "thine." *See* Immanuel Kant, The Meta-physics of Morals 68–79 (Mary Gregor trans., 1991).

3. For further analysis of hypothetical consent, see *infra* pp. 114, 118–19.

4. *See* Hess v. Pawloski, 274 United States Reports 352 (1927) (upholding "implied consent" as a basis for jurisdiction).

5. MacKenzie v. Hare, 239 United States Reports 299 (1915) (upholding Congressional statute to this effect).

6. Carlos S. Nino, *A Consensual Theory of Punishment*, 12 Philosophy and Public Affairs 289 (1983).

7. *See* John Locke, Two Treatises of Government 270–71 (P. Laslett ed., 1988): "Man . . . has not liberty to destroy himself . . . for Men being all the Workmanship of one Omnipotent, and infinitely wise maker . . . are his Property."

8. On the general point, see H.L.A. Hart, Law, Liberty, and Morality 30–34 (1963).

9. *See* Immanuel Kant, Groundwork of the Metaphysics of Morals (H.J. Paton trans., 1964).

10. John Locke, A Letter Concerning Toleration (J. Tully ed., 1983).

11. Roberto Unger, Knowledge and Politics 238–48 (1975).

12. Compare the German idea of the *Legalitätsprinzip*, which requires full enforcement of the law and is therefore hostile to plea bargaining. *See supra* Chapter 1 at p. 18.

13. Isaiah Berlin, *Two Concepts of Liberty*, in Isaiah Berlin, Four Essays on Liberty 122–31 (1969).

14. *Id.* at 131–134.

15. *See* the discussion of Kant's notion of autonomy in *infra* Chapter 9.

16. *See* M. Urofsky, A March of Liberty: A Constitutional History of the United States 443–45 (1988).

17. The Red Lily 75 (Modern Library trans. originally published 1894 as Le Lys Rouge).

18. Andrew Marvell, To His Coy Mistress Andrew Marvell: Complete Poetry (George def. Lord ed., 1968).

> Had we but world enough and time,
> This coyness, lady, were no crime.

19. Susan Estrich, Real Rape 43–47, 57, 86 (1987) (on dispensing with the requirement of corroboration).

20. Katie Roiphe, The Morning After: Sex, Fear, and Feminism on Campus (1993).

21. For further elaboration of this interpretation of Rawls, see George P. Fletcher, *Law and Morality: A Kantian Perspective*, 87 Columbia Law Review 533 (1987).

22. For more on the theory of desert, see *supra* Chapter 6.

8

Equality

Equality is at once the simplest and the most complex idea that shapes the evolution of the law. The simple idea is expressed in the maxims of political discourse. The Declaration of Independence proclaims: "All men [i.e., all people] are created equal." True, in 1776 the framers condoned slavery and the disenfranchisement of women. Nonetheless, the affirmation of human equality generated a standard thereafter for criticizing the shortcomings and inconsistencies of American politics.

Though we are committed, in principle, to the equality of all Americans [or all people?], there is something puzzling about our solemn declarations of human equality. "In what respect?" one is tempted to ask. Are they equally intelligent, strong, or beautiful? Obviously not. The only sense of "being created equal" that makes any sense is moral or religious. We are equal in the eyes of God. But what exactly does that mean? For one, the affirmation of equality implies that no one can maintain, convincingly, "I am intrinsically better than you are." That kind of claim was plausible for most of human history. It flourishes in societies that recognize aristocracy, nobility, or castes acquired at the time of birth. The claim of intrinsic superiority is the essence of racism and sexism.

Bruce Ackerman imagines a society in which everyone can claim, "I am as good as you are," and the claim is never adequately refuted.[1] What are the conditions that make this faith in humanity possible? There are, so far as I can tell, two sources of our commitment to equality.

One is the affirmation in the creation story of Genesis: "And God said, Let us make Humankind in our image, after our likeness. . . ."[2] The idea that humans are made in the image of God brings everyone's claim of human dignity to the same supreme level. The theme that "we are all God's children" reverberates in Western culture as an invitation to find a common humanity and a basis for mutual respect.

For those who are less religious, a second source in the philosophy of the Enlightenment yields the same commitment to equality. Immanuel Kant maintained that human dignity was a value beyond all price;[3] there could be no justification for intentionally sacrificing an innocent human life.[4] The implication of this supreme value attributed to human life is that all human beings are of equal dignity. If human life were not the supreme value, if it could be outweighed by a finite sum of dollars, then it is not clear that we could believe that all human beings were of equal dignity. For some people, the equivalent monetary value might be one billion dollars, for others, ten billion. There would be no reason to think that the same number of dollars outweighed the value of every individual's life. The exact price is less important than the inescapability of a price that varied from individual to individual.[5] If the price varied, as it seems it must, the clear implication would be that human beings are not of equal monetary value. The only way, then, to maintain the principle of equality is to make a commitment to the ultimate value of every human life. At the level of ultimate moral value, all human beings are equal.

The belief in human equality, then, establishes an ideal that motivates political reform. We can never achieve full equality of opportunity for all persons; and certainly we can never achieve the equal distribution of resources for all people in our society, not to mention the world as a whole. Yet there are always influential philosophers, such as John Rawls, who begin their work with the proposition that all social goods must be equally distributed unless "an unequal distribution . . . is to everyone's advantage."[6] Rawls himself draws on Kantian assumptions in order to maintain his zealous commitment to equality.[7] Admittedly, however, the belief in equality runs deeper than either the religious or the Kantian argument can justify. For many thinkers and social critics, equality is simply assumed. It need not be justified.

For the legal system, however, the matter is not so simple. No legal system, except perhaps the most rigorous commune or Israeli kibbutz, has ever sought to enforce strict equality among its subjects. And even in the commune, it would be difficult to prevent people from giving more gifts and doing more favors to their friends and loved ones than to relative strangers. Gift giving creates inequalities, but in response, one might argue: Equal treatment is not an ideal for personal relationships. The principle of equality typically enters into the law as a restraint on governmental action. The government may not discriminate against some people for the sake of others. As Dworkin puts it, the government owes everyone subject to its power "equal concern and respect."[8]

Despite the high-sounding invocation of equality in the Declaration of Independence, the 1787 American Constitution contained no reference whatsoever to the government's duty to treat all citizens equally.[9] The Bill of Rights enumerates a set of rights possessed by all persons subject to the government's power. There are other references in the body of the Constitution to the "privileges and immunities of citizens," but no mention of equality among citizens. The Civil War permanently changed the structure of the Constitution. The emancipation of the slaves brought with it three new amendments. The Thirteenth abolished "involuntary servitude" and the Fourteenth established the principle that no state may "deny to any person within its jurisdiction the equal protection of the laws." The Fifteenth secured voting rights to the newly emancipated Americans. There is still no provision that explicitly prohibits the federal government from discriminating unjustly, but the courts have no problem reading the principle of "equal protection of the laws" into the duty imposed on the federal government not to deny any of life, liberty, or property "without due process of law."[10]

A constitutional principle of equal treatment invests the courts with an enormous power to scrutinize and invalidate legislation. All laws discriminate, for all laws include some things and exclude others from their scope. Those outside the scope can claim that they are disadvantaged and therefore denied equal protection of the laws. Consider some examples. The law against homicide is limited to protecting living human beings. What about animals, fetuses, art objects, trees? Are they not discriminated against by being left out? The law of theft protects those who own objects, but in most states it does not protect people who provide services but are never paid. The latter group must sue under contract, but they do not receive the protection of the criminal law. Is this not discrimination?

And when we try to end discrimination against some, we end up discriminating against others. If ordinances require beepers in elevators to signal floors for the blind, we discriminate against the sighted who used to enjoy quiet elevator rides. Every law intervenes in social arrangements and creates new benefits and burdens. Those who bear the burdens can claim discrimination in violation of the equal protection clause. Whether they succeed in the courts is another story.

This area of law invites judicial deference to legislative judgments.[11] The courts assume that when the legislature carves up the world into those who profit and those who lose out under new legislation, the lawmakers generally know what they are doing. It would be difficult to generate a constitutional challenge against minimum ages for a driver's license or the right to buy cigarettes or to drink in a bar. Deference to legislative judgment also makes it difficult to challenge, on constitutional grounds, decisions about which classes of workers should receive social and economic benefits.[12] In these cases the Court requires only "plausible reasons for Congress's action."[13] This is known as the requirement of "minimum rationality." The statute's classification must be "reasonable in light of its purpose."[14] This is a standard with soft teeth but nonetheless one sharp enough to cut a swath through some deeply felt legislative schemes.

A good example is *Plyler v. Doe*,[15] a case that comes into the news every time there is an outbreak of sentiment against illegal aliens (also called, depending on your politics, "undocumented immigrants"). *Plyler* came to the Supreme Court because the state of Texas sought to deny the benefits of public education to children not "legally admitted" to the country. Californians who supported a similar measure in November 1994 argued that the purpose of their initiative was to discourage would-be immigrants from entering and remaining in the state illegally.[16] Despite an ostensible purpose of preserving educational resources for those lawfully in the state, the Supreme Court struck down the Texas law so far as it discriminated against children "on the basis of a legal characteristic over which children can have little control."[17] The children had no control over their parents' movements and therefore, the Court reasoned, they could not fairly be denied access to public education.

This is a complicated body of case law, and there is little to be inferred from isolated cases about when the Supreme Court will uphold or invalidate legislation on the ground that its classification is not "rationally" related to a legitimate state purpose.[18] Yet deference comes in degrees, and this phenomenon has led to some unusual judicial decisions. Since the late 1960s, the Supreme Court has developed a nuanced body of rules about when it will apply differing degrees of "scrutiny" to examining state and federal legislation.[19] Whenever the classification of the statute is premised on a "suspect classification," the Court applies "strict scrutiny" to the classification at issue. The paradigm for this kind of scrutiny is racial discrimination. "Strict scrutiny" means that whenever the statute or a judicial decision imposes a burden on a particular "race" (meaning presumably African, Asian, or Caucasian), the Court will give the responsible organ of government less deference than it would otherwise.

The principle of strict scrutiny applies most clearly to invidious racial discrimination in public facilities. In some applications of this strict standard, however, the element of race appears only in the background of the dispute. For example, the Supreme Court held that a state court denied a white mother equal protection of the laws after it deprived her of custody of her child because she had married a black man. She claimed that she was discriminated against relative to mothers who married white men or, generally, partners of the same race. The state court had reasoned that growing up in a mixed racial household would not be in the "best interests of the child." For those who accept the society's racial prejudice as a sociological fact, the state court had a plausible reason for its findings. Yet the Supreme Court reasoned that it could not "tolerate" private biases. These prejudices "may be outside the reach of the law, but the law cannot, directly or indirectly, give them effect."[20]

The intriguing feature of "strict scrutiny" is that it is not a rule of law that, in the ordinary way, confers rights and imposes duties on citizens. It is rather a rule directed exclusively to judges. It prescribes an attitude, a required posture toward the authority of state courts, Congress, and state legislatures. Strict scrutiny is a declaration to the effect: We should take a good hard look at the law in question. The implication is that in other cases, the Justices take a more casual approach toward the claim of unfair discrimination. There are some efforts in judicial language to translate this tough stand into legal language. Thus, the Court says, in cases of strict scrutiny, it will not uphold a statute unless it finds "a compelling governmental interest" in favor of the apparent discrimination.[21]

The treatment of categories other than race display, then, two basic problems. Will a nonracial category, such as gender, receive the same kind of "strict scrutiny" as racial classifications? And if it does not, how strong a governmental interest should be necessary to justify the classification? In recent years, the proper treatment of gender classification has received great attention. There is considerable agreement on the right judicial language, but less in its application. The reigning view is that gender classifications receive "heightened" or "intermediate" scrutiny, thus complicating the attitudes that the judges should display toward various classificatory schemes. Whatever the language, in the early 1980s, the Supreme Court upheld several legislative classifications protective of women that would be unthinkable in the area of race relations. In one case, the Court upheld the traditional practice of punishing statutory rape when committed against young women but not when committed against young men.[22] In another, it passed over an obvious discrimination in the draft that called young men but not young women to military service.[23] In the latter case, Justice Rehnquist wrote of Congress's authority over national defense: "perhaps in no other area has the Court accorded Congress greater deference."[24] The cases would, of course, have come out the other way if the classification had been based on race rather than gender. It is not clear that this difference lends itself to an explanation in the language of the degree of scrutiny the Court employs. Even if the scrutiny were superstrict, a majority of the Justices might find some purposes acceptable as to gender and sexual orientation that they would not find within the realm of imagination in the context of racial classification. [25]

Equality and Liberty

Political philosophers are fond of stressing the contradiction between the values of equality and liberty.[26] The more the society insists on equal treatment, the less people are free to do what they want to do. This may be true, but this tension is not particularly evident in the field of equal protection law. First, the Court has been wary of extending the principle of equal protection to matters that bear directly on the perpetuation of entrenched economic classes in American society. Differential funding for public schools—some local communities supporting their schools more and others supporting them less—will obviously have an impact on the distribution of wealth in the next generation. Yet the Court has refused to interfere in these funding practices, however much they may disadvantage some groups of children.[27] There is no restriction, then, on the liberty to pick a school, either public or private, that will further the relative chances of one's child for success. The important point is that the Court will not meddle in the greatest inequality of all—the inequality of opportunity due to the economic fortunes of one's family. To this extent, liberty interests—the freedom and the economic power to do what one wants to do—are fully compatible with the reigning interpretation of the equal protection clause of the Fourteenth Amendment.

The brand of equality promoted by the Supreme Court actually enhances freedom of association.[28] For example, ending school desegregation increased the opportunities for social contact with "other" Americans. By striking down statutes prohibiting interracial marriage, the Court increased the marriage options for everyone without any offsetting reduction in anyone's liberty.[29] Perhaps white segregationists could conceptualize their opposition to integrating the schools as the freedom not to come into contact with other races. But this claim of right, rejected by American history, is more in the nature of an asserted right to a certain environment in which other people behave according to one's preferences. It is not a claim of personal freedom to act or not to act in a particular way.

Despite the general effect of the equal protection clause, there is one area where the Court has begun in the 1990s to intrude heavily, though almost unwittingly, in a critical area of personal freedom. There is no institution more important to individual liberty than the criminal trial, where criminal defendants face the risk of imprisonment and perhaps even the death penalty. The cornerstone of the criminal trial is the jury. In the area of jury selection, the Court has begun to enforce principles of equality at the expense of the defendant's rights.

As early as 1880, the Supreme Court intervened in the process of jury selection to strike down, as a violation of equal protection of the laws, a statute prohibiting blacks from serving on juries.[30] Significantly, the defendant in the case was an African-American and he properly complained of being tried by a jury that the law required to be all white. Gradually, the Court invalidated other laws that restricted jury service. Today, virtually any discrimination against adult citizens in the composition of the pool or the venire—the list from which jurors are chosen— would be invalid. None of these changes in any way compromises the defendant's rights; indeed, they only improve the chances of a fair trial for members of minority groups.

The defendant's right to a fair trial enters a critical stage at the moment that jury selection begins. At that point, the prosecution and the defendant, together with the trial judge, interview prospective jurors and challenge those they regard as biased, or potentially biased. The judge decides whether there is "cause" to dismiss the potential juror from service in that case. After using these challenges for cause, both sides to the trial may invoke so-called peremptory challenges to remove jurors whom they suspect of bias but as to whom they cannot convince the judge that their intuitions are correct. The use of these peremptory challenges has now become the battleground for the tension between equality and liberty.

The problem is that both sides can use their peremptory challenges in a discriminatory manner. They can remove all blacks, all whites, all men, all Jews, all people who go to church, all people who read the *National Enquirer*, or any other group they think would be inclined to vote against their preferred outcome of the case. Of course, if prosecutors were engaged in the practice of using, in all cases, peremptory challenges against a particular group, then that practice would be tantamount to a law that precluded that group from jury service. As we have seen, laws of that sort are patently unconstitutional.[31]

In the 1986 *Batson* case, the Court began applying the principle of nondiscrimination in jury selection to particular cases, and that ushered in a new and uncertain jurisprudence. The prosecutor in *Batson* had dismissed four African-Americans without any apparent rationale except the likelihood that because of their race they would sympathize with a black defendant. When a pattern of discrimination emerges, the Court held, "the burden shifts to the State to come forward with a neutral explanation for challenging black jurors."[32] The Court reaffirmed the long-standing principle that "a defendant has no right to a 'petit jury composed in whole or in part of persons of his own race.'"[33] Yet, beginning in the *Batson* case, the Court undertook to supervise the tendency of lawyers—for now, just the prosecution—to engage in unfair or invidious discrimination in selecting the jury for particular cases.

The problem with speaking of discrimination in the selection of particular juries is that the activity is, by its nature, discriminatory. Lawyers want some people on the jury and not others. Now it is perfectly sensible to conclude, as did the Court in *Batson*, that when the prosecution discriminates against people who look like the defendant, the defendant is less likely to get a fair trial. This is not discrimination against the jurors who do not get to serve but against the defendant's interest in maintaining his liberty. This is another example of rulings that favor equality and liberty at the same time.

Yet *Batson* left in its wake a nagging problem. If the prosecution could not discriminate on the basis of race, did that mean the defense could not do so either? The two dissenters in *Batson*, Justices Burger and Rehnquist, anticipated the temptation to apply the principle of non-discrimination to the defense and found in this danger an argument against entering the field altogether. The problem of discrimination by the defense did not reach the Supreme Court until the winter of 1992. In a Georgia case that was structurally similar to the Rodney King trial, which was then gearing up in Los Angeles, a white defendant was charged with assaulting black victims. The Georgia prosecution sought a pretrial order preventing the defense from using peremptory challenges on the basis of race.[34] In that particular county, 43 percent of the population was African-American. A nondiscriminatory selection of the jury would have practically assured the participation of some black jurors. Of course, the defense would have preferred an all-white jury that might sympathize with a white man engaged in a racially motivated assault. In the end, as in the Simi Valley trial of the four police officers who beat up Rodney King, the defense secured a jury without a single African-American. This seemed unfair, but it was not easy for the Court to find a principle for fairly restricting the options of the defense to select the most sympathetic jury it could find.

Discrimination by the defense may seem unfair, but unfair to whom? To the prosecution? Americans are reluctant to recognize that the prosecution has rights under the Constitution; there is no liberty interest that is compromised when the prosecution loses the right to discriminate. Is it unfair to victims like Rodney King and those who identify with him? Indeed, it is, but American courts are just beginning to take the rights of victims seriously.[35] For want of a better theory, the Supreme Court formulated a curious view about why it should intervene to prohibit discrimination by the defense in jury selection. The discriminatory harm supposedly accrued to the jurors who could not serve. The majority of the Justices reconceptualized jury service from a duty of citizenship to a right of participation. Being denied this right on grounds of race began to appear comparable to the denial of the right to vote. In an important transition case, the Court commented, "Indeed, with the exception of voting, for most citizens the honor and privilege of jury duty is their most significant opportunity to participate in the democratic process."[36] The upshot of this reorientation was that in the summer of 1992, the Court held by five votes to four that the defense could not inflict this harm on potential jurors who were African-Americans by excluding them solely on the grounds of their race.[37] Notably, Justice Clarence Thomas wrote a separate opinion arguing that the decision would in the long run be deleterious to the liberty interests of black defendants. The decision implied that black defendants could no longer use their peremptory challenges against whites in order to secure a jury likely, on grounds of racial and cultural loyalty, to be sympathetic to them.[38] Their liberty was at stake, but the principle of equality took precedence.

The new philosophy of jury selection became disturbingly transparent in April 1994, when the Court ruled that neither prosecution nor defense could exclude men or women from a jury solely on the basis of their gender (or sex, as some people say).[39] In a suit to establish the defendant's paternity and obligation to pay child support, the state used nine of its ten peremptory challenges to remove male jurors. Its assumption was that women would be more likely to impose liability for child support. The defense engaged in the reverse tactic—striking the female candidates. Because there were more women in the pool, however, the jury consisted only of females and they found the defendant liable. On appeal to the Supreme Court, six Justices upheld the defendant's complaint that it was unfair, particularly in a paternity action to allow him to be judged by an all female jury.

The defendant won his appeal, but the opinion contains only a passing reference to the harm that discrimination caused the male defendant in this case. The Justices devote all of their rhetorical energy to a recitation of discriminatory practices toward women in the past. It is true that women gained the right to vote and to participate in juries later than did African-American men. It took the Nineteenth Amendment in 1920 to universalize the suffrage, and as of 1947, sixteen states still denied women the right to jury service. This discrimination, the Court reasons, was based on "stereotypical presumptions" about the competence and biases of women. These assumptions about men and women and their propensities "reflect and reinforce patterns of historical discrimination."[40] If lawyers rely on their intuitions about men and women, they supposedly reinforce the historical pattern of discrimination against women.

It is understandable, then, that the Court said almost nothing about whether it was fair to the defendant in this particular case to be tried by an all female jury. Implying that a women's jury would be partial to a female complainant would reinforce the stereotype that women think differently from men about certain issues. To avoid this tempting (and in my view reasonable) conclusion, the Court had to indulge in the assumption that the state violated the constitutional rights of the men who were excluded from serving on the jury. Of course, it is unclear why this defendant, if he received a fair and impartial trial, should secure a reversal of the judgment against him just because the rights of some other unnamed men were violated.

Curiously, in this line of cases, the most conservative Justices—

Scalia, Rehnquist, Thomas, and O'Connor—end up in the role of the defendant's champion. Those accused of crime should be able to maximize their options of a verdict in their favor by striking whomever they wish. In this situation, they favor liberty over equality. Yet the same judges often vote to curtail the rights of the accused. In the hierarchy of values in the 1990s, liberals and conservatives gravitate toward unfamiliar positions. For liberals, the imperative to extend equal protection to disadvantaged groups trumps the rights of criminal defendants. It is more important to root out stereotypes about women and ethnic groups than it is to protect the traditional options of the accused. For conservatives, the historically rooted conception of a fair trial does not surrender to the new egalitarian politics that seeks to ban "stereotypical presumptions that reflect and reinforce patterns of historical discrimination."[41]

The metamorphosis of jury selection provides a window on the power of egalitarian thinking to bring about fundamental changes in criminal procedure. Restrictions on the defense's options in jury selection obviously have an impact on the defendant's prospect of securing an acquittal; this is an instance, therefore, where the quest for equality does impinge on liberty—or at least on the likelihood that a criminal defendant will retain his liberty.

The political commitment to equality now threatens traditional attitudes toward freedom of speech. Catherine MacKinnon has developed a powerful new argument for restricting artistic and verbal expression that she believes threaten the dignity of women. The publishing and disseminating of sexually explicit materials, she claims, degrade women by treating them as sex objects and thus reinforce, as the Court said in the jury selection case, "patterns of historical discrimination."[42] Others make the same claim about hate speech directed against minorities that have suffered disempowerment in American society.[43] Thus, for good or for ill, the most prized liberty of all, freedom of speech, is under attack. This is the natural outgrowth of the deep American attachment to the principle that all men, all human beings, are created equal.

Punishment Negates Domination

The notion of equality has several antonyms or opposites. One opposite is unfair or invidious discrimination that leads to constitutional challenges under the equal-protection clause. This is a form of inequality that emanates from government action. Another antonym comes into focus when we think about the way private individuals generate inequalities in their relationships. When individuals come unjustly and improperly to dominate each other, the situation of inequality calls out for a legal remedy. Thus we hear the recurrent plea that the state should lend its efforts to groups, such as blacks, Hispanics, and women, who have historically suffered domination as well as discrimination. One version of this plea generates arguments for "affirmative action" in employment and in awarding governmental benefits, such as radio broadcast licenses.[44] These arguments are delicate and controversial, and they warrant full treatment in their own right.[45]

A relatively unexplored area of particularized inequality comes to the fore in criminal violence. The dominance gained by the criminal over his victim expresses itself in the victim's anxiety about recurrence of the crime. This fear is characteristic of many crimes, such as rape, mugging, and burglary, where the offender knows how to find the victim and implicitly threatens reenactment of the original crime. It is true as well in the case of blackmail, where the offender induces services or money in return for silence and is in a position to return at any time and demand additional payments.[46] Instilling fear is a mode of gaining dominance. Punishment counteracts this dominance by reducing the criminal to the position of the victim. When the criminal suffers as the victim suffered, one might argue, equality between the two is reestablished. By insisting on punishment, the victim's fellow citizens express solidarity and counteract the state of inequality induced by the crime.

Thus emerges an equality-based argument for criminal punishment. Immanuel Kant anticipated this argument by stressing the theme of equality—both as among offenders and as between victim and offender—in justifying punishment.[47] His hostility toward utilitarians stems largely from their willingness to deviate from the principle of equality in the interest of finding some benefit for the offender or for society.[48] The most extreme form of Kant's egalitarianism in punishment is expressed in the thought experiment of an island society about to disband. He imagines that as the citizens are ready to dissolve their society, there are still murderers who are condemned to die and still languishing in prison. What should they do about them? Kant insists that the murderers should be executed "so that each has done to him what his deeds deserve and blood guilt does not cling to the people."[49] Executing them seems to be pointless because no good could possibly follow. Kant's point is to justify punishment solely as a matter of justice, regardless whether anyone's safety or material welfare is thereby improved.

The failure to punish implies continuity of the criminal's dominance over the victim. When it fails to punish, the society becomes complicitous in this state of subservience and dominance. This is what Kant means, metaphorically, by "blood guilt" clinging to the people. They become guilty in the spilling of blood.[50] If the people and their government willfully refuse to invoke the traditional response to crime, they disassociate themselves from the victim. Abandoned, left alone, the victim readily feels betrayed by the system.

When the state fails to fulfill its duty to punish, all those who identify with the victim suffer a sense of discrimination and unequal treatment. This was the sentiment of the homosexual population in San Francisco which felt betrayed by the manslaughter conviction and mitigated penalty for Dan White in May 1979. White had killed Mayor George Moscone and gay leader Harvey Milk in cold blood, and yet the jury balked at convicting him for murder. This is the way African-Americans in Los Angeles felt after a Simi Valley jury acquitted the four police officers accused of maliciously beating Rodney King. And there are other classes of victims who often feel abandoned by a legal system that fails to punish the guilty.[51] The perceived discrimination, the apparent inequality, the sense of second-class citizenship—these assaults on the principle of equality readily erupt into violent protest.

One of the ways in which the principle of dominance expresses itself in criminal conduct is the recognition that victims should not be blamed for risking the occurrence of the crime. If Bernhard Goetz boards a subway train and sits down next to four rowdy youths, he is not to be blamed for being approached by youths who initiated a confrontation that resulted in violence.[52] If a woman goes jogging in Central Park at night, she is not to be faulted if she is attacked and raped. Although it is common in criminal trials to attack the victim, this practice runs contrary to the ethos of criminal responsibility. The criminal authors the situation that leads to dominance over the victim. Those who are preyed upon are in an essentially passive position; they are engaged merely in exercising their basic rights to live in private and move about in public.

The application of this egalitarian theme to criminal punishment is admittedly novel. It demonstrates the power of equality as a political and moral idea. This mode of thinking represents the "cutting edge" of legal thought today. A number of scholars are engaged in seeking to reinterpret issues of privacy and liberty in the language of equality. For example, the right to use contraception and the right to an abortion are generally understood in the law as grounded in the principle of privacy. The new interpretation is that rights to reproductive freedom are grounded in the principle of equality. The state's seizing control over issues of reproduction invariably generates a greater burden on women than on men.[53] As the argument goes, any system of regulation that has this kind of disparate impact on one gender should be open to challenge on grounds of equal protection of the laws. Similar arguments are advanced about the prohibitions of sexual intimacy that fall on particular groups, such as gay men.[54] To assess the value of this approach, we should turn to some themes, such as efficiency, privacy, and loyalty, that, as we shall see, have nonegalitarian implications. It may be that the commitment to equality is getting both stronger and weaker at the same time.

Notes

1. Bruce A. Ackerman, Social Justice in the Liberal State (1980).

2. *Genesis* 1:26

3. Immanuel Kant, Groundwork of the Metaphysics of Morals 102 (H.J. Paton trans., 1964).

4. Immanuel Kant, The Metaphysics of Morals 60 (Mary Gregor trans., 1991).

5. This is indeed the way tort law functions today. In an action for wrongful death, the value of the decedent's life is assessed according to life expectancy and earning capacity. This practice could be reconciled with human equality on the ground that it focuses on the damage caused by the death to the survivors.

6. John Rawls, A Theory of Justice 62 (1971). The difference principle, as discussed at p. 85 above, represents a form of justified inequality for it benefits the least advantaged class in the society.

7. See the discussion of genetic differences of ability *supra* pp. 121

8. Ronald Dworkin, Taking Rights Seriously 273 (1977).

9. But the 1787 Constitution did forbid the government's conferring titles of nobility. U.S. Const. art. I, § 9.

10. *See* Bolling v. Sharpe, 347 United States Reports 497 (1954).

11. For a discussion of deference, see *supra* pp. 72–73.

12. Railroad Retirement Bd. v. Fritz, 449 United States Reports 166 (1980).

13. *Id.* at 179.

14. *See* Laurence Tribe, American Constitutional Law 1440 (2d ed. 1987).

15. 457 United States Reports 202 (1982).

16. On November 8, 1994, California's voters endorsed Proposition 187 by an overwhelming margin. Because this provision seeks to deny routine medical care as well as access to public education to illegal or undocumented immigrants, we can expect the matter to remain open to legal debate for the rest of the decade.

17. 457 United States Reports at 220.

18. For example, as against equal protection as well as other arguments, the Court upheld Georgia's sodomy statute as applied to homosexuals, even though the Court hardly explained the purpose of the statute except as the enforcement of traditional conceptions of morality. Bowers v. Hardwick, 478 United States Reports 186 (1986).

19. *See* Gerald Gunther, Constitutional Law 601–646 (12th ed. 1991).

20. Palmore v. Sidoti, 466 United States Reports 429 (1984). (After the mother, Palmore, divorced Sidoti, the father, she married an African-American. Thereupon the court reversed its initial ruling awarding her custody.)

21. *Id.* at 432.

22. Michael M. v. Superior Court, 450 United States Reports 464 (1981).

23. Rostker v. Goldberg, 453 United States Reports 57 (1981).

24. *Id.* at 64–65.

25. For example, think about how the child custody issue posed above would come out if instead of beginning to live with a black man, the divorced

mother began living with a lesbian partner. For a recent example of judicial intolerance toward lesbian adoption, see In re Dana, 1995 New York Appellate Division LEXIS 3460 (decided April 1995), *rev'd* In the Matter of Jacob 1995 N.Y. LEXIS 3579 November 1995.

26. FRIEDRICH HAYEK, THE CONSTITUTION OF LIBERTY 85 (1960).

27. San Antonio School District v. Rodriguez, 411 United States Reports 1 (1973).

28. Herbert Wechsler would have preferred to rest the entire law of racial desegregation on the principle of freedom of association. See his controversial article, *Toward Neutral Principles of Constitutional Law*, 73 HARVARD LAW REVIEW 1 (1959).

29. *See* Loving v. Virginia, 388 United States Reports 1 (1967).

30. Strauder v. West Virginia, 100 United States Reports 303 (1880).

31. Swain v. Alabama, 380 United States Reports 202, 223–224 (1965).

32. Batson v. Kentucky, 476 United States Reports 79, 97 (1986).

33. *Id.* at 85. The principle dates to Strauder v. West Virginia, 100 United States Reports 303, 305 (1880).

34. For a detailed study of the Rodney King case, see GEORGE P. FLETCHER, WITH JUSTICE FOR SOME: VICTIMS' RIGHTS IN CRIMINAL TRIALS, Chapter Two (1995).

35. For more on this point, see *id.*

36. Powers v. Ohio, 499 United States Reports 400, 407 (1991).

37. Georgia v. McCollum, 112 Supreme Court Reports 2348 (1992).

38. *Id.* at 2360.

39. J.E.B. v. Alabama ex rel. T.B., 114 Supreme Court Reports 1419 (1994).

40. *Id.* at 1428.

41. *Id.*

42. *Id.*

43. Charles R. Lawrence III, *If He Hollers Let Him Go: Regulating Racist Speech on Campus*, 1990 DUKE LAW JOURNAL 431; Mari J. Matsuda, *Public Response to Racist Speech: Considering the Victim's Story*, 87 MICHIGAN LAW REVIEW 2320 (1989).

44. *See, e.g.,* Metro Broadcasting, Inc. v. FCC, 497 United States Reports 547 (1990) (upholding the practice of awarding broadcast licenses in order to promote greater minority participation in broadcasting).

45. *See, e.g.,* MICHAEL ROSENFELD, JUSTICE AND AFFIRMATIVE ACTION: A PHILOSOPHICAL AND CONSTITUTIONAL INQUIRY (1991); RACIAL PREFERENCE AND RACIAL JUSTICE: THE NEW AFFIRMATIVE ACTION CONTROVERSY (R. Nieli ed., 1991).

46. For further analysis of this theme, see George P. Fletcher, *Blackmail: The Paradigmatic Crime*, 141 UNIVERSITY OF PENNSYLVANIA LAW REVIEW 1617 (1993).

47. KANT, *supra* note 4, at 140–144.

48. *Id.* at 141: "The principle of punishment is a categorical imperative, and woe to him who crawls through the windings of eudaemonism in order to discover something that releases the criminal from punishment."

49. *Id.* at 142.

50. On the biblical origins of this idea, see Fletcher, *supra* note 34, at 202–203.

51. *See* Fletcher, *supra* note 34.

52. For more on this classic case, see GEORGE P. FLETCHER, A CRIME OF SELF-DEFENSE: BERNHARD GOETZ AND THE LAW ON TRIAL (1988).

53. Planned Parenthood for Southeastern Pennsylvania v. Casey, 112 Supreme Court Reports 2791, 2797 (1992) ("The ability of women to participate equally in the economic and social life of the nation has been facilitated by their ability to control their reproductive lives."); CASS SUNSTEIN, THE PARTIAL CONSTITUTION 272 (1993).

54. *See* Kendall Thomas, *Beyond the Privacy Principle*, 92 COLUMBIA LAW REVIEW 1431, 1510 (1992).

III

MORALITY IN
THE LAW

9

Morality

Judgments about the last four concepts discussed (justice, desert, consent, and equality) invariably raise questions of right and wrong, good and bad. For some theorists, the analysis of these value-loaded questions makes them aspects of morality. For other people, morality has a more limited domain. Surely it cannot be that every question of value raises an issue of morality. We praise a painting as beautiful, describe a film as interesting or entertaining, condemn a ballplayer as inept or a lawyer as unconvincing—none of these is commonly thought to be a moral judgment. Yet Dworkin assumes that there "is inevitably a moral dimension to an action at law. . . ."[1] This suggests that every time a claimant asserts a claim of equality or desert, the claim is based on morality as well as law. Here Dworkin's thesis seems to exceed the mark as much as the positivist thesis on the gulf between law and morality fails to capture the role of values in legal thinking.[2]

We shall try to make some headway on the relationship between law and morality by trying to figure out what "morality" is, what the closely related term "ethics" implies, and what might qualify as a "moral truth."

The Meaning of Morality

Virtually all Indo-European languages have developed a concept of "morality" based on the Latin root *mores* and a concept of "ethics" from the Greek root *ethike*. As the distinction has evolved in English, each of these terms has taken on special connotations. The Pope is said to be infallible when he pronounces ex cathedra on matters of faith and morals, but I have not heard it said that his domain includes ethics as well. Certain forms of sexual conduct generate what is called a "morals offense," but the same acts are not labeled "unethical." The term "unethical" seems to be more appropriately applied to breaches of relatively clear and teachable rules about relationships with others, particularly in the professional roles of lawyers and doctors. The American Bar Association is concerned about professional ethics, but apparently not concerned, as is the Pope, about the morals of lawyers.

The term "morality" rings right in certain phrases and not in others. Positivists balk at a moral approach to law, but can easily accept "legal ethics" as part of the legal system. The flourishing of the individual in his or her spiritual and intellectual entirety arguably poses a moral question. This might explain why self-regarding conduct, such as taking drugs, suicide, or sexual promiscuity might pose a moral problem (and bears a relation to issues of religious faith), but would hardly be discussed under the rubric of ethics.

The relationship between ethics and morality seems to run parallel to the distinction between honor and dignity. Ethics and honor attach to particular roles that we fill in our social and professional interactions with others. In these roles as student, teacher, lawyer, or judge, we perform correctly or incorrectly. If we breach the rules, we behave unethically and bring dishonor upon ourselves in our social roles. A judge who accepts bribes may retain her inherent dignity as a person, but she brings dishonor upon herself as judge. Dignity inheres in the individual, apart from his or her actions. "Human dignity is unassailable" reads the first line of Article One of the 1949 German Constitution. Ethical rules attach to roles, as do questions of honor and dishonor. Arguably, as ethics relates to honor, morality resembles dignity. The challenge to behave morally attaches to every individual, regardless of position and social role, and regardless of conventional social expectations.

Being clear about the meaning of morality, of course, does not solve any particular problem. We might agree about both the content and the scope of morality in general but disagree about how to classify the case at hand. For example, we might agree that lying to save a friend's life is a moral question, but disagree about the circumstances in which it is permissible to lie. Or we might agree that it is wrong to refer to Native Americans as Indians but disagree about whether this is a moral question (as opposed to a question of manners or of politics).

One approach to the meaning of morality is to ask: When and why do people use the term "moral?" What are they trying to say? In the English tradition, the use of "moral" signals a recognition that we are probably talking about an unenforceable claim or proposition. When a lawyer says, "My client has a moral right," our reaction is, "Oh! You mean, not enforceable." If she had meant that the right was enforceable under the law, she just would have said simply: "My client has a right." Generally, lawyers seek to have moral claims admitted into the inner realm of coercively enforced legal rights. Indeed, it is the aim of "moral" argument in the law to reform the law by bringing it into line with the "moral code" of society.

In the German approach to these issues, expressed most influentially in the eighteenth-century writings of Immanuel Kant, law and morality inhabit different conceptual spheres.[3] Law is addressed to external freedom, and morality to internal freedom. Law speaks to the relations between people in society; morality speaks to the struggle within each person between reason and desire. The twentieth-century version of this view is expressed in Gustav Radbruch's theory that actions and intentions carry different weights in law than they do in morality. Characteristically, the law requires some external event and relies on intention and internal sentiments as a guide to understanding the meaning of the external event. Accident and arson differ not in whether the house burns, but in the aims of the smoker who drops his cigarette. The difference between being kicked and being tripped—a distinction that, as Oliver Wendell Holmes Jr commented, "even a dog understands"[4]—lies in the attitude of the actor. The physical impact may be the same, but the quality of the act turns on the animus of the person extending his leg.

In the world of morality, according to the German tradition, the relationship between internal and external is transposed. What counts, morally, is whether the bond of love, friendship, or trust is breached or maintained. External events are not important in themselves. They have moral significance only so far as they provide evidence to confirm or disconfirm the inner sentiment. Forgetting an anniversary is significant only so far as it says something about the strength of the marriage. Even more serious events, such as helping a loved one who is terminally ill to commit suicide, must be embedded and understood in the context of the relationship between the people affected. It helps to be aware of these different ways of thinking about the scope of morality, but for our purposes we shall stick with the Anglo-American pattern of viewing morality as a set of rules about what is right and wrong, a code like the legal system but lacking a means of enforcement.

What Is Immoral?

If we assume that justice, desert, and rules of professional ethics are *not* part of morality, it is not easy to find a clear case of immoral behavior. What would it be? Many people associate morality with sex. But that is the area where there is the greatest disagreement about how we ought to live. One might argue that the Ten Commandments are a good guide to morality. But this is not true about all the commandments. Some of them—such as those prohibiting the making of graven images and remembering the Sabbath—have little to do with our intuitions of what morality is about.

Although we are not entirely sure where our moral judgments come from and how they have crystallized in our superego, most people would agree on the following propositions:

1. Do not exploit other people.
2. Do not inflict gratuitous suffering.
3. Do not cheat for the sake of receiving an undeserved benefit.
4. Do not lie unless you have a very good reason.

Of course, these prescriptions are vague, and that is probably why we can agree on them. The hard work of interpretation and application remains. Some people might assert a more precise list, such as:

1. Never lie.
2. Never torture.
3. Never take something that does not belong to you.
4. Always keep your promises.

Whether one adopts one list or another depends a lot on the arguments offered for these prescriptions. The two most common arguments for moral positions offered by lay people are God's command and conventional practice. Let us consider each of these in turn.

God's Command

Some people think that without God's permission (or prohibition) everything goes. Dostoyevsky's Grand Inquisitor is usually cited to back up the claims of "divine command morality," according to which God's command is both necessary and sufficient for moral action. If God commands Abraham to sacrifice his son Isaac, then this must be a moral act. Why? Because, as argued by the faithful, God is the ultimate source of truth.

Divine command morality is dubious on several grounds. Even within the biblical narrative there are counterindications.[5] In Abraham's debate with God about the destruction of Sodom and Gomorrah, Abraham appeals to a criterion of justice binding on God as "judge of the entire universe."[6] Also, God's commands are rarely obvious and free of the need for interpretation. There is debate today about whether the Seventh Commandment prohibits all killing or just murder—namely, unjustified or wrongful killing. It is by no means obvious what the Book of Leviticus means to prohibit when it prescribes: "Do not sleep with a man as you would with a woman."[7] (How would that be possible?). Interpreting the Bible is a process that requires moral sensitivity; a good interpretation is one that permits independently sound moral considerations to creep into the official reading of the Bible.

Further, the notion of morality is conceptually dependent or independent of God's will. If it is dependent, then the claim that "God's will is moral" is a purely analytic statement; it is true by definition, as is the statement, "A rectangle has four straight sides and four right angles." If morality is independent of God's will, then other problems arise. To paraphrase Socrates's challenge in the *Euthyphro*: Is an act moral because God wills it? Or does God will it because it is moral? Unless God is to be seen as acting arbitrarily, then the better view is that morality precedes and provides the basis for God's actions.

Convention

The logical problems associated with taking God as the supreme moral authority are repeated in the search for other definitive tests of morality. Some people reduce morality to mores, or the customs of society. The question always remains, however, whether we should trust our conventions as sound. Our collective experience with attitudes toward blacks, Jews, women, and homosexuals can only give us pause. A generation or two ago, it was "natural" to assume that blacks should go to different schools and hold inferior positions in society. Different but equally pernicious views concerning Jews, women, and gays have been the conventional wisdom of their age. So far as conventions inform our judgments about which groups are better and which worse, it is clear that they should not be trusted.

Yet there are some conventional bits of wisdom, stated abstractly, that do guide our moral thinking. Don't be selfish. It's better to give than to receive. You are your own best friend. Find the human within you. These and similar bits of wisdom have become banal precisely because they each capture a corner of the truth. Apart from these platitudes, it is unlikely that everyone would agree on our supposed social conventions. Not everyone agrees that incest should be taboo or that lying is bad. Even in supposedly doctrinaire or authoritarian societies, dissenters unexpectedly challenge received traditions. Moral leaders emerged under Communism to denounce that which had been accepted as truth, and prophetic critics have always come forward to challenge those who believe in Greek divinities or the Indian caste system.

Arguments based on either God's command or on society's conventions appeal to authority—the former the authority of a higher power, the latter the authority of the society expressed in a collective judgment. As we have seen, however, appeals to both sets of authorities can go awry. Their claims to moral wisdom must be tested against our judgments of what is "really" right and wrong. Fathoming the wellsprings of right and wrong is the task of critical as opposed to conventional morality. Two distinct theories of critical morality stand out as candidates for criticizing both conventional morality and the accepted practices of the legal system. The two theories—one English, one German—have in common their commitment to impartiality as the touchstone of moral thinking.

Impartial Moral Theories

Utilitarianism

The most common mode of moral reasoning in the Anglo-American tradition is cost/benefit analysis—the "balancing" of competing advantages and disadvantages of adopting particular courses of action. As the argument goes, all legal decisions (by individuals as well as courts) should be judged according to their consequences. The appropriate consequences to consider are those measured in human pain and pleasure. This way of thinking is reflected in the contemporary defense of necessity, which holds that violating the law is justified when it becomes necessary to serve a greater good. Aborting a fetus is justified if necessary to serve a greater good, such as the life or health of the mother. This defense hardly existed in the nineteenth century, but today, under the growing influence of cost/benefit analysis, it enjoys statutory recognition in almost every Western legal system.

The same mode of assessing consequences has reshaped our understanding of negligence in criminal and civil law. Negligence is understood as taking an unreasonable risk, sometimes called a substantial and unjustified risk of harm. Risks are reasonable or not, justified or not, depending on the dangers they pose and the benefits they offer. Driving fast will be classified as negligent or not, depending on its costs and benefits. As this method of balancing competing values teaches us, racing to a party should be treated less favorably than rushing to get a sick person to the hospital.

Many of the moral imperatives in the first list reflect the influence of balancing interests. "Do not cheat for the sake of receiving an undeserved benefit." The assumption seems to be that a deserved benefit would justify the nominal wrong of cheating. Or: "Do not lie unless you have a very good reason." A good reason is one that would outweigh the evil of lying. This kind of reasoning is common in a world in which all judgments are a matter of "trade-offs." In this world there are no absolutes, only precepts about balancing competing interests.

Yet these precepts are but a vulgar form of true utilitarianism, which expresses a commitment to improve the well-being of all sentient beings, that is, all living beings, including animals, who experience pleasure and pain. Since individuals seek to maximize pleasure and minimize pain, Jeremy Bentham argued in the late eighteenth century that societies should try to do the same.[8] The best social policy, therefore, is one that is likely to bring about what people seem to want—the greatest pleasure and least pain. It is as though the entire society acted as a single pleasure-seeking organism. The aim of social policy should be to maximize the *utility* of society, as measured by its pleasure and pain (its happiness), and thus the label utilitarian for those who follow Bentham.

Let us leave aside well-known problems of measuring happiness and assume that we can sum up the utility of diverse persons and compute what would be good for the society as a whole. The demand on each individual in the society is that she think of herself as having pleasures and pains that are important not because she feels them, but because they are felt by someone, anyone. The only thing that matters is that these pleasures and pains occur.

Utilitarianism, in this pure form, has much to recommend it. It teaches us that human happiness and suffering are relevant to moral action. It can easily account for lying when necessary to protect life or even to protect important relationships. The difficulty with utilitarianism is that the Benthamite calculus of pleasure and pain also generates some unpalatable results. It suggests that killing one innocent person would probably be all right to save two; if there is a net increase of pleasure over pain, more life is surely better than less. The same calculus implies that stealing from the rich would be all right to benefit the poor, for the pleasure to those starving would presumably be greater than the pain to the rich of losing redundant property. It even suggests that slavery in limited amounts would be desirable, for the pain to a few slaves might, in some cases, be less than the gain to their masters.

Some utilitarians struggle against these implications by limiting their claims of justification to the commonsense, traditional rules against harmful action. In the long run, these rules serve social utility, and we can easily see why. Avoiding various forms of aggression (homicide, rape, theft, etc.) certainly contributes to a more stable enjoyable way of life. But as many have argued, there is no reliable utilitarian argument to explain why individuals in times of stress should not violate the rules.[9] The principle of utility might explain why parents should be loyal to their children; but it cannot explain why if given the choice between saving my own child and the significantly more gifted child of my neighbor, I should save my own. Utilitarianism generates rules that are contingent on the computations of the moment.

Utilitarianism rests on an extreme form of altruism. That is, in making moral decisions, individuals must think first and foremost not about themselves but about the good for the collective organism called society. They may not rest their decisions on whether specific people bleed, but rather on bleeding in the abstract—disconnected from any particular artery in the society. It is as though the social organism truly had a common heart, a single nervous system, and a shared sensitivity to pleasure and pain.

The altruism of pure utilitarianism is hardly the version that we see applied in the day-to-day operation of the courts. The true utilitarian would be concerned about all of humankind, but national courts are interested exclusively in the welfare of the nation. American courts seek to maximize the welfare of Americans, or more limitedly, of the kind of people involved in the dispute. In a dispute about the liability of a manufacturer for a product causing harm to a consumer, the courts are likely to think primarily about the welfare of American consumers and less about either the national or world economy. Frequently, the courts are highly selective in choosing those whose welfare matters. Asked to justify a current provision prescribing "three strikes and you're out" (namely, life imprisonment for the third felony conviction), the true utilitarian would balance the increased security to the majority against the suffering of those who must spend added time behind bars. But American courts are more likely to consider the welfare of "society" as measured solely by the security benefits and monetary costs to the vast majority not threatened by the draconian punishment.[10] The compromise form of utilitarianism employed by the courts may be more workable than the pure mode fashioned by philosophers, but it is also less appealing as a moral standard of decision.

The Kantian Challenge

Utilitarianism is typically criticized for failing, in Ronald Dworkin's influential phrase, to "take rights seriously."[11] According to the Benthamite credo, individuals have rights only so far as those rights serve the public good. Jeremy Bentham summed up his position in the famous aphorism: "Rights are nonsense, and natural rights are nonsense upon stilts."[12] The rights protected under the Bill of Rights—free speech, religion, security in one's home, the privilege against self-incrimination—are hardly nonsense. Yet they would mean very little if we applied cost/benefit criteria and found that they give way when necessary for the collective good of society.

Utilitarians are also charged with failing to respect individual human dignity. Since individuals may be used and abused to serve the interests of others, individuals no longer function as the ultimate source of moral value. Those who oppose utilitarianism on these grounds typically turn to Immanuel Kant for support. To understand how Kant's views become relevant in this argument, we pause to consider the foundation of his critical moral theory.

Though a Lutheran Pietist by background, Immanuel Kant sought to deliver a basis for moral judgments that would appeal to enlightened secularists. He exacted of his reader only a belief in reason, a rational capacity to know the truth, independent of the passions and the inclinations of the body. Reason is expressed in what Kant calls a good will. And it is only the good will, he insists at the outset of his *Groundwork to the Metaphysics of Morals* (1785), that can generate a moral act. However noble the inclinations of the body, they lead us into excesses. Only the good will, driven by pure reason, is exempt from the risk of abuse.

But what is reason? Kant's definition is essentially negative. We know what reason is not, but not precisely what it is. It is not submission to bodily impulse. It is not the response of our organisms to external stimuli. Kant argues that there is some way of acting that transcends the impulse of the world around us and within us. Acting out of duty, Kant submits, is the only way of abstracting ourselves from the worldly influences that affect our sentiments. This higher, pure way of acting requires an attentive ear to the voice of reason.

The key to understanding Kant's system of thought lies in fathoming the links among the concepts of "reason," "duty," and "law." The connections are laid bare in a single sentence in the opening pages of the *Groundwork* in which Kant defines what he means by duty: "Duty is the necessity of an act out of respect for the law." The first part of this definition makes sense. Duty is a kind of necessity. If you know what your duty is, it seems that you are necessarily required to do it. The second part also makes sense. For at least in the natural sciences, the notion of necessity is connected to the idea of law. When we perceive the necessity of a cause inducing an effect, as when the spring sun melts the winter snow, we can formulate a law of physics.

In the field of moral conduct, however, the relevant form of necessity is within human control. The existence of the moral law does not automatically yield behavior in conformity with it. The kind of necessity that Kant had in mind for human conduct, the necessity of acting out of duty, is realized when one acts "out of respect for the law." Why should this be true? Respect or reverence (*Achtung*) in the Kantian sense is an expression of reason. Reverence for the law is an attitude that abstracts from the material world. So far as we are responsive to the sensual world, we cannot be acting solely on the basis of reason. Respect for the law, then, must be expressed as respect for the aspect of the law that is purely abstract, purely a matter of form, unattached to concrete facts in the sensual world. Kant termed this aspect of the law as the "ruledness" or "law-likeness" (*Gesetzlichkeit*) of the law.

This phrase—respect for the abstract ruledness or law-likeness of the law—provides the key move in generating Kant's famous categorical imperative: Never act on a maxim unless you can simultaneously will the maxim to be a universal law of nature.[13] If a maxim of action (what I say I am going to do) cannot be universalized, I cannot possibly be acting out of respect for the universal lawlike nature of my actions. A number of maxims readily fail the test. The maxim "I will kill you" cannot be universalized, for if everyone kills everyone else, no one is left alive and therefore I cannot act in the world, not to mention engaging in the act of killing another person. Similarly, "I will steal that car," cannot be universalized, for if stealing became the universal law of nature, the practice of taking other people's things at will would nullify the concept of property. If there is no property, alas, I cannot take a car *belonging* to another. Therefore I cannot act on my maxim to steal a car. These are easy cases, and significantly, most of the Ten Commandments, at least the negative prohibitions, find a rather easy defense under the principle prohibiting actions that cannot, in principle, be universalized.[14]

It is important to be precise, however, about what follows from the failure to universalize a maxim of action. An act of killing or stealing could never be moral. But abstaining from these actions—and this is the rub—is not automatically moral. The categorical imperative is formulated in the negative: never do such-and-such. Complying with the negative does not imply that the action is necessarily moral. The act must be done not only in compliance with the moral law, but out of respect for the lawlike nature of the action. The action must express the necessity of reason.

The second and third formulations of the moral law bring us closer to the affirmative nature of Kantian morality. From the first formulation of the categorical imperative, Kant derives the familiar principle that we should never treat anyone merely as a means, but always as an end in himself or herself. Human dignity is an absolute value, beyond all price; human dignity cannot be traded off, as we say today, as a means for achieving other ends. However difficult it is to fathom the distinction between means and ends, the notion of respecting someone's humanity as an end in itself lends some positive content to Kant's moral ideal. The critical idea behind his idea of humanity is that—like reason—it unites all human beings. Respecting the humanity of another is equivalent to respecting the humanity in oneself and vice versa. The man who engages a prostitute uses her as a means to an end and thereby expresses disrespect for humanity, as it is expressed in the two of them.

In its third formulation, Kant's conception of moral conduct is expressed as the union of positive and negative freedom. Positive freedom consists in submission to the moral law—in acting not just in conformity with the moral rule but out of respect for the law. And negative freedom implies that no sensual impulses have entered into the causal processes generating the action. The union of positive and negative freedom constitutes autonomy—the setting of a *nomos*, the moral law, *by* oneself and *for* oneself. These are rigorous demands for those who would be moral. It turns out that autonomy in this pure sense and moral action are logically possible, but not readily accessible to humans who suffer from constant tension with their sensual impulses. In the final pages of the

Groundwork Kant concedes that there is no way of proving that any particular human action, past or present, has ever been moral, i.e., an action expressing the autonomous necessity of reason rather than sensual impulse.[15] Moral action stands as an ideal that we should seek to attain, but our failure to attain it is hardly a great failing. It is in our nature as human beings that we unsuccessfully seek the moral.

In the end Kant's moral teaching demands purity from all of us. We are not free to affirm our particularity, to visit our friends because we love them, but rather to be moral, we must find the cause of our conduct in a realm of spirit abstracted from our worldly selves. Morality turns out to be a struggle of each person with himself to overcome the influences of personal attachment and sensual desire. This kind of morality rests on a yearning to think of human beings as agents wholly in control of themselves, who can act independently of their environment.

Kant's system breaks down when he turns from the theoretical grounding of morality to the resolution of practical conflict. He concluded in the *Groundwork* that promising without an intention to perform the promise under conditions of distress would violate the categorical imperative. He extrapolates that all forms of deception are impermissible. Lying can never be a moral act. For if lying were universalized, there would be no way of knowing who was telling the truth and who was not. Deception would no longer be possible. No one could tell a falsehood with the expectation of deceiving another. Therefore, lying, or telling a falsehood with the expectation of deceiving another, would be conceptually impossible.

In the most extreme application of this view, Kant offers the following example. Suppose a murderer pursues your friend and he takes refuge in your house. Let us say the scene is Paris in July 1944. The Gestapo agent knocks on the door and demands to know whether you are harboring Jews. According to the categorical imperative, you may not lie. For even if your telling the truth results in the death of your friend, the killing is not your act. The Gestapo are responsible for their heinous misdeeds; by telling the truth, you at least retain your integrity.

Who would want to live in a world in which it was wrong to lie to the Gestapo? That would be a world in which friendship was impossible, for surely the minimal condition of friendship is that one would do just about anything, which certainly includes lying to a murderer, in order to save the life of one's friend. There is something so obviously awry in Kant's thinking about lying that we hear the clock strike thirteen. It is hard to believe that the previous twelve bells intone a way of life that we should all follow.

Even if the innocent hiding in your home were not your friend, it would be permissible to lie in order to save his life. The doctrine of self-defense should come into play as a justification for using means, ordinarily illicit, in order to ward off an imminent attack against the person in hiding. If violent means are acceptable to fend off an unjust attack, then surely it could not be wrong to use words—even consciously false words—to achieve the same end. Yet the doctrine of self-defense has no place in Kant's moral system. He treats self-defense as a principle of the legal, not the moral order.[16] Self-defense speaks to the way people must resolve real conflicts in the real world.

Paradoxically, Kant thought he was delivering a firm grounding for the common moral precepts of his time. In the course of the *Groundwork*, he tries twice to bring to bear his abstract formulations of the categorical imperative to explain four concrete cases. These paradigmatically moral questions are whether it is permissible to commit suicide, whether one may make a promise with the intent not to perform it under particular circumstances, whether one is under a duty to develop one's talents, and whether one is under a duty to aid others in distress.[17]

The principle that one may act only on a maxim that one can will to be a universal law of nature supposedly leads to the conclusion that one may not commit suicide, that one may not make a promise without intention to perform, that one must develop one's talents and that one must aid others in distress. However great a thinker Kant was, the logical anomaly of his explaining these results has proved to be one of the more embarrassing passages in his life's work.[18] He sneaks in assumptions about human nature—that human beings have an impulse to live and a fear of being abandoned—in order to support his conclusions about suicide and the duty to aid others. These assumptions about human nature do not preclude universalization of the actor's maxim, but they do prevent human beings from "willing" their own demise or "willing" a state of isolation from others.

Kant's moral theory turns out to be an amalgam of the banal and the unattainable. Virtually all the maxims that provide the data for his moral theory find easy support in the Judeo-Christian tradition. Any child with a proper eighteenth-century European upbringing would subscribe to these Sunday school rules about killing, promising falsely, and helping others. The unattainable dimension of Kantian morality is the requirement of moral action itself, namely, that one must adhere to these maxims not as a nonthinking conformist but as a purely rational being. One must do the right thing for the right reason. Acting out of fear of divine punishment or of social censure is not moral. But the right reason—namely, acting for the sake of reason and duty alone—eludes the capacity of ordinary mortals.

Whatever its flaws, Kant's moral thinking has left an indelible mark on Western legal culture. His commitment to human dignity as a value beyond price, beyond trade-offs, is expressed in every legal system that takes individuals to be an ultimate source of value. The commitment to human dignity is expressed dramatically in the first article of the 1949 German Constitution, which provides: "Human Dignity is inviolable. It is the duty of all state organs to respect and protect it." This pervasive commitment to human dignity applies to everyone, both state organs and private individuals. The return to Kantian thinking provided postwar German legal culture with new foundations, respectful of human rights and the value of individuals.

The Kantian principle that no one should ever treat someone merely as a means to an end informs the Marxian concept of exploitation, which regularly reasserts itself in thinking about child labor, fair wages, and the role of workers in factory governance. Exploiting workers is to use them as tools, as instruments for one's own profit, rather than to respect them as participants in a joint enterprise. The moral assumption that exploitation is evil supports the demand for a legal right to an abortion; for, by forcing women to carry fetuses to term is to treat women's bodies as a means to other people's ends. The moral imperative to respect other people as ends in themselves underlies also the contemporary movement in the United States to impose stricter legal restraint on sexual harassment in the workplace. These are all instances in which versions of Kantian moral thinking come into play in legal analysis.

Kantian theory has also bequeathed some ideas to lawyers that they readily adapt for their own purposes. One common extension of Kantian thinking is expressed in the way we now talk about "autonomy." This term has lost its Kantian roots and become synonymous with liberty or with having many options at the time of making a decision. The social circumstances of our lives supposedly expand and restrict autonomy. In the original Kantian sense, however, autonomy is not an external feature of the environment in which we make decisions but an inner feature of acting that any person under any circumstances is capable of attaining. For moderns, autonomy is an expression of individual power relative to others. For Kant, autonomy is a sign rather of our commonality, of our participating in the universal dimension of pure reason.

Though autonomy may properly be used in different senses, we should note one rather clear misreading of Kant. Because Kant holds that the "pure will" is the highest good, he is often taken to believe that intentions are more important than actions. This is false. The will is not necessarily expressed in one's intentions. An intent to steal, for example, does not express the will. Nor does an intent to act kindly toward a friend in need. The will signals the demands of duty under the moral law. Intention is simply the inner quality of our actions, regardless of their moral merit. Also, Kant stresses that legal relations—unlike moral relations—are characterized by external compliance with norms; the inner mental state at the time of compliance is of secondary importance for the law.

Practical Morality and Spirituality

Neither utilitarian nor Kantian thought could have had an impact in legal analysis unless they first underwent a process of distortion and simplification. In their pure forms, neither of these critical moral theories provides guidance to practical people who must make decisions in the real world. Both of them confuse the perfection of the spirit with the problem of right and wrong in the world as we know it. Seeing why this is so requires some explanation.

Utilitarianism makes unrealistic demands on us. First, we must anticipate the consequences of our actions, which in most cases can be no more than a wild guess. In addition to this omniscience about the future, we are expected to be perfectly altruistic, thinking only about the welfare of the entire collective (all five billion people on the planet?) and not about ourselves or our loved ones first. Kant's moral theory makes the equally unrealistic demand that we act on the basis of reason alone, that our conduct be totally abstracted from the influences of the body and of the world around us. One theory as much as the other exacts a purity that is not of this world. Moral conduct becomes as much a part of our daily life as the perfect vacuum becomes the medium for experimental physics.

The purity exacted by both Bentham and Kant consists in imitating qualities of the divine. For Bentham, the quality of benevolence takes precedence, but it turns out that the theory demands the divine attribute of omniscience as well. The attribute of divine perfection that shapes Kant's thinking is the purity of reason, exercised without distraction by bodily impulses. However different their paths may be, Bentham and Kant share the Enlightenment impulse of grounding a moral theory in attributes of the human condition. In both cases, however, it turns out that the desired qualities are unattainable versions of God's perfection.

The critical moral theories of the Enlightenment, then, seek to perfect human behavior. Their aim is to challenge ordinary people to realize in their lives the qualities of reason, goodness, omnipotence, and benevolence that we attribute to divine perfection. This is best considered as a spiritual exercise, as *imitatio dei* (the imitation of God) rather than the development of criteria for guiding the lives of humble mortals. Only when these theories are simplified and distorted do they lend themselves to application in practical affairs and come to have an influence in legal thought.

We began this chapter with an inquiry about the relationship of law to morality. We conclude, inconclusively, with a recognition of the shortcomings in the two schools—utilitarianism and Kantian—that have dominated moral and legal philosophy for the last two hundred years. We know that moral thought influences legal thinking, but we are not sure exactly how much and in what form. In the following chapters, then, we consider two distinctive ways in which these general moral theories come into play in legal argument. The economic principle of efficiency has come to have a vast influence in legal thought. A careful look at the concept reveals that it is but an instance of the utilitarian arguments we have considered in this chapter. The ensuing chapter on loyalty illustrates a contemporary communitarian challenge to the impartial moral theories of both Bentham and Kant. The assessment of morality in the law ends with a chapter on consistency, for the final question must be whether these diverse moral outlooks and the differing perspectives offered in this book can be brought together in a single consistent view of legal phenomena.

Notes

1. Ronald Dworkin, Law's Empire 1 (1986).

2. *See* H.L.A. Hart, The Concept of Law 155–84 (2d ed. 1994). This is, properly speaking, an implication of positivism rather than a constituent element of the positive approach to law. *See supra* at pp. 33–34.

3. For further elaboration, see George P. Fletcher, *Law and Morality: A Kantian Perspective*, 87 Columbia Law Review 533 (1987).

4. Oliver Wendell Holmes, Jr., The Common Law 7 (Mark DeW. Howe ed., 1963).

5. On the independence of morality from religious duty, see the views of Yeshayahu Leibowitz, Judaism, Human Values, and the Jewish State (E. Goldman et al. trans., 1992).

6. *See supra* the discussion of this passage at pp. 79–80

7. *Leviticus* 20:13.

8. Jeremy Bentham, An Introduction to the Principles of Morals and Legislation 11–12 (J.H. Burns and H.L.A. Hart eds., 1970). ("By the principle of utility is meant that principle which approves or disapproves of every action whatsoever, according to the tendency which it appears to have to augment or diminish the happiness of the party whose interest is in question.").

9. For early critiques of so-called rule utilitarianism, see Richard Wasserstrom, The Judicial Decision: Toward A Theory of Legal Justification (1961). *Cf.* David Lyons, Forms and Limits of Utilitarianism (1965).

10. Rummel v. Estelle, 445 United States Reports 263 (1980) (upholding life sentence imposed after third nonviolent felony conviction). *But see* Solem v. Helm, 463 United States Reports 277 (1983) (striking down as unconstitutional a life sentence, without possibility of parole, after seventh conviction for a nonviolent felony).

11. *See* Ronald Dworkin, Taking Rights Seriously (1977).

12. Jeremy Bentham, *Anarchical Fallacies*, in 2 The Works of Jeremy Bentham 489, 501 (John Bowring ed., 1962).

13. Immanuel Kant, Groundwork To The Metaphysics Of Morals (H.J. Paton trans., 1964).

14. Note that the prohibition against adultery finds a similar justification. If everyone is sleeping with everyone else's spouse, it would be hard to understand the concept of marriage. If there were no concept of marriage, I could not contemplate sleeping with someone else's wife.

15. Kant, *supra* note 13, at 116–17.

16. *See supra* note 3.

17. KANT, *supra* note 13, at 17–22.

18. See the critique offered in ROBERT PAUL WOLFF, THE AUTONOMY OF REASON: A COMMENTARY ON KANT'S GROUNDWORK OF THE METAPHYSIC OF MORALS 163–73 (1986).

10

Efficiency

Traditional ideas of justice and morality in the law now face a radical challenge from economists and economically trained lawyers. Every good law school faculty now includes at least one scholar trained in a field called "law & economics" (for short, L&E).[1] A novel form of interdisciplinary research has become a movement. There are some areas, such as antitrust and unfair competition law, where economic understanding is indispensable. But the devotees of L&E make their most challenging contribution in other fields of law where economics has had, until recently, no apparent bearing. The battleground for the new way of thinking about law has been torts or accident law.

The insight that initiated this challenge was Yale Law Professor Guido Calabresi's reconceptualizing the field of accident law and its goals. He began by noting that both accidents and accident prevention generate costs that can be measured in a single common denomination of dollars and cents.[2] Accidents cost money, as reflected in the dollar sign that juries place on the victims' physical and emotional harm, medical bills, lost wages, and pain and suffering. Accident prevention also costs money—the funds expended, for example, on making cars, airplanes, and microwave ovens safer. These, plus the costs of adminstering the legal system, constitute the total costs of accidents. The aim of tort law, Calabresi inferred, should be to minimize the sum of these costs. As expressed in economic language, the goal of tort law should be to bring about an *optimum* number of accidents. This optimum is reached at the equilibrium point when the marginal cost of one more accident exactly equals the marginal cost of preventing that accident. An optimum number of accidents is also considered the efficient solution to the accident problem.

These terms "optimum" and "efficient" are now common parlance in the law. The courts have yet to go over to the new language, but there are many teachers of law who think that efficiency is the *summum bonum*, the supreme good, of legal arrangements. Though they are loathe to identify their theories as "normative" as opposed to "positive" and scientific, the advocates of efficiency espouse a new morality for the law—or at least a new mode of expressing the principles of utilitarian morality.

The quest for efficiency has led to efforts to restructure, or at least reinterpret, the traditional criteria for making one person pay for harm that he causes to another. Submerged in this search for efficiency is the recognition that economics itself consists of diverse schools of thought. There is far more conflict and contradiction in economic theory than the advocates of L&E are willing to concede. Explicating this conflict of ideas is the task of this chapter.

Voluntary Markets and Pareto Efficiency

Efficiency—like so many of the terms we have considered in this book—signifies different things to different people. One influential notion of efficiency derives from the ideal of trading in a frictionless market. Let us take a closer look at the meaning of allocating goods and services efficiently.

Imagine that the goods of society are distributed to the members of society in a more or less equal way. Yet the goods are different. Some people have television sets, others have shoes, and still others have sugar, and others, tobacco. As life begins in this imaginary society, the players realize that they have different goods. The one with shoes realizes that he would like a TV set, and the possessor of the TV senses immediately that she would like some shoes. The two of them consider a trade and begin negotiating. Eventually they will agree on a "price" for the TV set in the currency of shoes, say five pairs of shoes for one 19-inch color set. The two parties exchange the goods. The exchange is based on consent, freely given, informed by knowledge of all the available alternatives.

Now what do we want to say about the impact of this exchange on the welfare of these parties? Have they merely exchanged an "equal" amount of goods, leaving them in exactly the same situation they were in before the exchange? Or are they, as a result of the trade, better off, happier in some sense? Recall Aristotle's view that the exchange is a form of commutative justice: the traded goods are equal in value and therefore no one is better or worse off as a result of the exchange.[3] Modern economic theory departs radically from this premise of equality in the exchange. The guiding assumption today is that both sides benefit from the exchange. If they would not benefit, economists now say, they would have no incentive for making the trade. The party who gets the shoes values five pairs of shoes more than she values a television set. The party who gets the TV set prefers it to five pairs of shoes. Both parties, therefore, are better off. Their "utilities," viewed subjectively, are enhanced.

The trade makes the world better off so far as it makes at least one of the parties better off and it makes no one worse off. This is the definition of a *Pareto-superior move*, a trade that benefits at least one and harms no one. Our trade of a TV set for shoes was a Pareto-superior move for both sides. Note that in the economic view of the world, if parties have the same stack of goods in front of them, trade occurs only because the trading partners have different sets of preferences. They are individuals, with different tastes and desires. If everyone were alike, if we all valued shoes and TV sets in exactly the same way, there would no incentive for trade. There would be no point to trading goods if we did not gain something. The economist begins by noting that trade does in fact take place in the real world. His theory of Pareto-superior moves explains what we observe in the marketplace.

Now note what happens when the possessor of tobacco wants to trade his stock for a TV set. He goes to a TV owner and offers her an amount of tobacco. She responds that she despises tobacco and that in fact you would have to pay her to take it. What should the tobaccoholder do? He has two ways of obtaining a TV set. He can search around for other parties who are willing to trade something for tobacco (shoes will work) or possibly sugar, that he can use to entice the TV holder into selling a TV set. Or he can wait until someone who likes tobacco comes into possession of a TV set. The world would be much simpler for the tobaccoholder if everyone used an intermediate, common commodity that everyone liked. That common denominator is called money. If they had a common currency, say dollars, everyone would trade first for dollars then use the dollars to buy what they really wanted.

The assumptions that underline that simple version of a market are very important. First, everyone participates with an initial set of property rights. They could not trade if they were uncertain about what they owned. Second, each of them is an idiosyncratic individual, each having different tastes and preferences. And third, each is capable of consenting to voluntary transfers that will transplant their property rights to others. The first and third assumptions illustrate how the market and the legal system interact. Without a legal regime specifying who owns what and a system for transferring rights, the market could not operate. Without these basic rights firmly secured, there can be no market. This principle is becoming clear to Eastern Europeans who are struggling to make the transition from a Communist order in which the state owned almost everything to a market economy based on private ownership.

Sooner or later the market transactions in our imaginary society of shoes and TV sets will come to an end. When they do—that is, where there is no longer the possibility of making a Pareto-superior move—the resulting equilibrium is called a *Pareto-optimal* state. This is the optimal point beyond which trading cannot improve the welfare of these two participants. Trading will cease until either new goods are brought into the game or the preferences of one of the parties suddenly change and thus create the possibility of a new Pareto-superior transaction.

This model of economic relations carries with it certain points of avowed ignorance. As a matter of principle, economists claim that there is nothing to know economically about the relative merits of different Pareto-optimal states. The Pareto-optimal state might be a roughly equal distribution or it might be a situation in which one player possesses all the goods; in neither case would a move be possible that would leave no one worse off. All of these Pareto-optimal states are equally efficient in the sense that no readjustment of the goods can bring about a better state of affairs. Optimality or efficiency in this economic sense has nothing to do with the justice or the desirability of the distribution.

Another point of avowed ignorance is the quantitative extent of the gain that occurs from each trade. We know that when the shoeholder and the TV possessor trade, each makes himself better off. But we do not know how much better off each becomes. Nor can we say whether one gains more than the other. The reason for this limitation is that utility in economics is entirely subjective. It depends on how much individuals are actually willing to pay for the goods they want. The precise way of stating this assumption is: no interpersonal comparison of utilities. The most we can do is derive a map of utilities for each person and that map is based on choices he or she actually makes.

As it stands, this pure version of the market could not possibly be of relevance to the law. Its underlying principle is the sovereignty and autonomy of every player in the market. The market is voluntary; its supreme principle is consent. But the law is coercive. The market depends on decentralized, uncoordinated decisions, but the law stands for centralized decision making. In order to achieve relevance to lawyers and policy makers, the system of Pareto efficiency had to undergo a transformation that would enable it to appeal to partisans of coercive intervention. How this transformation occurred is the tale we now tell.

Kaldor/Hicks and Collective Efficiency

The beginnings of the transformation took hold in the late 1930s when a British economist, Nicholas Kaldor, turned his mind to a problem that national legislatures have often confronted.[4] May they make a legislative change that will benefit the economy as a whole even if the change implies that a certain group in the society will lose? The specific problem was the 19th-century debate in Britain about the Corn Laws, the protective tariffs that shielded British farmers from foreign competition. A similar debate occurred recently in the United States about our joining the North American Free Trade Association. Participating in the tariff-reduction program of NAFTA might be good for the country as a whole but certain producers would lose out to cheaper Mexican imports.

Kaldor argued that abolishing the Corn Laws was a Pareto-superior move in the modified sense that the gains to the country as a whole from free trade were likely to be sufficiently great to outweigh the loss to some corn farmers.[5] Kaldor believed that the winners could have purchased the right to remove the tariffs from the farmers and still have gains left over. That they *could* have purchased the right (but did not) meant that the move was Pareto-superior in a modified sense. Another economist, J. R. Hicks, quickly extended the argument to all market impediments.[6]

There is nothing surprising about the aim of these arguments. Free market economics imply general social benefits from free trade. Economists in this tradition are naturally opposed to tariffs and other impediments to competition. They understandably favored the repeal of the Corn Laws and other protective tariffs. An economist truly committed to free trade would think of the gains from tariffs as illegitimate, reaped by the grain farmers at the expense of the rest of society. Ending this illegitimate state of affairs is hardly a basis for thinking (even hypothetically) about compensation. There would be no more reason for Kaldor and Hicks to favor compensation for the farmers who would lose under the repeal of the Corn Laws than it would have been appropriate for abolitionists to pay compensations to the slaveholders who lost their human property under Abraham Lincoln's Emancipation Proclamation. Yet for some reason, it seemed important to Kaldor and Hicks to reconcile the abolition of a tariff with the principles of Pareto efficiency. This led them to inquire whether the society as a whole stood to gain enough from the increase in free trade to pay off (hypothetically) the farmers who benefited from the tariffs.

It is sometimes said that hard cases make bad law: This is an instance in which an easy economic problem (abolishing restraints on free trade) generated a dubious moral principle. Kaldor's and Hick's ruminations about the Corn Laws transformed the Pareto principle of efficiency into an instrument for legislation and judicial policy making. The Kaldor/Hicks test, as it is now formulated, holds that any reallocation of property rights is acceptable so long as it is generates more gain to the winners than loss to the losers. This means that, in principle, the winners could compensate the losers and still have a gain left over. The emphasis here is on "could compensate"; they need not actually make the transfer for the change to be Pareto superior under the Kaldor/Hicks test.

To see how the Kaldor/Hicks test works in practice, let us return to our example of trading shoes for a television set. Suppose that the parties could not communicate with each other, but that some third party (call it the State) knew that party *A* wanted a TV set and that she was willing to pay five sets of shoes as compensation. The third party also knew that *B* was willing to accept five pairs of shoes for a TV set. This means that under the Kaldor/Hicks test, the state would be engaging in a Pareto-superior move by taking the TV set from *B* and giving it to *A*. *A* could compensate *B* for the set, and under ideal economic conditions, she would simply have bought the set from *B*. But in our imaginary situation, the parties are unable to trade and therefore the state must do it for them.

Now you might wonder why the state should not at the same time take five pairs of shoes from *A* and give them to *B*. Perhaps it should. But the fact is that under the Kaldor/Hicks test, as interpreted in the school of L&E, *A* need not compensate *B* for the TV set. Herein lies the trick. In the original example of voluntary trading, the two transactions were conceptually linked: TV set for shoes, and shoes for the TV set. The only basis we have for saying the trade made the parties better off is that they actually made the trade. Yet under the Kaldor/Hicks test of hypothetical trading, the single transaction splits into two. Moving the TV set from one party to the other is one move toward efficiency in the Kaldor/Hicks sense, and moving the shoes in the opposite direction is another move toward efficiency.

Of course, you might be puzzled by all this. It seems very unfair to take the TV set from *B* and give it to *A* free of charge. If you confronted an advocate of the Kaldor/Hicks test with this problem, the conversation might go like this:

Skeptic: How can you do that? Take from one person and give to another? Do you think you're Robin Hood?

Advocate: I'm merely reallocating goods so that people who enjoy them more get to use them. You admit if *A* had to compensate *B*, she would go ahead and buy the set and *B* would take the five pair of shoes for the TV set. Does not this show that *A* would enjoy that particular TV set more than *B* does?

Skeptic: Yes, it is clear that *A* and *B* would trade if they could. But without the actual trade, how do you know that *A* would actually pay five pairs of shoes for the set? Also, isn't it unfair for *B* not to get paid for the TV set?

Advocate: I'm stipulating that *A* would pay five pairs of shoes for the TV. After all, it's my example. As far as fairness goes, that is a problem of distribution not of efficiency.

Skeptic: But in real life, you cannot stipulate how much *A* would be willing to pay. If you ask *A* how much she would pay (when she does not have to pay), she will, of course, exaggerate her willingness to pay. The only way you can know how much *A* would pay would be, as a good economist, to watch what she does, not what she says.

Advocate: How about looking at what some other person would pay for a TV set in a situation in which trading was possible?

Skeptic: You cannot do that. After all, the assumption of your "science" is that everyone has a distinct and different set of preferences. There are no other traders just like *A* and *B*.[7]

The advocate of the Kaldor/Hicks test has undoubtedly manipulated the idea of Pareto superiority to make it suitable for the law. Kaldor originally advocated eliminating a restraint on free competition on the ground that it would benefit the society as a whole more than it would harm one segment of the society. The current advocate of Kaldor's revision of Pareto's principle now seeks to reallocate property rights when it is more efficient to do so. There is method in this manipulation. The Kaldor/Hicks test converts a principle of voluntary market transactions into a standard for judicial intervention. Using the Kaldor/Hicks test, courts can redefine property rights "from time to time as the relative values of different uses of land change."[8]

As a result of the Kaldor/Hicks revision, the concept of efficiency takes on a new meaning. Efficiency is no longer synonymous with the workings of a perfect market. It becomes equivalent to a utilitarian standard justifying intervention in the market and in property rights when the benefits outweigh the burdens of intervention. Suppose, for example, that a railroad emits sparks and thereby destroys the property of a farmer with land abutting the railroad right of way. It appears that the railroad's sparks are encroaching upon the farmer's land and therefore the farmer should be compensated for the resulting damage. But the Kaldor/Hicks test suggests a different answer. The relevant question becomes whether the railroad gains more from emitting sparks than the value of the loss to the farmer. As we will discuss later, the market could decide that question if the market is able to function properly between the parties. If the market does not work, then the Kaldor/Hicks test would require a court to assess which of the parties would make more valuable use of the land. That question turns out to be equivalent to determining which of the parties would pay more for the right to use the strip of (the farmer's) land potentially affected by the railroad's sparks.

As applied in cases of this sort, the Kaldor/Hicks test merely restates the utilitarian principle that in a dispute about property rights, the courts should make the decision that would promote the interests of society as a whole. Awarding the disputed land to the railroad or the farmer serves the interest of society if the use of the land goes to the party who makes better use of it, with "better use" measured by the economic rewards of railroading or farming. The only difference between the utilitarian and the advocate of the Kaldor/Hicks test is that the former relies upon the standard of happiness and the latter relies on a standard implicit in a hypothetical willingness to pay for the disputed resource.

American law professors have been receptive to economic analysis of the Kaldor/Hicks variety because the culture of American law has long had strong ties to utilitarian thought. The devotee of L&E writes in a long line of theorists who think that all legal institutions should serve the interests of society—or at least of American society. Yet we have traced a remarkable transformation. The discussion begins with Pareto's principles of efficiency, grounded in the values of secure property rights, individual choice, and the necessity of voluntary transactions. In light of Kaldor's modest amendment, later generalized to cover all property rights, we end up with a theory of legal intervention that permits the periodic redefinition of property rights for the sake of a collective vision of efficiency. A theory of individual supremacy ends up as a philosophy of group supremacy. This is a remarkable metamorphosis. Any theory that can successfully obfuscate the difference between individual sovereignty in the market and the dominance of group interests in coercive decision making will surely gain a large number of followers.

Pigovian Efficiency

The preceding tale of transformation is not nearly as dramatic as another story that began to unfold at The University of Chicago in the early 1960s. Since the late nineteenth century, the courts have occasionally relied on free-market principles as a justification for liability in cases like that of the railroad spark. These are cases of "externalities," typified by pollution and other burdens on society that the entrepreneur imposes on others.[9] The basic claim has been that the law should serve to perfect the market by making each enterprise pay the full costs of production. Firms have to pay for the costs of capital and labor, but they do not have to pay for the social costs, such as sparks, air pollution, and noise, of the factories and machines they operate. According to the economic argument for liability, the free market cannot work properly unless these externalities are charged to the producers who generate them. Internalizing the social costs by forcing the entrepreneur to pay for them leads to an efficient allocation of resources. The injuring firm's liability costs are subsequently passed on to consumers in the form of higher prices. Consumers make the ultimate decision of allocative efficiency by purchasing those commodities that, in view of their costs of production and their harmful effects on others, best satisfy their preferences.

To see how this works in practice, think about the way that the flying of supersonic airplanes inflicts noise on the surrounding area as an externality. If the airline is not liable for the harm caused by its sonic booms, the price of a ticket will be lower and consumers will purchase "too much" supersonic travel. If the price of a ticket reflects the harm inflicted on people in the flight path (i.e., the externality is internalized), the price will correctly reflect its social desirability. Consumer sovereignty will then yield the most efficient satisfaction of everyone's preferences—and the victims will be no worse off, for they will be compensated for suffering the noise. The assumption, of course, is that some sum of money can make up for the disturbance of the ear-splitting noise.

Calabresi developed the same argument for the externality represented by automobile accidents.[10] The harm that cars do to pedestrians and bicyclists is a social cost of producing and driving cars. By holding manufacturers (and drivers?) liable for accidents, the law could internalize the social costs of accidents in the price of cars. Consumers would then decide whether a vehicle as risky as the automobile is worth the cost. If manufacturers are not liable for accidents, the price of cars is lower and consumers invest more in cars than in safer modes of transport. The policy of nonliability functions, in effect, as a subsidy to automobile manufacturers and distorts the free-market system as a mechanism for the efficient allocation of resources.

The distortion of the market results from subsidizing some producers at the expense of others. Any form of subsidy, whether it be for wages, machines, or the social consequences of production, has the effect of supporting weaker producers. The contrary principle is: Each industry must pay its own way. Lord Bramwell developed an argument of this sort in imposing liability against a railroad for emitting sparks and destroying an abutting farmer's crops. There was no doubt in his mind that the sparks were an externality of railroading, not of farming.[11] There was no reason for the farmer to subsidize the railroad by bearing the loss himself. For those who believe in market efficiency, subsidies are an evil. The function of the law should be to eliminate the natural subsidy that occurs when industries cause harmful side effects and they are not legally liable; the function of liability is to insure that each industry pays its way.

This principle, now associated with the writing of English economist Arthur C. Pigou in the early twentieth century,[12] has had a great impact on the law. It is the reigning view of externalities in the courts. It is an eminently sensible way of thinking about applying economic principles in legal analysis. The influential doctrine of "enterprise liability" seems also to be based on the idea that each enterprise in society should bear the cost in human suffering it inflicts on the unwary. Because of the Pigovian principle and its related doctrines in the law, we have witnessed an enormous expansion of products liability (i.e., when products cause injuries to consumers) over the last three or four decades. The expansion has been so great that many politicians now claim that American business is now less competitive with foreign producers who are not subject to the same demanding rules of products liability. Until the 1960s, this was the only theory in town. It seemed obvious that the way to internalize the social costs of industrial enterprises was to make them pay for the harm they cause.

Note the way in which the latter argument of efficiency differs from the Kaldor/Hicks standard of efficiency. The Pigovian claim is simply: Let the market work. Incorporate the social costs into the price and let the consumers decide what they want and how much they are willing to pay for it. There is no need in this market-based method to make a centralized cost/benefit judgment, no call for a common denominator for expressing the value of competing interests. The process of internalizing the social costs of production need not assume what the economists call the "interpersonal comparison of utilities," a process implicit in reducing the competing interests to a common standard of measurement. The market works on the assumption of consumer sovereignty: Each consumer is considered to be unique. Though we can rank her utilities and preferences, we cannot compare them quantitatively or qualitatively with the utilities (or preferences, pleasures, or pains) of anybody else. The great appeal of the Pigovian theory is that it demands fewer assumptions. All we need to assume is that consumers will make consistent decisions about what they want. Or so it seems.

The Coasian Reaction

Nothing makes academic waves more than a refutation of received wisdom. In the early 1960s, when the Pigovian theory reigned as dogma in the analysis of tort liability, Ronald Coase, an economist at the University of Chicago, burst on the scene with his article *The Problem of Social Cost*.[13] In 1963 Aaron Director, one of the early leaders in the nascent field of L&E, walked into class at the University of Chicago Law School and made the prescient announcement: this article will change the way lawyers think about law. He was right, at least about the way academic lawyers think about externalities.

Coase's basic claim is that what Pigou said "ain't necessarily so." Imposing liability against polluters and other injuring firms is not the only way to achieve efficiency in the allocation of resources. Coase has two basic strategies for countering Pigou. Both strategies depend on shifting the focus of economic analysis from decisions by consumers to potential decisions by victims. The first strategy is worked out in speculations about potential "bribes"[14] by victims to prevent impending harm. Suppose that unlike the example of supersonic air travel above, there are no impediments to the victims bargaining with enterprises that injure them. To take Coase's example, a rancher must decide whether to let the *n*th (say, the third) steer graze on his property. If so, the steer will roam and cause harm to the neighboring farmer. Does economic efficiency require that the rancher pay for the harm? Pigou would say "yes," in order to avoid the victims' (the farmer and his customers) "subsidizing"[15] the cost of beef by absorbing the damage done by the third steer. The gist of Coase's response is that the only relevant economic question is whether the rancher grazes the third steer or not, and that, he showed, was a function not of the liability rule, but exclusively of the relative value of the steer to the rancher and the damage to the farmer's crops.

There are only four relevant cases. In cases I and II, the steer can generate $300 in revenue for the rancher, and the crop damage is $200. In cases III and IV, the figures are reversed: $200 for the rancher and $300 damage to the farmer.

Case I. *Premises*: $300 gain for rancher; $200 loss for farmer; according to the law, the rancher is liable for the damage by the steer.
Consequence: Rancher grazes the steer and pays farmer $200 in damage costs. He retains $100 of the gain.

Case II. *Premises*: $300 gain for rancher; $200 loss for farmer; according to the law, rancher is *not* liable for the damage.
Consequence: Rancher will obviously graze the steer because he nets the full $300.

Case III. *Premises*: $200 gain for rancher; $300 loss for farmer; according to the law, rancher is liable for damage.
Consequence: Rancher will *not* graze the steer because his loss in liability costs to farmer ($300) would be greater than the potential gain ($200) from the steer.

Case IV. *Premises*: $200 gain for rancher; $300 loss for farmer; ACcording to the law, rancher is not liable for damage.
Consequence: Even though rancher is not liable for the damage, negotiations between rancher and farmer will result in the steer's *not* grazing. It will be worth it to farmer to offer rancher more than $200 but less than $300 (the loss that would occur from grazing) to induce rancher not to graze the steer, and it will be in rancher's interest to accept some sum greater than $200 from farmer in place of the $200 he could earn from grazing the steer.

This is all there is to the Coase theorem. In cases I and II, the steer grazes; in cases III and IV, it does not. This is a consequence not of liability but of the economic consequence to the rancher and the farmer of the steer's grazing. If it is worth it to the rancher and farmer to have the steer graze, it will graze; if not, it will not graze. It goes without saying the same method applies to any conflict over whether a single resource, such as land or air, should be used in one way or another. You could play out the same argument in a dispute about smoking in restaurants or industrial pollution. The only assumptions necessary are that parties seek gain, that they are able to bargain with each other, and that they have full information about alternatives in the market.

The only move in this demonstration that might puzzle the non-economist is the resolution of case IV: farmer will bribe rancher not to graze the steer if the numbers so dictate. The rancher will accept the bribe and hold back the steer. It seems unfair that a potential victim should have to pay "protection" to someone who might injure him. It is indeed unfair, but the premise of the economic argument is that fairness is irrelevant. It is efficient for the potential victim to pay not to be injured, and efficiency is the only value at stake.

Though this brief demonstration is sufficient to prove Coase's theorem, his classic article is devoted largely to a second attack on Pigou. It seems very important to Coase to undermine the judgments that courts routinely make about who causes what. The point of this attack is clear. Pigovian analysis presupposes that we can determine which enterprises cause which injuries. We can carry out the task that Calabresi dubbed "cost accounting."[16] If there is no way to know whether the cause of sonic booms is flying supersonic planes or the failure of affected people to use thicker glass in their windows, then there is no way of applying the Pigovian principle to concrete cases. A little skepticism enables us to perceive the victim as a causal factor in his own suffering. After all, if the farmer insisted on planting next to the railroad, then of course the crops would be destroyed by spark-induced fires. If pedestrians walk near the highway, then they participate in bringing on accidents with cars. If it takes two to tango, then according to Coase, it takes two to create pollution, an accident, or, indeed, any externality. The victim is as much of a cause as the industrial enterprise.

Though this causal nihilism is not a necessary part of the economic proof of Coase's theorem, it is a part of the general attack on the Pigovian tradition. The function of this attack, it seems, is to undermine confidence in making judgments about whether manufacturing automobiles causes accidents, or, indeed, whether factories emitting smoke cause air pollution. Despite the vigor of Coase's critique, however, the Pigovian principle has had far more influence in the development of the law than has the Coase theorem. First, the Pigovian principle applies in nonideal as well as ideal bargaining conditions between injurer and noninjurer. The Coase theorem does not apply in the case of supersonic travel because the costs of bargaining (organizing and communicating with the affected class) are insuperable. Coase has created an elegant theory limited to ideal conditions. He attempts to adjust his model to reality by noting that the costs of bargaining (transactions costs) will enter into the analysis of negotiating parties whether to make a deal. For example, the farmer in case IV will not bribe the rancher if the transactions costs are more than $100, for in that case he cannot gain anything by paying the rancher his minimum of $200. (The fee to the rancher plus the transactions costs will be greater than the damage that the steer would do.)

The Pigovian theorem will continue to reign in the courts so long as the bench is staffed by lawyers rather than economists. In addition to its more ready applicability, the Pigovian theorem dovetails well with the commonsense judgment that he who causes harm without justification ought to pay for it. "Making industry pay its way" appears to be a principle of fairness as well as efficiency. Coase will never succeed in the courts, because his view of efficiency is incompatible with elementary principles of fairness. It boggles the noneconomic mind to expect the farmer to pay the rancher to keep his steer from grazing.

The remarkable feature of Coase's theorem is that it has any impact at all. His theorem that the rule of liability does not matter under ideal conditions runs parallel to the model of voluntary bargaining under Pareto's principles. As the latter could not have impact without undergoing a transformation, so Coase's theorem could not guide legal thought unless it became a rationale for coercive legal intervention. A theory about the irrelevance of law might be exciting in the ideal world of economic models, but it is surely of little utility in the real world of legal conflict. The great mystery, therefore, is how the Coase theorem underwent a metamorphosis from a critique of Pigou's theory into a tool for analyzing liability in real cases of economic conflict.

Coase himself had virtually nothing to do with this transformation. The critical work came from those, like Richard Posner and the legions of L&E supporters, who saw in Coase an implicit endorsement of the market for solving legal problems. The steps in this reasoning can be broken down into these:

1. Under ideal conditions, the market will produce efficient results.
2. Efficiency is good.
3. Where the market does not operate perfectly (e.g., the problem of the supersonic air travel), the courts should intervene.
4. What should the courts do? They should allocate liability in an effort to generate the result that a free market would generate if it could operate.
5. Why should courts do this? Because efficiency is good. (See step 2 above.)

There we have it. A plausible defense for converting the Coase theorem into a standard for resolving concrete disputes: Mimic the market by assigning rights and liabilities. This particular manipulation of economic ideas should not come as a surprise. It replicates the intellectual history that led from Pareto's principles of bargaining under ideal conditions to coercive intervention under the Kaldor/Hicks test.

It is worth pinpointing the fallacy in the argument that courts should mimic the market. We must distinguish between two senses or conceptions of efficiency that have run through this chapter. One form of efficiency is built into a model of trading under ideal circumstances. If trading continues to the point that no further trade is possible without making someone worse off, then the resulting state of affairs is Pareto-optimal and, by definition, efficient. All that efficiency means in this context (as well as in step two above) is that people get what they want. It is tautologically true that under ideal circumstances, the market will produce efficient results; it will give people what they want. This is an example of what Rawls calls pure procedural justice.[17] If the game is played according to the rules, the outcome will, as a matter of logical necessity, be right.

A totally distinct form of efficiency derives from making cost/benefit judgments about whether the benefits to passengers of flying the SST outweigh its costs to people in the flight path. Flying a supersonic airplane is efficient in this sense if its benefits outweigh its costs. There is no market mechanism, no ideal game, for determining the balance of competing goods and bads of supersonic flight. Ideal markets cannot be inefficient, but whoever makes a centralized judgment of efficiency in this situation might make a mistake and opt for an inefficient outcome. Ideal markets cannot be wrong, but centralized decisions can be, and they often are. In Rawls's terms, this is an instance not of pure but of imperfect procedural justice.[18] I want to distinguish between these two conceptions of efficiency by calling the first M-efficiency (M for market) and the second, C-efficiency (C for centralized). The first depends on the hidden hand of a decentralized market; the second, on the heavy hand of a single decision maker (or committee) that makes an assessment of competing costs and benefits.

If efficiency is good, it is good in these two different senses. M-efficiency is good because people get what they want; C-efficiency is good because it generates a net surplus of benefit over cost. The former is a libertarian value; the latter, good because it is better for society, collectively, to have more rather than less. The fallacy in the demonstration above is the shift between these two meanings of efficiency. Step 2 is based on M-efficiency; step 4 on C-efficiency. The effort to mimic the market turns out to consist in centralized cost/benefit decisions. The pretense of mimicking the market, therefore, converts a libertarian value into a utilitarian standard for maximizing the welfare of the group.

Methods and Insights

The concept of efficiency suffers internal contradictions, but as we shall see in the final chapter, these contradictions may be no worse than those that infect the legal culture as a whole. Despite their obfuscation of the political and moral issues at stake, economists have brought great insights to the law and have stimulated debate about the foundations of liability. I group their contribution under the heading of "morality in the law" for their propositions are a form of moral argument. Either they argue in the libertarian tradition that individual autonomy and consent are supreme values; or they replicate, in a quite different language, the interventionist arguments of utilitarians.

The major difference between the economic and the philosophical style of argument lies less in substance and more in method. The philosophical style of this book expresses a primary commitment to clarity and conceptual analysis. Understanding differences and distinctions is a prime goal. In contrast, the methods of economists are functional rather than analytic. Their style of argument trades on perceiving similarities rather than differences. A typical economic argument is that a tax exemption is functionally equivalent to a grant-in-aid from the government. The similarity consists in the economic consequences of, say, a $1000 tax exemption and a $1000 grant in aid. The notion of "subsidy" is used rather freely in a similar way to describe any reduction of liability that runs counter to an assumed base line. Supporters of Pigovian theory would say that not requiring industry to pay for externalities is, in effect, to subsidize industry. Because they regard the assignment of externalities as a more fluid issue, supporters of the Coase theorem deny the charge of subsidization.

Calabresi is adept at spotting functional similarities. He claims that both contract rights against specific people and rights to use things should be called property rights.[19] Lawyers have spent centuries trying to clarify the distinction between rights in personam (against particular people) and rights in rem (against the entire world), but this distinction gets lost in a single stroke of the economist's pen. Calabresi also claims that the term "liability" should cover the case of a plaintiff who is denied recovery. We ordinarily say in this case that there is no liability, but Calabresi and many people influenced by him would say that the plaintiff is "liable" for his own injuries.[20] The impact of this careless speech is to camouflage the difference between getting stuck with a loss and being able to shift the loss to someone else.

Economic theorists of law are lumpers rather than splitters. They see similarities but downplay conceptual differences. They blur the meaning of causation, of property, and of liability. Other concepts fall as well to the impulse to see functional similarities. The distinction between corrective and distributive justice gets erased in the economist's dividing the world into questions of efficiency and questions of distribution. The latter category includes both corrective and distributive justice.

The impact of economic analysis on the law reminds us of the way legal realists systematically misused the language of discretion in order to make a valuable point about judicial creativity.[21] The realists too were lumpers rather than splitters. They grouped together decisions by administrative agencies, decisions by police on the beat, verdicts by juries, and judicial decisions under the law. All of these turned out to be discretionary. Arguments of lumping generate a temporary sense of understanding: "Ah," says the student, "now I see a functional relationship I did not see before." The price of this understanding is widespread debasing of the language. Without a precise language, careful thought and argument come to an end.

Economic analysis of the law displays virtues as well as vices. The tension between these views and those who believe strongly that accident law should be about justice rather than efficiency has enormously enriched legal debate. Yet the most serious ramification of the L&E movement has been the pretense that L&E is simply an extension of the neutral, nonpolitical science called "positive economics." In this chapter I have attempted to show that though the argument begins in the methods of descriptive economics, it ends up by taking a stand on controversial moral and political principles of individual rights and group interests.

The supposed neutrality of L&E correlates in time with the emergence in the late 1970s of a large school of avowedly political scholars who campaigned under the banner of "Critical Legal Studies" (CLS).[22] It's hard to know whether L&E itself triggered the CLS reaction, but the pretense of an apolitical science in law might well have had (and properly should have had) this effect. The central thrust of CLS is that political commitments play a greater role in the life of the law than ordinarily assumed. In recent years the CLS movement itself has fragmented into conflicting political camps, some arguing as feminists for women's interests, others stressing the significance of race and gender in thinking about legal issues.

The political reaction against the pseudoscience of economic analysis coincides with a renewed debate about the possibility of impartial thinking in morality and public affairs. The universal and impartial ambitions of Bentham and Kant have given way to a renewed appreciation for local and partial commitments. These, of course, are the commitments that drive political action. They support the aims of previously disempowered groups—such as gays and lesbians, ethnic minorities, and women—to assert themselves as "communities" with rights of their own. The new challenge for American law is to fathom the relationship between individuals and the groups from which they derive their identity.

Notes

1. For general treatment of the field, see RICHARD POSNER, ECONOMIC ANALYSIS OF THE LAW (3d ed. 1976); A.M. POLINSKY, AN INTRODUCTION TO LAW

AND ECONOMICS (2nd ed. 1989); ROBERT COOTER & THOMAS ULEN, LAW AND ECONOMICS (1988).

2. *See* GUIDO CALABRESI, THE COSTS OF ACCIDENTS: A LEGAL AND ECONOMIC ANALYSIS (1971).

3. *See supra* p. 94 note 18.

4. Nicholas Kaldor, *Welfare Propositions of Economics and Interpersonal Comparisons of Utility*, 49 ECONOMICS JOURNAL 549 (1939).

5. *Id.*

6. Cecil R. Hicks, *The Foundations of Welfare Economics*, 49 ECONOMICS JOURNAL 696 (1939).

7. This argument, admittedly, leaves out of consideration the possibility of measuring preferences across a large group of people by observing how they behave in the markets where there is choice between two versions of a single commodity. For example, if smokers are willing, on average, to pay ten percent more to dine in restaurants where smoking is permitted (as an exception to the norm), then we have a rough idea how much particular smokers are willing to pay to light up after a meal. This rough guide hardly works to establish the quantitative difference in utility between any two persons competing for the use of single space for the purpose of smoking or breathing smoke-free air.

8. POSNER, *supra* note 1, at 47.

9. An externality is defined as a cost or benefit of production that does not enter into the producer's decisions about how much to produce.

10. *See* Guido Calabresi, *The Decision for Accidents: An Approach to Nonfault Allocation of Costs*, 78 HARVARD LAW REVIEW 713 (1965).

11. Vaughan v. Taff Vale Railway, 157 English Reports 1351 (Exch. Ch. 1860).

12. The first edition of THE ECONOMICS OF WELFARE was published in 1920.

13. 3 JOURNAL OF LAW AND ECONOMICS 1 (1960).

14. Economists often use terms like "bribe" in unusual ways. The kind of bribe they have in mind is simply a payment designed to produce a desired form of behavior. *See infra* the discussion at pp. 169–70 on the functional method in economic thinking.

15. The comment in note 14 *supra* is applicable as well to the use of "subsidy" in economic jargon.

16. *See* Calabresi, *supra* note 10, at 720.

17. JOHN RAWLS, A THEORY OF JUSTICE 85–87 (1971). See the discussion *supra* pp. 81–82.

18. RAWLS, *supra* note 17, at 85–86.

19. Guido Calabresi and A. Douglas Malamed, *Property Rules, Liability Rules, and Inalienability: One View of the Cathedral*, 85 HARVARD LAW REVIEW 1089 (1972).

20. *See* JULES COLEMAN, RISKS AND WRONGS 230–32 (1993).

21. *See* discussion *supra* pp. 52–53.

22. *See generally*, ROBERTO M. UNGER, CRITICAL STUDIES MOVEMENT (1986); MARK KELMAN, A GUIDE TO CRITICAL LEGAL STUDIES (1987).

11

Loyalty

Few ideas have grasped the imagination of twentieth-century lawyers more firmly than the now pervasive principle of privacy. If we cast a glance at the prior state of the law in 1900, both here and abroad, we can hardly find an explicit reference to the principle that individuals should be left alone. The idea is not found in the great codifications of nineteenth-century Europe. It was not then known in Asian legal cultures, and it had yet to find elaboration in Anglo-American law.

In the course of this century, the idea of privacy has taken hold both as a basis for tort recovery and as a principle of constitutional law that commends itself to the diverse lines of thought in Western jurisprudence. The common law tort, breach of privacy, traces its roots to the classic article by Brandeis and Warren, published just before the dawn of the century.[1] Although the German Civil Code, which came into force in 1900, does not contain a provision on privacy or related concepts, the German courts interpreted the open-ended tort provision of the Code to include a "right to personality" (*personalité, Persönlichkeit*). This is the phrase that has come to be the Continental equivalent to our notion of privacy.

At the constitutional level, the right to privacy (or personality) has become a standard figure in the pantheon of basic human rights. The 1949 German Constitution recognizes that "everyone has a right to the flourishing of his or her personality."[2] The European Convention on Human Rights, adopted in the same year, recognizes the right to a "private life" (*vie privée*).[3] And as is well known, the U. S. Supreme Court has found a right to privacy embedded in constitutional provisions that recognize the right of the individual to be left alone.

Neither the word "autonomy" nor the word "privacy" appears in the Constitution or the Bill of Rights, but there are many provisions that suggest a private sphere of action exempt from regulation by the state.[4] In one of the critical turns in constitutional jurisprudence, the Supreme Court recognized in 1965 that the principle of privacy, underlying these diverse provisions of the Bill of Rights, should insulate the sale and use of contraceptives from the state's supervision.[5] After this initial foray, the Court extended the shield of privacy to protect unmarried lovers[6] and then in the famous case *Roe v. Wade* to cover abortions under certain circumstances.[7] Yet it became clear, in time, that the idea of privacy implicit here was not an implication of the relationship between the pregnant woman and her lover. Biological fathers had no rights to veto a woman's decision for or against reproduction.[8] The notion of privacy seemed to be one of physical space. Just as the home is off limits unless there is a strong social interest to the contrary so, too, is a woman's womb.

This implicit emphasis on private space rather than on private relationships may have contributed to one of the Court's most oft-derided decisions of the last fifty years. In 1986 the Court held that the emergent principle of privacy did not encompass homosexual relationships.[9] This decision effectively stymied the possibility of developing some general principle of relational privacy.

There was a time, early in the century, when the Supreme Court recognized the autonomy of certain relationships, in particular, voluntary contracts.[10] That idea—known as "freedom of contract"—has suffered widespread criticism, particularly when it is asserted as a principle of constitutional law.[11] Implicitly today, the courts still recognize some relationships as standing apart from the state's regulatory power. The family has always had this appeal.[12] Indeed the German constitution explicitly recognizes the family as a constitutional value.[13] The U.S. Supreme Court seemingly protected the traditional family unit against the claim of a third party for visitation rights with a child he had fathered in an adulterous relationship with the wife.[14] Yet there has been no general effort in legal theory to extend the notion of privacy to particular relationships. In this chapter I propose a general principle for exempting certain relationships, which I call generally relationships of loyalty, from the state's regulatory power.

The Value of Loyalty

We value privacy, but it is hardly a moral value. Whether privacy becomes moral depends a great deal on what one does in the space left unregulated and unsupervised. Privacy, being left alone, is itself neither good nor bad. Loyalty, by contrast, communicates the moral value of remaining steadfast to friends, lovers, families, organizations, political movements, and nations. We search for loyalty in all those with whom we seek to build personal, business, or political relationships.

Loyalty is expressed in relationships. There is always the other to whom one is loyal. What this loyalty means is that if a third party tempted one out of the relationship, the loyal would refuse the temptation. A loyal lover is one who rejects the temptation to shift his love to a third person. A loyal citizen is one who refuses to join the enemy when his people or nation are in difficulty. Treason—the prime case of disloyalty—is defined in the Constitution as "adhering to the enemy, giving them aid and comfort." Loyalty exacts the sacrifice of self-interest. A loyal friend is one who stands by the other even at some personal cost. A loyal business or political associate is one you can count on even when the going gets rough.

Loyalties make possible friendships, marriages, families, organizations, and nations. But acting loyally also benefits the actor. The loyal express their authenticity by recognizing their ties to others. The loyal become fully themselves in recognizing the way their bonds with others limit their freedom of choice. In a highly individualistic society, of course, loyalty has its critics. Loyalties, the critics insist, express the dead hand of history. There is no reason why being born into a family or nation should generate any particular obligation toward others with a common fate. There is no reason, by like token, why a long friendship entails a duty to keep it alive and flourishing. Like every other moral value, loyalty invites its fair share of dissent.

The law, particularly Anglo-American law, is loathe to recognize duties that derive exclusively from birth or personal history. The notable exception is the crime of treason, which is applicable only to citizens or permanent residents of the United States, not to foreigners. Choice or consent—some voluntary act—seems to be essential to the Anglo-American view of legal duty. Parents have duties toward their children, for they choose to bring them into the world. But children have no legal duties to their parents, not even to support them if they are incapable of earning their own livelihood. The argument is that children do not choose their parents, and therefore there is no moral basis for a duty to care for them. Yet other legal systems do recognize the duty of children to provide for elderly, impoverished parents. The new Russian constitution, for example, carries forward the communitarian spirit of their culture by explicitly recognizing this filial duty.[15]

True, Anglo-American law recognizes duties of loyalty when the duty rests on choice and contract. Fiduciary duty is a matter of loyalty; it is an obligation to put first the interests of the company or the individual toward whom one must act as a fiduciary. Lawyers are under duties of loyalty toward their clients. They must treat their interests as paramount and protect the secrets of the relationship. These examples of contractual loyalty differ fundamentally from, say, the duty of children to support their parents. The latter is a duty rooted not in choice and consent, but in birth and blood.

In a sensible approach to loyalty, the state permits the flourishing of a morality of standing by others. The state stays its hand in deference to a sphere of private relationships. The courts can do this by not enforcing duties that run contrary to existing duties of loyalty. A good example of this protective attitude is exempting people in certain relationships from the duty to testify against each other. A wife may choose not to testify against a husband, and vice versa.[16] Many writers advocate extending this exemption to other relationships within the family and some even to relationships between friends. The law permits, therefore, persons who are close to each other to choose to remain silent rather than testify and harm someone dear to them. The processes of justice suffer, of course, for the courts must thereby forego valuable evidence, but the relationships thereby protected prosper.

The recognition of privacy as a separate sphere illustrates the treatment that should be accorded to relationships of loyalty. Another example of the proper deference to the value of loyalty is the nearly universal attitude toward inheritance. Even though strict egalitarians object to transmitting wealth from one generation to another, the practice survives everywhere. Even the Communist regimes dared not eliminate it. Leaving property to another at death is a way of expressing a bond with the recipient. Writing wills permits people to express their loyalties to some and not to others. It is an important institution, not simply because it protects freedom to dispose of property. The possibility of transmitting wealth across generations is important because it permits personal loyalties to flourish.[17]

It is important to note that neither of these institutions—exemptions from testifying and the right to transmit wealth—rests explicitly on the value of loyalty. My claim is that the recognition of loyalty as a moral value is implicit in the legal institutions. The mode of interpretation used resembles the arguments of economists who contend that the pursuit of efficiency is implicit in the legal practices they observe.[18]

Loyalty cannot trump all conflicting values. Members of organized crime families may be guilty of criminal conspiracy even if their way of life rests heavily on an ethic of unquestioning personal loyalty. Yet the value of loyalty often captures one important side of many disputes. I turn now to two hotly contested areas of the law where the value of loyalty enables us to understand what is at stake in the dispute.

Surrogate Motherhood

In a surrogacy contract, a woman commits herself, for a fee, to let herself be artificially inseminated, to carry a child to term, and then to surrender the child to the other contracting party, thereby forfeiting all her parental rights. The problems that attend these contracts are well-illustrated by the saga of Mary Beth Whitehead in the 1980s. Ms. Whitehead, a mother of two and homemaker of uncertain income, responded to an ad in a local New Jersey newspaper and learned, upon contact with a fertility center in Manhattan, that she could earn $10,000 by acting as a surrogate, giving birth to a healthy child without deformities, and surrendering the child to the child's biological father and his wife. If she did not deliver the goods—a healthy child—she would receive only one thousand dollars for her time and trouble.[19] The parties with whom she eventually contracted were William and Elizabeth Stern, both with advanced university degrees, and with an income in the uppermost percentiles of American society.

People who believe strongly in contract see nothing wrong with arrangements of this sort. They give full vent to the parties' autonomy and capacity for rational self-governance. Promises and contracts are binding because we all assume that competent adults can commit their personalities to an agreement and thus sacrifice the freedom to change their minds. Though contracts are an important vehicle of economic development, it is extraordinary that one can sacrifice one's future freedom for the sake of present advantage. This is the basis of the recurrent Faustian metaphor of pacts with the devil; for the sake of present fame or fortune, one commits oneself to a price that one hopes will never come due. Contracts glorify the capacity for individual commitment, but they also represent the means by which individuals sell themselves into slavery. Philosophers like John Stuart Mill who revere contract as an expression of freedom also recognize the overweening importance of preserving freedom in the future.[20] No one should be able to go too far in selling his or her future for the sake of present compensation. And how far is "too" far? Mill thought that contracts of slavery went too far, as did the commitments of women who entered into polygamous marriages. In the law today, we say that these unconscionable arrangements are void as violations of "public policy."[21]

In the arrangement between Whitehead and the Sterns, something was bound to go wrong, for no one told the hospital about the plan to surrender the child.[22] The sensible way to execute an adoption from birth is to have the baby removed immediately, without coming into contact with the mother. But after giving birth in late March 1986 to the little girl Sarah, later known as Baby M, Mary Beth received her child in her arms and like any other mother in the ward she nursed her, ogled her, and began to love her. She left the hospital a few days later with the child she naturally and predictably came to regard as her own. The transfer to the Sterns was supposed to take place three days after birth, away from public view, at the Whiteheads' home.

The arrangement was clearly designed with some concern for what other people would think. There may have been an element of shame, for the suspicion came easily that the Whiteheads, the Sterns, and the lawyers had devised a scheme that reduced babies to a commodity, something to be bought and sold. More likely they were concerned about possible criminal prosecution[23] and whether the contract to deliver a healthy child in return for $10,000 would hold up in court.

The Whiteheads did deliver the child as promised, despite Mary Beth's feeling that as a result of giving up her child her life "wasn't worth anything . . . [she] was no longer worthy of being [a] mother [to her other two children]."[24] But there followed over a year of extraordinary pulling and tearing at the child the Whiteheads called Sarah and the Sterns, Melissa (whence the name Baby M).[25] The day after giving up the child, Mary Beth walked into the Sterns' home and managed, somehow, to walk out with her Sarah.[26] The Sterns tried legal remedies to get their Melissa back, but the Whiteheads fled with the child to Florida. A court order, secured in Florida,[27] put the Sterns back in custody and the Whiteheads were reduced to fighting in the New Jersey courts to eke out whatever rights might be left to them. As the dust was settling, the child was adapting to life with the Sterns and this fact in itself tended to strengthen their case that they could provide a better home for Baby M.

If the contract turned out to be valid, however, there would be no discussion in court about who had a superior moral claim to Baby M or who could provide a better home for the child. The contract would terminate the mother's claims forever. Therefore the judges of New Jersey had first to ponder how far people should be able to go in trading their future lives and the fate of children in return for present advantage. It is not hard to imagine arrangements close to the Whitehead-Stern contract that would be obviously void as a violation of public policy. Suppose that the Sterns want a son and they therefore introduced a term in the surrogacy contract that required Whitehead to have an abortion if the fetus tested female. This condition would be void on several grounds. The courts would not countenance an agreement that discriminated against the birth of girls, and further the notion that a woman would be compelled to abort a fetus would be so clearly unconscionable that the discussion would have been brief. There is not much difference, however, between requiring a woman to abort a fetus and mandating that she abandon her child. It is indeed more difficult to contemplate the loss of the born child, particularly if it is foreseen that the mother will possess and nurture the infant for a few days after birth.

Nonetheless the New Jersey trial court came to the surprising conclusion that, indeed, contract ruled the matter: The mother's rights were

to be terminated forever. The judge carried out a hasty adoption cere-
mony in chambers; Elizabeth Stern replaced Mary Beth Whitehead as
the legal mother of the child. The New Jersey Supreme Court brought
the state to its senses. The seven justices unanimously reversed the trial
court and held that the agreement violated the basic principles of law
and justice in the state.[28] Conceiving children and determining custody,
even before conception, is not within the autonomy of contracting
parties.

In the court's characterization of the surrogacy agreement, the natural parents determined the custody of child even before it is conceived. If
a contract for this purpose were valid, it would usurp the judicial function of deciding whether custody with the natural mother or the natural
father better serves the best interests of the child. There are other problems as well. The contract seeks to terminate a mother's rights even
before the child comes into existence. It violates the premise that
wherever possible children should grow up nurtured by both their natural parents. "Worst of all, however," the court continues, "is the contract's total disregard for the best interests of the child."[29] Where the
biological parents do not live together, as was the case with William
Stern and Mary Beth Whitehead, the courts must intervene to make this
decision about the child's welfare.

In the first days of a child's life, it is fanciful for a court to try to
determine whether she would flourish more in one family or another.
There is no way to project alternative lives into the future without the
intrusion of the crass forms of social and economic bias. How could a
court balance the love and devotion of the natural mother against the
wealth, education, and worldly sophistication of the father? Should it
matter that the Sterns had divergent ethnic and religious backgrounds?
That the Whiteheads' finances were in difficulty at the time of trial? That
Mary Beth Whitehead had already successfully (whatever that means)
reared two children?

Better courts have thoughtfully distanced themselves from attempting in this way to divine the advantages and disadvantages of alternative
modes of life. In the end, there is no more sure guide to the child's
welfare than the commitment felt by the natural mother. The mother's
loyalty sustains the child more deeply than the supposedly objective
factors of wealth, opportunity, and lifestyle.[30]

The New Jersey Supreme Court adopted a peculiar way of talking
about a mother's claim to care for her own child. The question was
supposedly one of the mother's "right to the companionship of her
child."[31] American lawyers and judges commonly phrase every issue as
an expression of individual rights, but I take it that the dominant
thought motivating mothers like Mary Beth Whitehead is not the notion
of right, but of duty. The mother of Baby M felt compelled to care for her
offspring. Her attachment, her sense of loyalty, to the child that she

brought to term defined the course she had to take. To speak of a "right to the companionship of her child" is to treat a mother's most basic impulse as little more than an interest in being amused.

The father's donating his sperm does not generate a duty of comparable force. It would be ludicrous for a father to sue a sperm bank to force disclosure of the identity of a child born of his sperm used in artificial insemination. He could not plausibly claim a loyalty to the child solely on the basis of his genetic transmission. The mother's loyalty is grounded not just in biology, but in the experiential connection of carrying the child to term and nurturing it after birth.[32]

The evil of the surrogacy contract is aptly formulated in the language of loyalty. The contract to bear a child for another family requires a mother to act disloyally toward her own offspring. And it is an act of disloyalty that has permanent consequences of estrangement and self-alienation. It is, indeed, comparable to a contract prior to conception that if the fetus is not of a particular gender, the mother will terminate the pregnancy. As it would be unconscionable to force a woman to go through with an abortion, it would be equally wrong to force a woman to carry out an agreement made before she held the child in her arms. Contracts are no more than useful instruments for furthering human designs. Where they rivet people in arrangements with consequences disastrous to their self-esteem, they are to be disregarded.

The Free Exercise of Religion

In the modern, secular world, one might wonder about the wisdom of the First Amendment, which appears to privilege the exercise of religion over other expressions of human belief and commitment. Why should society tolerate religious diversity but not other forms of unconventional conduct? Why should those who rest on the biblical Sabbath be able to claim special attention and accommodation, while those who want to play golf on Wednesdays have no basis to demand Wednesdays off? One approach to religion, mandated by a commitment to equality, is to treat activities in its name neither better nor worse than any other activity. The alternative is to accord religious activities special treatment, to create an exception in the laws for those who believe they may not work on the Sabbath, should not send their children to public school, should not serve in the military, or should not receive blood transfusions.

When religious groups claim on religious grounds a right to *abstain* from work, school, the military, or medical treatment, their claims are generally honored. Since 1943 the Supreme Court has been receptive to these arguments saying "no": We will not do what the others do. The case law began with a dramatic overturning of precedent, in which the Court decided in the middle of World War II that the children of Jehovah's Witnesses could abstain from saluting the flag.[33] By bringing a number of challenges to the courts, the Jehovah's Witnesses won exemptions from an array of statutes that, they say, require idolatrous practices. Now they need not salute the flag. They need not stand for the national anthem.[34] They need not carry patriotic messages on their license plates.[35] A second group that has said "no," Sabbatarians—those who refuse to work on Saturdays—has also won numerous victories in the Supreme Court. Sabbatarians need not give up unemployment compensation if they refuse to accept jobs that require work on Saturdays.[36] The same policy applies to Christians who refuse to work on Sundays[37] and presumably would extend to Muslims who refuse to work on Fridays.

As a third religious group saying "no," the members of an Amish community in Wisconsin refused to send their children to a public high school that, they feared, would educate them in ways foreign to the community's traditional religious culture.[38] The children were in the community's public school until the age of fourteen, but state law demanded education until the age of sixteen. The Amish wanted their children not only to avoid the secular influences of a public high school, but to settle down in early adolescence to the adult roles of farming and homemaking prescribed for them in the community's traditional way of life. Like the Jehovah's Witnesses in the controversy over saluting the flag, the Amish relied upon their own interpretation of Scripture. Though all Christians accept the passage in Paul's Epistle to the Romans, "be not conformed to this world . . . ,"[39] the Amish insist on a literal reading that requires them to separate themselves from the surrounding American culture and devote themselves to a simple agricultural life suffused with religious thought and devotion.[40] The Amish won their case for special treatment in the Supreme Court.[41]

Religious liberty becomes more problematic when religious groups assert the right not only to abstain from certain behavior but also to engage in action forbidden to people outside the religious group. As to activities such as practicing polygamy, using otherwise prohibited drugs in religious worship, or sacrificing little animals on the altar, they claim a right to an exemption from the law. They want to say, "Yes, I can do this even though it is forbidden to others." The first time the question came before the Supreme Court, the Justices held that Mormons could not claim an exemption from laws prohibiting polygamy.[42] Orthodox Jews fared badly before the Court when they wanted to keep their stores open on Sunday in contravention of Sunday closing laws. They made the perfectly sensible claim that because their religion required them to abstain from work on Saturdays, they deserved an exception from the law mandating that others close on Sundays.[43] When the Santeria religion sought recently to reintroduce animal sacrifice in Hialeah, Florida, the townspeople reacted in horror. They passed an ordinance barring the "ritual sacrifice" of animals. On the side of the Santeria, it should be said, animal sacrifice is a practice clearly rooted in the Old Testament. This would have been a very difficult case for the Court were it not for the appearance of discrimination in Hialeah's passing an ordinance aimed at the Santeria practice. The Supreme Court struck down the local ordinance without addressing the question whether, had the ordinance already been in place, another group could claim an exemption in order to slaughter animals on the altar of their church.[44]

The most provocative claims for special treatment are those based on the use of drugs. Timothy Leary did not get far in the courts when he claimed that he had founded a new religion based on the grand principle "Tune in, turn on, and drop out." His using dope as a ritual act was subject to the ordinary rules of the criminal law.[45] The problem is more delicate, however, when couched as a ritual act of using peyote in the Native American Church. When a couple of drug counselors in Oregon admitted to using peyote in Native American rituals, they lost their jobs, whereupon they applied for unemployment compensation. In view of the reason for their dismissal, the compensation was denied. The counselors sued on the ground they should not have been penalized for exercising their religion. The Supreme Court turned down their complaint without apparent qualms.[46] At the time of this decision in 1990, it seemed there was little life left even in the principle of accommodating those who wished, like the Jehovah's Witnesses, the Sabbatarians, and the Amish, just to say "no" to the demands of the secular world. Yet Congress thereupon intervened with a statute that appeared to rescue the prior pattern of Supreme Court case law.[47]

The free exercise clause represents a frontal attack on the principle of applying the laws equally to everyone. What is so special about religious claims that they generate exemptions from statutes that apply neutrally to everyone?[48] If someone says, my religion requires me to smoke pot, we are not likely to chuckle behind his back. Why? The philosophical essence of religion eludes us, for no single criterion compels us to classify group activities as religious or not. A number of practices invoke religious associations: belief in God, acceptance of a revealed text, a regular form of worship, a quest for the ultimate truth about the origin and purpose of human existence. Yet committing ourselves to a list like this introduces the bias of our historical situation. These are the factors that characterize Judaism, Christianity, and Islam, and therefore we are inclined to think that they are essential constituents of the religious life.

There is no way to make headway on the constitutional concept of religion without first developing a theory about why the Constitution should wish to defer to religious commitments. The present tendency on the Court and among scholars is to think that the psychological intensity of religious beliefs requires us to accord these beliefs special protection. Forcing people to act contrary to their religious beliefs imposes a certain sort of harm, and this harm must be balanced against the state's interest in securing universal compliance, say, with a law prohibiting polygamy, requiring attendance in school, or imposing military or prison discipline. The conventional mode of analyzing free-exercise claims requires that the Court first establish whether the claimant sincerely holds the religious view asserted and then, on the other side of the ledger, whether, in the mode of strict scrutiny, the state has a "compelling interest" that outweighs the religious claim.

This way of thinking is deeply flawed. First, the intensity of belief cannot provide the relevant test for religious beliefs; for, many beliefs are as strongly held as those characteristic of the great religions.[49] The Court in the Amish case captured the problem in this example:

> Thus, if the Amish asserted their claims because of their subjective evaluation and rejection of the contemporary secular values accepted by the majority, much as Thoreau rejected the social values of his time and isolated himself at Walden Pond, their claims would not rest on a religious basis. Thoreau's choice was philosophical and personal rather than religious, and such belief does not rise to the demands of the Religion Clauses.[50]

The analogy is strained, for Thoreau had no reason to seek refuge in the Constitution; there was nothing illegal about his return to nature. But let us suppose, if we could, that we had a case of someone holding personal commitments as deep as Thoreau's that required deviation not only from social but from legal norms. It would be difficult to say, as a psychological matter, that their commitments would be less strong than those imposed by the recognized religions. Yet the Constitution protects only religious beliefs, and therefore there must be some account of these beliefs that is both plausible and adequate to explain why religiously motivated conduct is singled out for preferred treatment.

An additional flaw runs through the conventional way of thinking about free-exercise exemptions. If the claimant really could make out a claim of religious commitment that should prevail over secular legal obligations, it is hard to imagine why an interest of the state— compelling or otherwise—should outweigh the religious commitment. Antigone defied the law of Athens, as proclaimed by Creon, and buried her fallen brother Polyneices.[51] Imagine Creon arguing with Antigone about whether the community's interest in civic solidarity should prevail over her loyalties to her dead brother and to Hades, the god of the nether world. Creon could well argue that the state's interest was compelling, to which Antigone would properly respond, in the contemporary idiom: "Creon, you just don't get it." Hades's law required her to bury her dead brother. There was no room in her mental calculus for balancing competing interests.

We need an account of religious commitment that goes beyond the recognition of the psychological weight of these commitments and explains why these commitments should prevail over secular law. The imperative of loyalty to a higher power provides the most compelling account of our deferring to religious obligations. The religious life, as we know it in the West, is based on the individual's having loyalties to a transcendental authority. These loyalties preclude giving wholehearted allegiance to a secular authority. One must "render unto Caesar the things which are Caesar's; and unto God the things which are God's."[52] Antigone must render unto Creon that which is Creon's, and unto Hades that which belongs to Hades.

These loyalties are directed toward the divine voice, but they cannot simply express a vision that God exists and has spoken to the believer. These aberrant claims about communication with God are more likely to be taken as a sign of mental illness than as an expression of an orientation worthy of constitutional protection.[53] In order for a claim of higher loyalty to be plausible, it must be embedded in a community practice. There must be others who hear the same voice and there must be, in recited legends or in a written text, some objective manifestation of what the higher power demands of his loyal followers. The loyalty to God then becomes interwoven with loyalty to a community and fidelity to a tradition. It is not an accident that in those cases in which the Court has recognized a religious exemption, the claimant has always rested his or her claim on a biblical passage, most of them in the Ten Commandments. The relevant passages instruct believers not to worship graven images, to keep the Sabbath, not to kill, not "to conform to this world." Where the religious claim has no biblical foundation, as Leary's claim to use drugs, the courts readily dismiss the claim as ill founded.

The fundamental error, I submit, is the assumption that religious belief can be reduced to intensely and sincerely held beliefs that the believers label religious. Religious beliefs, so far as they are to be taken seriously, arise in congregations or communities of believers. They represent a submission to an external authority that commands obedience. They are expressed not only in views about the world, but in shared, interdependent rituals based on the those views. Prophets calling in the wilderness may indeed hear the voice of God, but standing alone, they cannot be expected to be honored in their own land.[54] Abraham may indeed have been commanded by God to sacrifice his son,[55] but if he had committed the deed, he should not have expected his homicide to be treated as the free exercise of religion.[56]

The Challenge of Loyalty

The principle that unites our study of surrogacy contracts and the free exercise of religion is simply put: The state should not force people to act disloyally. It should not force mothers to abandon their children, and it should not force believers to act disloyally toward God and their religious communities. In both cases, the most appealing examples are those where the individual simply says "No. I won't give up the child; I won't work on the Sabbath; I won't serve in the military; I won't send my children to public school." Honoring the decision, however, to say "no" flies in the face of other respected values in the legal culture. Surrogate mothers put loyalty to their children ahead of their contractual duties, duties to which they fully consented at an earlier point in time. The religious put their loyalty to God ahead of their duty to submit to laws equally applied to everyone. These matters remain controversial precisely because they expose the fault lines of our inconsistent legal premises.

Loyalty bears strong ties to the notion of law. The root for "law" is the Latin *"lex,"* which has also generated the French terms *"loi"* [law] and *"loy*auté" [loyalty]. A legitimate child was once known as a "loyal child" and good money was called "loyal money." Loyal behavior is law-like. It follows the inner law of the person. It renders us consistent and authentic. The opposite is the person without character, unstable, changing with the whims of the moment.

The interesting linguistic feature of loyalty is that like privacy, the concept reveals a strong connection to the English and French sounds that denote it. Many other European languages have cognate versions of "loyalty" of "loyauté" and they all draw on the same Latin root. German has *Loyalität* as well as its own word *Treu*. The latter has the connotation of "fidelity" and the language obviously needs both ideas. The root for "truthfulness" also generates words, such as the Hebrew *ne-eman*, that are close to "loyalty" but not exactly the same. The peculiar features of "loyalty" are in fact captured in this particular word.

The moral value of loyalty represents a challenge to the principles of autonomous and binding consent on the one hand and to those of equality on the other. At another level, the loyal person rejects the morality expressed in both Kantianism and utilitarianism. Loyalty is a form of partiality, a willingness to be closer to some than to others. The loyal have no qualms about helping friends more than they do strangers.[57] The loyal would unhesitatingly lie in order to save the life of a loved one in danger. The loyal also think more in the language of duty than of rights. Loyalty as a virtue reflects an older, premodern ethic that recognizes the influences of birth and experience on our duties to others.

The survival of loyalty in modern legal culture reminds us that this culture, like the earth's surface, is best understood as a layered accumulation of diverse influences and historic deposits. Both equality and loyalty—impartial morality and partial morality—have left their traces in the legal culture. Unfortunately, the sediments of these ideas have not mixed readily and settled into a harmonious whole.

Notes

1. Louis Brandeis and Samuel Warren, *The Right of Privacy*, 4 HARVARD LAW REVIEW 193 (1890).

2. GRUNDGESETZ [Constitution] art. 2, § 1.

3. European Convention on Human Rights art. 8, § 1.

4. In addition to guaranteeing the free exercise of religion, the First Amendment prohibits the state from passing laws "abridging the freedom of speech." The Third Amendment prohibits the quartering of soldiers in private homes; the Fourth Amendment prohibits unreasonable searches and seizures. The Privilege Against Self-Incrimination in the Fifth Amendment expresses the autonomy of individuals by requiring that all testimony prejudicial to one's liberty be fully voluntary.

5. Griswold v. Connecticut, 381 United States Reports 479 (1965) (relying on the "penumbra" to the First, Third, Fourth, and Fifth Amendments).

6. Eisenstadt v. Baird, 405 United States Reports 438 (1972).

7. Roe v. Wade, 410 United States Reports 113 (1973) (holding that a state may not forbid abortions until the final three months of pregnancy).

8. Planned Parenthood v. Danforth, 428 United States Reports 52 (1976) (outlawing requirement of spousal consent). The point is affirmed in Planned Parenthood v. Casey, 112 Supreme Court Reports 2791, 2826–31 (1992) (outlawing requirement of spousal notification).

9. Bowers v. Hardwick, 478 United States Reports 186 (1986).

10. Lochner v. New York, 198 United States Reports 45 (1905).

11. GERALD GUNTHER, CONSTITUTIONAL LAW 445 (12th ed. 1991): "Rejection of the Lochner heritage is a common starting point for modern Justices."

12. Striking down an Oregon law requiring all children to attend public school, the Supreme Court wrote: "[T]he child is not the mere creature of the state; those who nurture him and direct his destiny have the right, coupled with the high duty, to recognize and prepare him for additional obligations." Pierce v. Society of Sisters, 268 United States Reports 510, 535 (1925).

13. GRUNDGESETZ [Constitution] art. 6, § 1.6(1).

14. Michael H. v. Gerald D., 491 United States Reports 110 (1989).

15. Russian Constitution art.

16. For further details, see GEORGE P. FLETCHER, LOYALTY: AN ESSAY ON THE MORALITY OF RELATIONSHIPS 79–82 (1993).

17. For further details, see *id.* 87–89.

18. *See* RICHARD A. POSNER, ECONOMIC ANALYSIS OF LAW (4th ed. 1992).

19. My description of the case draws on the opinion of the New Jersey Supreme Court in In the Matter of Baby M, 109 New Jersey Reports 396, 537 Atlantic Reports 2d 1227 (1988), and the book written by Mary Beth Whitehead, in collaboration with a journalist, M. WHITEHEAD & L. SCHWARTZ-NOBEL, A MOTHER'S STORY (1989).

20. *See* JOHN STUART MILL, ON LIBERTY (1859).

21. *See* E. ALLAN FARNSWORTH, CONTRACTS 323–39 (2d ed. 1990).

22. As reported in WHITEHEAD & SCHWARTZ-NOBEL, *supra* note 19, at 17.

23. The court reviews the New Jersey statutes punishing giving or paying

money in connection with an adoption, New Jersey Statutes Annotated 9:3-54a. 109 New Jersey Reports at 423–27.

24. WHITEHEAD & SCHWARTZ-NOBEL, *supra* note 19, at 26.

25. I leave out some of the details of the story that were highlighted in the popular press. It seems to be irrelevant whether Elizabeth Stern had sensible medical grounds for refusing to bear her own child. Nor does it seem important that William Stern is the son of Holocaust survivors and therefore particularly concerned about continuing his blood line.

26. According to the opinion of the Court, she threatened suicide and said that she would return the child in a week. 109 New Jersey Reports at 415.

27. According to the account in WHITEHEAD & SCHWARTZ-NOBEL, *supra* note 19, the Florida court order was fraudulent. I am not in a position to verify this claim.

28. 109 New Jersey Reports 396 (1988).

29. *Id.* at 437.

30. *See* J. GOLDSTEIN, ET AL., BEYOND THE BEST INTERESTS OF THE CHILD 16–17 (1973); *see also* J. GOLDSTEIN ET AL., BEFORE THE BEST INTERESTS OF THE CHILD (1979).

31. 109 New Jersey Reports at 450.

32. I leave aside the difficult problems raised by ova donors and other high-tech variations.

33. West Virginia Board of Education v. Barnette, 319 United States Reports 624 (1943).

34. Sheldon v. Fannin, 221 Federal Supplement Reports 766 (District of Arizona 1963).

35. *See* Wooley v. Maynard, 430 United States Reports 705 (1977) (not required to use New Hampshire license plates that read "Live Free or Die"). *See also* Thomas v. Review Board of Indiana Employment Security Div., 450 United States Reports 707 (1981) (Jehovah's Witness could receive unemployment compensation even though he quit his job because he did not want to participate in the armaments industry).

36. The primary winners under this line of cases have been Seventh Day Adventists. *See* Sherbert v. Verner, 374 United States Reports 398 (1963); Hobbie v. Unemployment Appeals Commission of Florida, 480 United States Reports 136 (1987).

37. *See* Frazee v. Illinois Department of Employment Security, 489 United States Reports 829 (1989).

38. Wisconsin v. Yoder, 406 United States Reports 205 (1972).

39. *Romans* 12:2.

40. Justice Douglas concurred in a separate opinion stressing the right of the children to decide for themselves whether they would attend public high school. 406 United States Reports at 241 (1972).

41. Quakers and other Protestant pacifists did not have to litigate claims of conscientious objection from military service; the Selective Service statute itself recognized an exemption. *See* Gillette v. United States Reports, 401 United States Reports 437, 443 note 8 (1971).

42. Reynolds v. United States, 98 United States Reports 145 (1879).

43. Braunfield v. Brown, 366 United States Reports 599 (1961).

44. Church of Lukumi Babalu Aye, Inc. v. City of Hialeah, 113 Supreme Court Reports 2217 (1993).

45. Leary v. United States, 383 Federal Reports 2d 851 (1967).

46. Department of Human Resources of Oregon v. Smith, 494 United States Reports 872 (1990).

47. Religious Freedom Restoration Act of 1993, 42 UNITED STATES CODE §§ 1988 2000 bb. et seq.

48. Commentators have noted a tension between the two religion clauses of the First Amendment. Privileging religious claims under the "free exercise" clause arguably represents an "establishment" of religion. The only way to avoid this conflict is to deny special treatment of religious claims. *See* Philip Kurland, *Of Church and State and the Supreme Court*, 29 UNIVERSITY OF CHICAGO LAW REVIEW 1 (1961); DAVID RICHARDS, TOLERATION AND THE CONSTITUTION 129–33 (1986).

49. In giving his view of why conscientious objector status should be extended to humanists as well as religious believers, Justice Harlan wrote, "[T]he common denominator must be the intensity of moral conviction with which the belief is held." Welsh v. United States, 398 United States Reports 333, 358 (1970) (Harlan, J. concurring).

50. 406 United States Reports at 216.

51. *See* SOPHOCLES, ANTIGONE (E.F. Warling trans., Penguin ed. 1947).

52. *Matthew* 22:21.

53. One of the few articles in the literature that shares this view of the religious life is Perry Dane's student comment, *Religious Exemptions under the Free Exercise Clause: A Model of Competing Authorities*, 90 YALE LAW JOURNAL 350 (1980).

54. *See Matthew* 13:57.

55. *Genesis* 22:2.

56. For a more thorough treatment of this body of law, see FLETCHER, *supra* note 16, at 36–40, 69–75.

57. Recall the second definition of justice offered in Plato's Republic: justice consists in doing good to friends and harm to enemies. REPUBLIC I, 332a–b. In the city imagined by Socrates, the guardians must be raised in religious beliefs that give them a particular sense of loyalty and duty to their city. *Id.* at III, 414b–e.

12

Consistency

Outsiders to a legal culture generally assume that the law is reducible to a set of well-defined rules. A more sophisticated view would include in the law principles, policies, and other standards that influence decision making. Even insiders schooled in the law treat the legal system as a consistent and coherent set of ideas. It is uncommon to argue, as I do in this concluding chapter, that modern legal cultures are torn in conflicting directions by irreconcilable premises.

Each of the concepts traced in this book spawns a school of thought. Devotees of Rawlsian justice are at odds with those who believe in desert. The advocates of efficiency collide with those who take the demands of fairness, justice, and equal treatment as their starting points. Some people think that individual rights are critical; others seek to promote the welfare of the group as a whole. There is hardly an issue in the law that invites resolution without tapping into these deeper debates.

As legal debates reduce to irreconcilable premises, so do attempts to fashion a morality of the law. Moral debate remains open-ended and inconclusive. There is no end to the conflict between those who side with Bentham's utilitarianism as opposed to Kant's theory of duties to respect human dignity. And both of these schools of "liberal" impartial morality are now embattled against critics who urge a communitarian morality, typified by the argument in favor of loyalty as a moral value. The law is suffused with a moral debate that is not likely to end in the quiet of a universal consensus.

That there are divergent sources of legal thought led Robert Cover to generate a picture of lawmaking or "jurisgenerative" thought springing up from the roots of the legal culture. New ideas keep coming forth but not all of them endure. At the higher levels of thought and decision, some of these schools survive and others are slain.[1] Yet a surprising number of conflicting and inconsistent schools do coexist without falling into open warfare for supremacy.[2]

What is the harm of inconsistency and contradiction? The postmodern mind seems to delight in mixing and mismatching. This is done in law as well as architecture. Yet lawyers also think of themselves as rational analysts. So far as they are committed to rationality, lawyers would have to be concerned about the paradoxes that lie latent in legal thought. Let us look at one of these contradictions hidden in the verbiage of legal reasoning.

A Sample Paradox

Perhaps more than other areas, the law of torts is rent by inconsistent starting points on how to think about allocating losses that occur in accidents. Here we see the advocates of justice, morality, consent, and efficiency all plying their methods. Traditionalists support a theory of corrective justice in tort law; one faction of moderns has hit upon efficiency (as understood in the Kaldor/Hicks test) as the proper goal of tort law. To illustrate the conflict, let us consider the proper interpretation of the rule to be as follows: Someone who creates a risk should be liable only if his negligent conduct causes the plaintiff's harm.

Judges ordinarily instruct juries that defendants must pay for the harm they caused if they failed to act as a reasonable person would have acted under the circumstances.[3] Academics draw on an opinion by Judge Learned Hand to interpret this standard of negligent conduct in the language of expected costs and benefits.[4] Under this test, now standard in the academic literature, a risk is thought to be unreasonable or negligent only if the cost of running the risk exceeded the benefits of doing so. The court's or jury's assessment of these expected values is retrospective or ex post in the sense that the question is how the risks should have appeared to the actor at the time of his acting.

Some writers interpret this standard according to criteria of justice;[5] others, according to a principle of efficiency.[6] As a matter of justice or desert, those who act in a way beneficial to society deserve an exemption from liability for the harm they cause. As a matter of efficiency, an act justified on cost/benefit grounds provides a model for others to imitate; if the imitation is successful, then society will be better off. A true utilitarian would be concerned, however, not just about whether the defendant's act provided a model for others but about whether the court's decision itself would produce a greater social benefit than cost. It is more and more common for courts to think that their purpose in deciding cases is not only to judge the case before them but to promote socially desirable goals for the future. Thus there is a serious conflict between judging a defendant's behavior, retrospectively, and deciding in the public interest, prospectively.

If we take a careful look at this tension, we will find that interweaving retrospective and prospective considerations in decision making generates a serious paradox. According to the Learned Hand test, if the expected benefits of an act or omission (the money a defendant saves by not acting to prevent an accident) exceed its expected costs (the risk of injury), the act or omission is regarded as reasonable and therefore nonnegligent. Suppose that the costs to a hotel of not stationing a lifeguard at its pool are 50.[7] This figure represents the risks of drowning and other injury that might be avoided if the guard were present. Suppose the benefits of taking this risk—saving money and keeping down room costs—are 40. Given these figures, the risk should be judged as unreasonable, and under the standard of negligence, the hotel should be liable for injuries that a guard could have prevented. This seems like a straightforward analysis of a negligence problem.

The contemporary literature of tort law, however, stresses a number of benefits that flow directly from the decision to impose liability. These are the benefits of compensation, risk distribution, and deterrence.[8] If hotelkeepers in the future expect the pattern of liability to continue, they will either hire lifeguards, or they will routinely provide compensation for victims injured when no lifeguard is present. If they regard compensation as the cheaper alternative, they will in effect provide insurance for those persons injured in their pools. Presumably, they would raise rates and charge guests "a premium" to cover the risk of drowning on their premises. This form of "compulsory insurance" generates the benefit known in the tort literature as loss (or risk) distribution. The benefit of insurance, whether voluntary or compulsory, is that it prevents catastrophic losses from falling on particular individuals and families.[9]

Let us estimate this additional benefit of imposing liability to be 20. This figure represents the value of the consequences that are likely to flow from the decision, as discounted appropriately by the probability of their occurrence. Let us see what happens if we allow this additional benefit to bear upon the analysis of a particular case. The starting point for the argument is that the hotel is negligent; the overall costs of taking the risk and not hiring a guard exceed the benefits 50 to 40. A rational court would reason as follows:

1. The conduct is negligent and therefore we impose liability.

2. If we impose liability, we generate an additional benefit of 20, and therefore, ex ante, the benefits of the actor's taking the risk (and

being held liable) are 60. If the benefits exceed the costs, the conduct appears, overall, to be reasonable. If it is reasonable, there is no liability.

3. If there is no liability, we do not incur the benefit of risk distribution, and therefore the costs exceed the benefits 50 to 40. The conduct is negligent and we should impose liability.

4. Same as 2.

5. Same as 3.

Interweaving the benefits of liability with the retrospective analysis of the risk generates this endless circle. The inclusion of the consequences of the decision invariably destabilizes the results of the retrospective assessment of the risk. The same paradox arises in the analysis of necessity or lesser evils as a defense, both in criminal and in tort cases. To take a routine problem of justification, suppose that the cost of running a red light—represented by the risk of an accident—is 40; the benefit of getting a sick person to the hospital is 50. On these numbers, the cost-efficient act is obviously to violate the traffic laws by running the red light.

In looking at the problem ex ante from the time of decision, a court might sensibly conclude that additional social costs would accrue from acquitting someone who intentionally runs a red light. The acquittal might encourage other people to be lax in their observance of traffic rules. Hasty calculations by other drivers that their acts were justified might endanger public safety. Let us represent the expected social cost of acquitting this particular driver as 20. This cost will not arise if the driver is convicted and fined.

If the costs and benefits of running the red light are assessed purely retrospectively, it seems clear that the act is justified. If, however, the court considers the consequences of its decision to acquit, then we end up in the same endless circle of destabilization. The reasoning of a rational court would go like this:

1. The costs of running the red light are 40; the benefits are 50. Therefore we should regard the act as justified and acquit the defendant.

2. If we acquit, we will encourage lax observance of the law thereby incurring, ex ante, an additional cost of 20. The overall costs of running the red light (and not being held liable) will therefore exceed the benefits, 60 to 50. Therefore the conduct is not justified and we should convict.

3. If we convict, we will not incur the cost of 20. Therefore, the benefits of running the red light exceed the costs, 50 to 40. We should acquit.

The circle loops back on itself. If the court concludes that it should acquit, it generates a conclusive argument for conviction; if it concludes that it should convict, it cannot escape the conclusion that the act is justified and therefore the defendant should be acquitted. The destabilization results from interweaving the consequences of the decision itself with the retrospective assessment of the merits of the decision.

Resolving the Paradox

Now what should we say about a paradox of this sort? How serious is it? When he heard about Russell's paradox of "the class consisting of all classes that are not members of themselves,"[10] the German mathematician Gottlob Frege said that the foundations of arithmetic, as he had understood them, had collapsed. Mathematics could not proceed until the paradox was resolved by finding a way to avoid the self-reference in Russell's paradox.

In the face of paradox, a rigorous discipline comes to a halt. Until the contradiction or paradox is resolved, the foundations of the discipline remain shaken. Yet thinking about paradoxes has proven to be a productive source of innovation, particularly in mathematics. Zeno's paradox of the race between Achilles and the tortoise (Achilles can never pass the tortoise because he must always first run half the distance remaining between them) eventually generated the theory of the limit. An infinitesimal distance became equivalent to no distance (which meant that the faster Achilles could catch up with the slower tortoise). The contradictions that arise from dividing by zero[11] led to a less glamorous but necessary innovation, namely prohibiting division by zero. The mathematical mind could not rest without these resolutions. The notion of living with contradictions is anathema to the logical mind.[12]

But the law has none of these qualities possessed by mathematics. It is neither rigorous nor logical. Lawyers pride themselves on the attitude captured in Holmes's quip: "The life of the law has been experience rather than logic."[13] Lawyers and judges are not shocked by the shifting premises of their thought. Sometimes they reason in the language of efficiency and utility; sometimes in the idiom of rights, autonomy, and equality. Sometimes they are concerned about the dignity of the individual; sometimes about the welfare of the group. The oracles of the law eschew ideology. They quote Emerson: "Consistency is the hobgoblin of little minds."[14] The supreme values of the law are flexibility and adaptability. To remain free to adapt to the demands of experience, jurists cultivate a pantheon of values ready to respond to the call of the moment.

Yet no one who takes pride in rational thought can confront a contradiction indifferently. The life of the law may not be logic, but unresolved contradictions would initiate its demise. When paradoxes block our way, the imperative of consistency requires their resolution.

For the paradox just surveyed, there are in fact two paths to a solution. The beginnings of a solution lie in recognizing the difference between the consequences of the act being judged and the consequences of the act of judging. As elaborated in the work of Wasserstrom,[15] Rawls,[16] and Hart,[17] the distinction between rule making and rule application has crystallized in the philosophical literature. Rule making addresses itself ex ante to a general category of cases; rule application focuses ex post on the fitting of the rule to a particular set of facts. In the philosophical literature, this distinction illuminates the difference between the purposes of a system of sanctions in general and the meaning of the sanction as applied in a particular case. At the level of the system as a whole, punishment may have a deterrent, rehabilitative, or retributive purpose; in the particular case, it has the significance of sanctioning the wrong done. The purposes of tort law include compensation, deterrence, and risk distribution. In the particular case, however, the significance of the tort remedy is that it provides compensation for the harm suffered by the plaintiff.

For our purposes, the advantage of this fundamental distinction is that it keeps distinct (1) the costs and benefits of the rule as a whole and (2) the costs and benefits of the act assessed in a particular case. The formation of the rule of lesser evils, for example, would include all the considerations of fairness and utility that might make this rule sound. The costs of inducing others to be lax in their cost/benefit analysis (represented as 20 in our discussion) would bear on the contours of this general rule. If these costs were too high, the court might adopt a narrow rule of lesser evils. Similarly, the benefits of risk distribution would bear upon the design of the general tort remedy. These systemic costs and benefits should not intrude, however, into the analysis of whether a particular act falls under the rule being applied.

The major difficulty with this two-stage decision process is that it induces courts self-consciously to engage in a legislative function. It might be possible for a court to develop the applicable rule on the basis of general principles implicit in the legal system. Yet a court that overtly assessed the costs and benefits of a proposed rule would be functioning as a legislature. In a democratic society based upon the separation of powers, we shall continue to be troubled by the fine line between the courts' refining the law and their usurping of the function of elected officials.

Now, it may be the case that courts routinely distinguish between the making of rules and the applying of them, even though they do not always signal the stage of their analysis. There is some evidence, particularly in the necessity cases, that courts have decided against particular litigants for fear of the general consequences of recognizing the insti-

tution of necessity as a defense to nominally criminal behavior.[18] Yet
there is something significant in the courts themselves not getting
tripped up on the horns of this paradox. If they are confused, the confusion is one they can live with.

A paradox can bring to the fore a deep problem in legal theory. This
particular paradox highlights the dangers of using the consequences of a
decision as a rationale for a decision that must include a retrospective
component. A radical solution of the paradox would require courts to
disregard the consequences of their decisions altogether. There are many
voices for this position heard independently of the logical issue posed
here. The classical theories of private law[19] and criminal law support the
view that courts should focus exclusively on the merits of the case before
them. The retributive theory of punishment holds that punishment is
justified solely on the basis of retrospective assessment of the actor's
wrongdoing and culpability.

There are, then, two paths to the resolution of the paradox. We face
a choice either to empower the courts to make rules and then apply
them or to challenge the authority of the courts to think prospectively as
they are making decisions in particular cases. The choice depends on
whether we want courts to deviate from the classical model of separation
of powers and exercise, overtly, a rule-making function. The paradox
arises precisely because we prefer to suppress this delicate question of
political theory.

Our capacity to tolerate contradictions and to live with inconsistent
values expresses a commitment to pluralism in American law. Our discourse shows an unusual attachment to "reasonableness," and we show
an aversion to the European notion of Right and its suggestions that
there is always a single right answer. The common denominator of
reasonableness suggests that there is more than one right answer. One
reasonable answer might trace its roots to the values of corrective or
retributive justice; another, to the values of efficiency or deterrence. One
reasonable answer might stress our commitment to impartiality and
equality; another, to partiality and loyalty. The spirit of American law
may lie precisely in its capacity to absorb conflicting premises and a wide
range of starting points for legal debate. We search for a consensus, but
the diversity of values expressed in our basic concepts ensures that the
debate will not soon end.

Notes

1. Robert Cover, *Foreword: Nomos and Narrative*, 97 Harvard Law Review 4 (1983).

2. For reflections on conflicting paradigms of legal thought, see George P.
Fletcher, *Corrective Justice for Moderns*, 106 Harvard Law Review 1658 (1993).

(review of JULES COLEMAN, RISKS AND WRONGS (1992)); George P. Flecther, *Fairness and Utility in Tort Theory*, 85 HARVARD LAW REVIEW 537 (1972).

3. W. PAGE KEETON ET AL., PROSSER AND KEATON ON THE LAW OF TORTS 358 (5th ed. 1984).

4. The test originates in United States v. Carroll Towing Co., 159 Federal Reports 2d 169, 193 (2d Circuit 1947).

5. *See, e.g.,* Ronald Dworkin, *Hard Cases*, in RONALD DWORKIN, TAKING RIGHTS SERIOUSLY 81 (1977).

6. Richard A. Posner, *A Theory of Negligence*, 1 JOURNAL OF LEGAL STUDIES 19 (1972).

7. This example is discussed *supra* at pp. 87–88.

8. *See* GUIDO CALABRESI, THE COSTS OF ACCIDENTS 39–67 (1970).

9. *Id.* at 39.

10. For a popular discussion of this paradox, see DOUGLAS HOFSTADTER, GODEL, ESCHER, BACH: AN ETERNAL GOLDEN BRAID 15–19 (1979).

11. Consider the nominally correct proof that $2 = 1$. Let $x = 1$. Multiplying by x, $x^2 = x$. If we subtract 1 from both sides, we get: $x^2 - 1 = x - 1$. By factoring $x^2 - 1$ into $(x + 1)(x - 1)$, we can divide both sides of the equation by $(x - 1)$, and thus: $x + 1 = 1$. Recalling the premise that $x = 1$, and substituting 1 for x, it follows that $2 = 1$. The contradiction arises from dividing by $(x - 1)$ or 0.

12. For more on paradoxes in mathematics and in the law, see George P. Fletcher, *Paradoxes in Legal Thought*, 85 COLUMBIA LAW REVIEW 1263 (1985).

13. OLIVER WENDELL HOLMES, JR., THE COMMON LAW 1 (1881).

14. Ralph Waldo Emerson, *Self Reliance*, in ESSAYS AND OTHER WRITINGS OF RALPH WALDO EMERSON 152 (1940) (the quote in full: "A foolish consistency is the hobgoblin of little minds, adored by little statesmen and philosophers and divines.").

15. *See* RICHARD WASSERSTROM, THE JUDICIAL DECISION 138–71 (1961).

16. *See* John Rawls, *Two Concepts of Rules*, 64 PHILOSOPHICAL REVIEW 3 (1955).

17. *See* H.L.A. Hart, *Prolegomenon to the Principles of Punishment*, in H.L.A. HART, PUNISHMENT AND RESPONSIBILITY 1, 19–23 (1968).

18. *See, e.g.,* People v. Unger, 66 Illinois 2d 333, 362 Northeast 2d 319 (1977); People v. Lovercamp, 118 California Reporter 110 (4th Dist. 1974).

19. The paradigm of reciprocity represents an effort to state this classical view of private law. *See Fairness and Utility in Tort Theory, supra* note 2, at 543–56; ERNEST WEINRIB, THE IDEA OF PRIVATE LAW (1995).

Dramatis Personae

Ackerman, Bruce A., 1943– . Sterling Professor of Law and Political Science at Yale, Ackerman studied at Harvard College and Yale Law School. He clerked for Judge Friendly of the U.S. Court of Appeals, Second Circuit and Judge Harlan of the U.S. Supreme Court. His important books include *Social Justice in the Liberal State* (1980) and *We The People: Foundations* (1991).

Aristotle, 384–322 B.C.E. Widely regarded, along with Plato, as one of the two most influential philosophers in the West, Aristotle was born in Stagira, Macedonia. At 17, he entered Plato's Academy in Athens and remained until Plato died. In 335 B.C.E. Aristotle founded a school, the Lyceum, on the outskirts of Athens and there built the first great library. His work that figures prominently in this book is *The Nicomachean Ethics*, an unparalleled exploration of the intricacies of human motivation and morality.

Bentham, Jeremy, 1748–1832. Considered the principal author of the moral theory known as utilitarianism and the father of modern legal positivism, Bentham was born in London, studied law under Blackstone at Oxford, and then embarked on a career as a social and political reformer. He criticized theories of natural law and social contract, legal fictions, and other abstractions that lacked firm empirical grounding. The issues on which Bentham's views had a dramatic effect are still the foundation of the liberal agenda—use of birth control, elimination of capital punishment, sexual freedom, welfare for the poor and animal rights. After his death, Bentham's body was embalmed and is located at a college he founded, University College London, where his body with a wax head is occasionally displayed.

197

Berlin, Isaiah, 1909– . Born in Russia and educated at Corpus Christi College at Oxford, Berlin became one of the most important philosophers in post-war Britain. His classic essay *Two Concepts of Liberty*, discussed in this book, continues to generate controversy and new interpretations.

Blackstone, William, 1723–1780. Author of one of the most important legal treatises written in the English language, *Commentaries on the Laws of England*, Blackstone was born in London, educated at Oxford, and thereafter became the first professor in Britain to lecture, at Oxford, on English rather than Roman law. From 1761 to 1770 he served as a member of Parliament. His four volume *Commentaries* became the standard text for studying law in the American colonies.

Bork, Robert Heron, 1927– . Perhaps best known for his controversial and unsuccessful nomination to the Supreme Court, Judge Bork first enjoyed productive careers in private practice and then as a professor at Yale Law School. From 1973–77, he served as the U.S. Solicitor General. In 1982, President Reagan appointed him to the U.S. Court of Appeals, District of Columbia Circuit. After the nomination fight in 1987, Bork resigned from the Court of Appeals and became a Resident Scholar at the American Enterprise Institute. He then published a best-selling book about his conservative judicial philosophy, *The Tempting of America: The Political Seduction of the Law* (1990).

Brandeis, Louis Dembitz, 1856–1940. Born in Louisville, Kentucky, Brandeis studied law at Harvard and reputedly received the highest grades in the school's history. President Wilson nominated him to the Supreme Court. Brandeis's reputation as an attorney for the "people" in opposition to special interest groups and his being the first Jewish nominee to the Court generated a protracted confirmation battle. Finally confirmed in 1916, Brandeis served 22 years on the Court.

Burger, Warren Earl, 1907– . Coming to maturity under difficult circumstances in St. Paul, Minnesota, Burger sold life insurance and attended evening classes at the school now called the Mitchell College of Law. After serving as Assistant Attorney General of the Justice Department, Civil Division, he was appointed to the U.S. Court of Appeals for District of Columbia. President Nixon nominated him as Chief Justice of the Supreme Court, where he served as a leading conservative voice for 17 years.

Calabresi, Guido, 1932– . Born in Italy, Calabresi came to the United States as a youth and distinguished himself as a student at Yale College, as a Rhodes Scholar at Oxford, and at Yale Law School. He clerked for Justice Hugo Black in the 1958–59 term and then returned to Yale to teach law. His early articles laid the foundations of the Law and Economics movement. His most influential work, cited frequently in this book, is *The Costs of Accidents: A Legal and Economic Analysis* (1971). He served as Dean of Yale Law School from 1985 to 1994, at which time President Clinton appointed him as a judge of the federal Court of Appeals, Second Circuit.

Cardozo, Benjamin Nathan, 1870–1938. Born in New York City, a descendant of Sephardic Jews, Cardozo entered Columbia University at the age of 15 and graduated with honors in 1889. He entered Columbia Law School in 1891 and was admitted to the New York Bar in the same year without a law degree.

Following 23 years in private practice, Cardozo was elected to the New York Supreme Court and that same year was appointed to the New York Court of Appeals. In 1932 President Herbert Hoover appointed him to the Supreme Court, where he served another six years prior to his death. Cardozo is best known for his elegant and florid opinions written as a judge on the New York Court of Appeals.

Coase, Ronald Harry, 1910– . Born and educated as an economist in England, Coase has made an indelible impression on legal studies with his famous Coase theorem, first formulated in the *Journal of Law and Economics* in 1961. Coase received the Nobel Prize in 1991 for his work on theory of the firm.

Coke, Sir Edward, 1552–1634. Born in Mileham, England, Coke became the dominant legal figure of the seventeenth century. A judge, he fought for the supremacy of the English common law over royal prerogative, a position that landed him in frontal conflict with King James I. His most influential work is the four-volume treatise, *Institutes of the Lawes of England* (publication beginning in 1628).

Dan-Cohen, Meir, 1949– . Author of an influential article on criminal theory, "Decision Rules and Conduct Rules: On Acoustic Separation in Criminal Law," 97 *Harvard Law Review* 625 (1984), Dan-Cohen was born in Lodz, Poland, and immigrated to Israel as a child. He studied law at the Hebrew University in Jerusalem, where he was chief editor of the Law Review. He received his doctorate from Yale in 1981 and began teaching at the University of California at Berkeley in 1977.

Director, Aaron, 1901– . One of the founders of the Law and Economics movement, Director graduated from Yale in 1924 and began teaching economics at the University of Chicago in 1931. Later he moved to the University of Chicago Law School and educated generations of future lawyers in the foundations of price theory and the economic view of law. After retirement, he became a Senior Fellow at the Hoover Institute in Palo Alto, California.

Dworkin, Ronald, 1931– . Born in Worcester, Massachusetts, Dworkin received undergraduate degrees from Harvard in 1953 and from Oxford in 1955, and his law degree from Harvard in 1957. After a spell in private practice, he began teaching law and legal philosophy at Yale in 1962. In 1969, he succeeded H.L.A. Hart as Professor of Jurisprudence at Oxford and since 1977 has also taught at New York University Law School. He is generally regarded as one of the leading philosophers of law in the English-speaking world. His most important book is *Law's Empire* (1986).

Estrich, Susan, 1952– . Now the Robert Kingsley Professor of Law and Political Science at the University of Southern California, Estrich has pursued an unusual career in law and politics. After graduating in 1977 from Harvard Law School, she clerked for two years, including one year for Justice Stevens of the U.S. Supreme Court. She started teaching criminal law at Harvard in 1981 and managed to generate, for the first time, serious academic and political interest in the law of rape. In 1984, she was the Senior Policy Advisor for the Mondale-Ferraro Campaign and in 1988 she was the Campaign Manager for the Dukakis-Bentsen ticket.

Frankfurter, Felix, 1882–1965.   Born in Vienna, Austria, of Jewish parents, Frankfurter immigrated to the United States in his youth. After graduating from City College and Harvard Law School, Frankfurter entered private practice, became an assistant U.S. Attorney and served in the War Department in Washington. In 1914, he returned to Harvard to teach. In 1939 President Roosevelt appointed him to replace Benjamin Cardozo on the Supreme Court, where he served until 1962 as an intellectual force and leading exponent of judicial restraint. Frankfurter is remembered as well for his support of liberal causes: his defense of Sacco and Vanzetti, his support of the NAACP as well as Zionism, and his contribution to the founding of the ACLU.

Frege, Gottlob, 1848–1925.   Considered the founder of modern logic and the philosophy of mathematics, Frege was born and educated in Germany. He taught all his adult life in the Mathematics Department in Jena.

Greenawalt, Kent, 1936– .   After graduating from Swarthmore in 1958 and Oxford in 1960, Professor Greenawalt attended Columbia Law School where he was editor-in-chief of the Law Review. After graduation, he clerked for Supreme Court Justice John M. Harlan and was an attorney for the Lawyers Committee for Civil Rights in Jackson, Mississippi. In 1965, Greenawalt joined the faculty at Columbia Law School. From 1971–72 he was Deputy U.S. Solicitor General. His many books include *Speech, Crime, and the Uses of Language* (1989), and *Private Consciences and Public Reasons* (1995).

Hand, Learned, 1872–1961.   Educated at Harvard, Hand was named to the U.S. Court of Appeals, Second Circuit, in 1924. From 1939 to 1951 he served as Chief Judge. His opinions were influential in shaping the law of anti-trust as well as the law of torts.

Hart, Herbert Lionel Adolphus, 1907–1992.   Though he began his career as a barrister, Hart became the most important legal philosopher of his generation. He was appointed professor of jurisprudence at Oxford in 1955 and held that position until 1968. Hart was the first legal philosopher to bring to bear the powerful tools of conceptual and linguistic analysis developed by the analytic philosophers such as Ludwig Wittgenstein and G. E. Moore. In his path-breaking book *The Concept of Law* (1961), Hart develops a sophisticated view of positivism and finds a middle position between legal realists who are skeptical of the significance of rules in law and formalists who espouse an almost mechanical jurisprudence.

Hayek, Friedrich, 1899–1992.   Born and educated in Vienna, Hayek became a leading theorist of laissez-faire, free-market economics. He was a joint recipient of the Nobel Prize for Economics in 1974. Governmental intrusion and even collective action such as unions were anathema to his overriding commitment to individual freedom. Hayek's best known work is probably *The Road to Serfdom*, published in 1944.

Hegel, Georg Wilhelm Friedrich, 1770–1831.   Born and educated in Stuttgart, Germany, Hegel held a variety of posts that enabled him to develop a body of work that has had a lasting impact on the history of ideas. Though difficult to penetrate, his work influenced Karl Marx and Friedrich Engels and continues to tantalize thinkers looking for a new insight on the relationship of the human subject to the world around it. Hegel's leading books are *The Philosophy of Right* (1821) and *The Phenomenology of Spirit* (1807).

Hicks, John Richard, 1904–1989.   Born and educated in England, Hicks taught at various universities in his home country. He and Kenneth Arrow jointly received the Nobel prize in Economics in 1972. His magnum opus *A Theory of Economic History* appeared in 1969.

Hillel, First century Before the Common Era.   One of the leading rabbis of the *Talmud*, Hillel is well known for his apodictic wisdom and his teachings of leniency in the interpretation of the law. When asked to summarize the essence of Jewish law in one sentence, he replied with a version of the Golden Rule: Do not do unto others that which you would not have them do unto you.

Hobbes, Thomas, 1588–1679.   As developed in his most famous book *Leviathan* (1651), Hobbes's political philosophy responds to humanity's general insecurity and fear of violent death. He spent the last seven years of his life writing his autobiography in both Latin prose and verse, as well as publishing a translation of the *Iliad* and *Odyssey*.

Hohfeld, Wesley, 1879–1918.   After nine years teaching at Stanford Law School, Hohfeld accepted an appointment at Yale Law School in 1914 and taught there until his untimely death in 1918. His landmark contribution to jurisprudence consists in the eight categories of jural relations developed in his article on "fundamental legal conceptions," published in the *Yale Law Journal* in 1913.

Holmes, Oliver Wendell, Jr., 1841–1935.   After graduating from Harvard as the class poet in 1861, Holmes served in the Massachusetts Volunteers during the Civil War and was wounded three times. After having studied and taught law at Harvard, he brought together several of his lectures in his influential book, *The Common Law* (1881), which enjoyed a reputation as a seminal work in jurisprudence and was translated into many languages. Holmes served as judge of the Massachusetts Supreme Judicial Council, where he wrote over 1000 opinions. In 1902 President Theodore Roosevelt nominated Holmes to the Supreme Court, where he served as a leading voice until he reached the age of 90.

Kaldor, Nicholas, 1907–1986.   A leading economist of the twentieth century, Kaldor was born in Budapest and then emigrated to England, where he taught at Cambridge and advised the British government on taxation and economic issues. In 1974, he became the Baron Kaldor of Newham.

Kant, Immanuel, 1724–1804.   His work now studied all over the world, Kant lived his entire life in Königsberg, Prussia. He taught and lectured in various capacities until he was 74 years old. At the age of 55 he published his magnum opus *The Critique of Pure Reason* (1779). His major work on ethics, *The Groundwork of the Metaphysics of Morals* appeared six years later, and his philosophy of law took form in his later years in *The Metaphysics of Morals* (1797).

Kelsen, Hans, 1881–1973.   A leading legal philosopher of the twentieth century, Kelsen was born in Prague, taught legal philosophy in Vienna and fled Nazi persecution for the United States in 1940. He became a Professor of Political Science at the University of California at Berkeley in 1945. In *The Pure Theory of Law* (1934), Kelsen set out his positivist theory that the entire legal system derives from a hypothetical norm, the *Grundnorm*, that confers validity on the norms applied in practice.

King, Martin Luther, Jr., 1929–1968.   Perhaps the greatest leader in the fight to end racial discrimination in twentieth-century America, King championed the theory and practice of nonviolent resistance to evil. As a Christian minister and a spell-binding speaker, he commanded a unique moral authority in his time. He received the Nobel Peace prize in 1964. While giving a speech in Memphis, Tennessee, he fell to an assassin's bullet.

Llewellyn, Karl Nickerson, 1893–1962.   A founder and leader of the school called legal realism, Llewellyn was one of the most colorful legal personalities of his time. After having served in the German Army in World War I and having written a book about the common law system of precedent in German, he returned to the United States to teach law at Columbia and the University of Chicago. He was a pioneer of the study of the law in action as opposed to the law on the books. Together with an anthropologist E. Adamson Hoebel, he lived for a spell with Cheyenne Indians and together they wrote *The Cheyenne Way* (1941). In the last decade of his life, he became a co-author of the Uniform Commercial Code.

Locke, John, 1632–1704.   After his education at Oxford, Locke became the personal physician of Lord Ashley, earl of Shaftesbury who involved Locke in the political affairs and philosophical debates of the day. Fearing a treason prosecution, Locke fled to Holland, where he began to write seriously. His *Two Treatises of Government* (1690) and *A Letter Concerning Toleration* (1690) are considered landmarks in modern political theory.

Luhmann, Niklas, 1927– .   Born in Luneberg, Germany, Luhmann was educated at the University of Freiburg in Breisgau and Harvard. After a career as a lawyer, he became, in 1968, a professor of sociology at the University of Bielefeld. His debates with Jürgen Habermas in the 1970s and 1980s about systems theory and moral truth occupied the center of German intellectual life in that period.

MacKinnon, Catharine A., 1946– .   One of the leading feminist legal scholars, Mackinnon graduated from Smith College in 1969 and Yale Law School in 1977. She has taught at various law schools, currently as a tenured professor at the University of Michigan. Her theoretical work and her advocacy have been pivotal in developing contemporary policies toward sexual harassment. In recent years she has focussed her energies on generating a view of pornography as demeaning and discriminatory toward women. Her most recent book is *Only Words* (1993).

Marshall, John, 1755–1835.   Considered the founder of the American system of constitutional law, Chief Justice John Marshall was born in a log cabin in Germantown, Virginia. He fought at Valley Forge as a member of the Virginia Regiment. From 1799 to 1800, Marshall successfully ran for congress, was appointed secretary of state and then became, by presidential appointment, the second Chief Justice of the Supreme Court. He is most famous for his opinion in *Marbury v. Madison* (1803), which established the power of the Court to declare acts of Congress void as a violation of the Constitution (the power known as "judicial review").

Mill, John Stuart, 1806–1873. Widely regarded as the leading intellect of nineteenth-century England, Mill received his education at home from his father James Mill. By the age of 8, he had read several classic Greek works of history as well as six of Plato's dialogues, all in Greek. At age 15, he read Bentham's work and later said that all of his beliefs and theories suddenly fell into place around the unifying conception of the principle of utility. Mill's two most influential works are *Utilitarianism* (1863) and *On Liberty* (1859), championing individual freedom against governmental restraints.

Montesquieu, Charles-Louis de Secondat, 1689–1755. A French political philosopher whose work advocated the separation of powers and thus had a major influence on the drafting of our Constitution, Montesquieu led a privileged life of traveling and writing. His magnum opus is *The Spirit of the Law* (1748).

Morris, Herbert, 1929– . One of the first American scholars to apply contemporary philosophical techniques to the philosophy of law, Morris now teaches criminal law and the philosophy of literature as professor emeritus at the University of California at Los Angeles. His most influential article on the philosophy of law, "Persons and Punishment," generated great interest in retributive theories of punishment.

Nozick, Robert, 1938– . A leading contemporary political philosopher, Nozick was born in Brooklyn and educated at Columbia, Princeton, and Oxford. He has taught philosophy at Harvard since 1969. His first book *Anarchy, State, and Utopia* (1974) won the National Book Award in 1975.

O'Connor, Sandra Day. 1930– . The first woman to serve on the Supreme Court, Justice O'Connor was born in Texas and educated at Stanford. She began her legal career as an assistant attorney general in Arizona. In 1969, she was elected to the Arizona State Senate where in 1973 she became the first female in the nation to be the majority leader of a state senate. In 1981, President Reagan appointed her to the Supreme Court.

Packer, Herbert L., 1925–1972. A leading professor of criminal law in his generation, Packer was educated at Yale and taught primarily at Stanford. His most important book is *The Limits of the Criminal Sanction* (1958).

Pareto, Vilfredo, 1848–1923. Well known for the economic terms that carry his name, Pareto was born in Paris and educated in Italy. In 1892 Pareto accepted the chair of political economy at the University of Lausanne, Switzerland.

Pigou, Arthur Cecil, 1877–1959. A leading economist of his time, Pigou was born and educated in England. He taught political economy primarily at Kings College, Cambridge, where he made a lasting contribution to the theory of welfare economics.

Plato, 429 B.C.E.–347 B.C.E. Along with Aristotle the most important philosopher in the Western tradition, Plato taught at the Academy in Athens. His early work carries forward the inspiration of Socrates, who died in 399 B.C.E. Plato's work is generally divided into three periods. His early Dialogues, including *Euthyphro, Apology, Crito, Protagoras,* and *Gorgias,* introduce Socrates who is depicted as ever challenging false claims of knowledge. The middle dialogues include *The Republic,* which addresses the problem of justice and the ideal organization of the state. The late dialogues include *The Laws*, which presents a comprehensive approach to legal institutions.

Posner, Richard A., 1939– . Now Chief Judge on the federal Court of Appeals, Seventh Circuit, Posner has had a distinguished academic career as an advocate of the economic analysis of law. After graduating from Harvard Law School, he clerked for Supreme Court Justice William Brennan from 1962 to 1963 and then practiced law in various government positions. He began teaching at Stanford in 1968 and then moved to the University of Chicago, where he continues to teach as a senior lecturer. Among his books that have received considerable attention are the *Economic Analysis of Law* (4th ed. 1992) and *Sex and Reason* (1992).

Radbruch, Gustav, 1878–1949. A leading German legal philosopher of the twentieth century, Radbruch belonged to the generation for whom the crisis of National Socialism was a decisive experience. Before the rise of Hitler, he was a professor in Königsberg, Hiedelberg and Kiel and also served as Minister of Justice from 1921–23. In the post-war phase of his work, he advocated a strong natural law perspective and insisted that the innate purpose of law was to seek justice.

Rawls, John, 1921– . Author of the influential *A Theory of Justice* (1971), Rawls is credited with having revived the study of political philosophy in England and the United States. He studied and taught at Princeton and several other universities before accepting a professorship at Harvard in 1962. In the last quarter century, Rawls has fine-tuned and revised his original theory and recently published *Political Liberalism* (1993).

Raz, Joseph, 1939– . A leading contemporary legal philosopher, Raz received his early education in Israel and then assumed residence at Oxford, first as a student, then as tutor, and finally in 1985 as professor of philosophy of law. He also teaches on a regular basis at Columbia Law School. His most recent books are *The Morality of Freedom* (1986) and *Ethics in the Public Domain* (1995).

Rehnquist, William Hubbs, 1924– . Now Chief Justice of the Supreme Court, Rehnquist received his initial appointment to the Court from President Nixon in 1971. He came to his judicial role from a career as a lawyer and activist in the Goldwater wing of the Republican Party.

Russell, Bertrand Arthur William, 1872–1970. A paragon of the philosophical life, Russell spent his early years working on the foundation of mathematics. The *Principia Mathematica* (1902) written in collaboration with Alfred North Whitehead, was the great achievement of this period. In his long and productive life, Russell wrote on virtually every aspect of philosophy and expressed himself, often in controversial ways, on the political and moral issues of his time. In 1950, he received the Nobel Prize for Literature.

Sandel, Michael J., 1953– . A professor at Harvard University, Department of Government since 1980, Sandel is widely credited with reviving interest in communitarian thinking with his critique of Rawls's views in *Liberalism and the Limits of Justice* (1982).

Scalia, Antonin, 1936– . A Justice on the Supreme Court since 1986, Scalia held a variety of governmental and teaching positions before being appointed, in 1982, to the U.S. Court of Appeals. He is generally regarded as the leading intellectual voice among the conservative Justices now on the Court. In 1995 he delivered the prestigious Tanner Lectures at Princeton.

Searle, John, 1932– .   A leading American philosopher of language, Searle was educated at the University of Wisconsin and at Oxford, as a Rhodes Scholar. In 1959, he started teaching philosophy at Berkeley. In 1971, he served as an advisor to President Nixon on student unrest at universities. One of his more influential books is *Speech Acts* (1969).

Socrates, 470 B.C.–399 B.C.   Our view of Socrates comes mostly, but not entirely, from accounts of him in Plato's writings. Plato depicts him as a roving philosopher who engages in dialogues with others who believe that they have knowledge about various matters. Through the dialogue, Socrates eventually reveals to the interlocutor that his view is unsound. As described in Plato's *Apology*, as well as *Crito* and *Phaedo*, Socrates was tried and convicted for corruption of young men and subverting their faith in conventional morality. Socrates declined an opportunity to escape into exile and took the hemlock to end his life.

Thoreau, Henry David, 1817–1862.   Thoreau's most famous work *Walden* (1854) is considered one of the enduring masterpieces of American literature. It recounts the two years in which Thoreau retreated from the corrupt, materialistic society, which for Thoreau had become a spiritual void, and lived by himself in a cabin he built on the edge of Walden Pond in the woods of Massachusetts. His essay "Civil Obedience" (1849) reported his experience in being imprisoned for refusing to pay a tax that he thought would promote slavery.

Unger, Roberto. Born circa 1950.   A professor at Harvard Law School since 1971, Unger is a leading voice in the Critical Legal Studies movement. His lectures and his first book *Knowledge and Politics* (1974) had a strong impact on his contemporaries.

Wasserstrom, Richard A. 1936– .   A distinguished philosopher and lawyer who has litigated civil rights cases as will as written on moral philosophy, Wasserstrom now teaches at the University of California in Santa Cruz. His most notable work on legal philosophy is *The Judicial Decision* (1961).

Zeno of Alea.   A pupil and advocate of Parmenides, this Greek philosopher was born circa 490 B.C.E. Zeno is most famous for his paradoxes of time, space, number, motion, and infinity which are contained in the one book of his that has survived and from which we have only fragments.

Index

Abortion, 13, 35
Abstract review, 20
Accident law. *See* Efficiency
Ackerman, Bruce, 121, 197
Act/omission distinction, 3–4
Aknia, Oven of (talmudic discussion), 67–68
Antioch College Code, 115–16
Aristotle. *See also* Desert; Efficiency; Justice
 categories of justice, 80
 corrective justice, 88–92, 93*n* 18
 equal exchange, 156–57
 excuses, 105
 in general, 197
 involuntary actions, 106
 risk, 90
 scientific law, 41*n* 15
Austin, John, 40

Baby M, 177–78
Bentham, Jeremy, 38, 152, 153*n* 8. *See also* Morality; Utilitarianism
Berlin, Isaiah, 114, 198
Bible
 animal sacrifice, 181
 conduct and fortune, 95–96
 creation story, 122
 higher law, 26*n* 4

justice as blind, 91
sodomy, 153*n* 7
source of law, criticized as, 74*n* 6
source of morality, 141–44
Ten Commandments, 181, 183
universal justice, 79–80
Blackmun, Justice Harry, 74*n* 6
Blackstone, William, 63, 69, 71, 198
Bork, Judge Robert, 26*n* 15, 198
Brandeis, Justice Louis, 69, 172, 198
Burger, Justice Warren, 198
Byron, Lord, 115

Calabresi, Guido, 40*n* 5, 155, 163, 169, 198
Capital punishment
 arbitrariness of, 24
 Council of Europe, 20
 cruel and unusual punishment, 23
 in Hungary, 23–25, 27*n* 23
 retributive justice, 24
Capitalism, 16
Cardozo, Justice Benjamin, 13, 69, 198–99
Ceteris paribus, 57–58
Civil disobedience, 16
Coase, Ronald, 164–67, 169, 199
Coke, Sir Edward, 34, 38, 199
Communitarianism, 86, 174, 188